D0931314

ISBN: 0–8054–2502–0
4225–02

THE CHURCHBOOK

A Treasury of Materials and Methods

By

GAINES S. DOBBINS, A.M., Th.D., D.D., LL.D.
Former Dean, School of Religious Education
Southern Baptist Theological Seminary
Louisville, Kentucky

BROADMAN PRESS
NASHVILLE, TENNESSEE

To
My Students Who Have Gone Out
To Be Good Ministers of Jesus Christ

Contents

Foreword

A thoughtful businessman remarked that he had discovered a new reason for believing that a church is a divine institution. "No other enterprise," he said, "could survive if managed so haphazardly." But this picture of a church as a poorly run affair is becoming increasingly less true. Ministers are receiving training in church administration as part of their theological education. Businessmen and women are bringing to lay offices in the church their executive ability and experience. A church is much more than a business enterprise, but the practical affairs which it is called upon to deal with are of high importance and should be efficiently handled.

This volume is the outgrowth of many years of teaching in the field of church administration. On the alert to discover and make available to his classes new ideas and workable plans, useful forms and time-saving devices, thought-provoking suggestions and creative proposals, the author has sought to report, record, revise, edit, and reproduce materials year by year that students could file in their notebooks for immediate evaluation and study and for adaptation and use in their pastorates.

Insistent demand has arisen for the publishing of these notebook materials in permanent form. This book is, therefore, sent forth in the spirit of sharing, that a lifetime of accumulation of carefully selected materials, systematically organized, may be greatly useful to an ever-widening circle of students, ministers in service, officers and leaders in the churches, and all others charged with responsibility for phases of church work for which they need guidance.

Acknowledgment is gratefully made of indebtedness to publishers and individuals for materials used in whole or in part, in original form or as edited. Without this generous aid and permission, the book would of course have been impossible.

A Church Getting Well Started

A church, like an individual, is fortunate to have been well born. Like an individual, a church is fortunate to have been well nourished in its early years. In all its vicissitudes, through prosperity and hardships, a church is fortunate to have had a sound pattern of development.

Happy is the church that has a good location—in a community of opportunity and need, with a field that is not overcrowded, on property which permits expansion, in a building that facilitates worship and work. The "rugged individualism" characteristic of American Christianity encouraged the planting of churches with a minimum of planning. The result was that some communities were overchurched, while others were underchurched. Frequently churches were built too close together. Sometimes they were located according to the wishes of an influential family, with little regard for the convenience of the majority. Again, churches were often loosely organized, almost no attention being given to such important matters as constitution and by-laws, rules of order, covenant relationships, doctrinal bases.

The New Testament is, of course, the sole, sufficient, and authoritative rule of faith and practice for a church that rejects ecclesiastical rule. Yet, as in the case of basic doctrine, there is need for systematic statement of polity and practice based on New Testament principles. A Baptist church is under no compulsion to take other churches into account when it is instituted, to organize according to any traditional procedure, to adopt a covenant and articles of faith, to formulate constitution and by-laws, to co-operate with its denomination, to observe the amenities of comity with other religious bodies; but to do so, without abridging its freedom or violating its conscience, is to make its own future more secure and to demonstrate the spirit of Christ, who said, "This is my commandment, That ye love one another, even as I have loved you" (John 15:12); and of Paul, who admonished, "But let all things be done decently and in order" (1 Corinthians 14:40).

DETERMINING THE NEED OF A CHURCH

When is a new church needed? America is noted for its many churches, and some communities are obviously overchurched; yet occasions for the instituting of new churches constantly arise. We assume that wherever there are people, the church is needed. Social, moral, and spiritual poverty inevitably characterize a churchless community. There remain many communities which have been thus poverty stricken for years. New communities throughout the nation are constantly being formed where new churches should be organized. Population shifts sometimes leave churches without a supporting constituency; hence, the site of the church should be moved. Sometimes changed conditions make advisable the uniting of two near-by churches, which may necessitate a change of location.

The formation of a new church is a matter of grave moment. Questions such as these should be carefully canvassed:

Is there a definable community within which the church would be located? What are its boundaries? What is its present population? Is the population trend toward or away from the community?

What are the prospects of success? Is there a reasonably strong nucleus of like-minded Christians sufficient to give the new church its initial support? Is there enough favorable sentiment to warrant the church's beginning? What would be the probable consequences if the church were not established? What consequences might follow should such a church be instituted and then struggle on without adequate support to ultimate failure?

DETERMINING THE LOCATION OF A CHURCH

A church's future is often bound up with its physical location. A church, rightly located, has many advantages; wrongly located, it is under a serious handicap. Wisdom and unselfishness of a high order are required in the location of a new church. Such questions as these should be asked and answered:

Is the church location maximally accessible? Is it near the main highways of travel? Would it be difficult to reach at any season of the year? Is it too far from the main body of people whom it would reach? Will it probably remain accessible through the long future?

Is the location desirable? Is the neighborhood substantial? Is the property suitable? Will the services be reasonably free from distractions and disturbances? Will the people have a sense of pride in the church as it grows and the building expands? Has due regard been given to its proximity of other churches? Has the counsel of other churches been sought?

FORECASTING THE FUTURE OF A CHURCH

An inescapable element of human uncertainty enters into the formation of a church as in any other human enterprise. Divine guidance through prayer should be sought at every step of a church's beginning. This guidance is not ordinarily apart from the exercise of good judgment based on study and conference. Such questions as these arise:

Is the new church a part of a larger plan? In pioneer days there could scarcely have been an over-all strategy of church location. After these years of development and experience, however, to neglect or ignore such plans is to invite distress or failure. Has the denomination with which the proposed church is affiliated a "planning board" or its equivalent? Is there a committee of the local association charged with responsibility for aiding new churches? Is there a county or city zoning commission which regulates or recommends the location of buildings? Have any or all of these agencies been consulted?

Will the new church render an increasing service? A church will usually either grow or die. Its growth will depend largely upon its opportunity to reach and serve people. What are the prospects of population increase? What areas of need will call for and respond to its services? What leadership and equipment will be required if it is to challenge the interest and support of the people? Does it seem humanly possible that the new church can supply this type of leadership and facilities?

ENTERING INTO FORMAL ORGANIZATION

Agreement having been reached that the new church shall be instituted, after careful and prayerful consideration as indicated, steps will be taken looking toward formal organization. There are no fixed rules or procedures, but experience and common sense will indicate the necessity of foresight in getting the church off to a good start. Here again certain questions are confronted:

When shall the church be constituted? The constituent group may have been operating as a mission, under the sponsorship of a mother church; or the group may have been meeting together in unorganized fashion. Are they now ready to form themselves into an independent church? If so, announcement should be made publicly and a program formulated for the occasion.

How shall the church be constituted? On the occasion of the church's inauguration, after prayer for guidance, a resolution may be read stating the purpose of the group to form a church, setting forth briefly their common convictions in certain articles of faith and pledging themselves to the faithful performance of certain duties and availing themselves of certain privileges as indicated in a solemn covenant. Simple constitution and by-laws may be read, establishing orderly processes of guidance and government in the conduct of the church's affairs. Upon adoption of this comprehensive resolution by motion and vote, the church will be declared constituted and named. Prayer for strength and wisdom and fruitage would then, of course, be offered. The names and credentials of charter members will be read, who will thus constitute *ipso facto* a church with all the rights, powers, and privileges pertaining thereto.

BECOMING A PART OF THE LARGER FELLOWSHIP

A church thus constituted after the New Testament pattern is local, independent, autonomous; at the same time it is universal in scope, cooperative in obligation, and interdependent in relationships. In Baptist polity it has the right and the duty of fellowship with other churches of like faith and order in a district association, then more broadly in a state convention or general association, then still more extensively in a regional convention, and finally in a world-embracing alliance. A church is free to accept or to reject its privileges and obligations of fellowship and cooperation, and it surrenders none of its freedoms if it becomes a part of this ever-enlarging household of faith, but refusal to participate would cut it off from sources of life and power.

The church, when duly constituted, should make application for membership in its district association. Certified by the association, it may send duly accredited messengers to this body and to the larger bodies in accordance with the terms which have been agreed upon. Its financial contributions to the causes represented in the Cooperative Program enable the church to fulfil its mission at home and abroad. These questions arise:

Does the church understand its worldwide significance? From its inception a church should be made deeply conscious of its place in the kingdom program of Christ. Does it realize that the missionary commissions of Christ are not optional but mandatory? Has it caught the vision of world need and world responsibility? Is it prepared to share its resources, however meager, with others "from Jerusalem . . . unto the uttermost part"?

Does the church accept both its independence and its interdependence? Its independence is a precious heritage and must be jealously guarded. Yet its interdependence is equally precious and should be proudly claimed. Within a democratic Christian fellowship there is room for "many men of many minds" who are held together, not by legal enactments or man-made creedal statements, but by common commitment to the New Testament as their sole guide in matters of faith and practice.

Historically, Baptists have not required subscription to a creed or to articles of faith as a condition of joining a church, or of a church belonging to an association of churches, or of ordination of deacons or ministers.

Broken fellowship may be recognized and declared when essential New Testament principles have been violated, but within the gospel framework, "where the Spirit of the Lord is, there is liberty" (2 Corinthians 3:17). Persecution of any sort, for any reason, is abhorrent to the individual Christian and to any organized body of true Christians. Statements of faith are chiefly valuable as giving clarity and cohesion to those who already believe what these articles undertake to state, because they have first accepted the Scriptures from which the statements have been systematically gathered.

COVENANTING WITH FELLOW CHRISTIANS FOR COMMON ENDS

A covenant is "a solemn and binding undertaking to do something or get something done." In the very nature of the case it must be entered into voluntarily. From time immemorial men and women have covenanted with one another. Early in Baptist history church covenants appeared, a given form of which became generally approved. Often candidates for church membership know nothing of the "church covenant" until after they have been received. If the covenant is to be taken seriously, should it not be presented and explained beforehand? If it is a mere formality, the occasional public reading of the covenant becomes all but meaningless. Here is a form of covenant widely employed in Baptist churches which would form a beautiful and meaningful pledge of allegiance on the part of each member coming into the church if accepted voluntarily and seriously.

OUR CHURCH COVENANT

Having been led, as we believe, by the Spirit of God, to receive the Lord Jesus Christ as our Saviour, and on the profession of our faith having been baptized in the name of the Father, and of the Son, and of the Holy Spirit, we do now in the presence of God, angels, and this assembly, most solemnly and joyfully enter into covenant with one another, as one body in Christ.

For the Advancement of This Church

We engage, therefore, by the aid of the Holy Spirit, to walk together in Christian love; to strive for the advancement of this church, in knowledge, holiness, and comfort; to promote its prosperity and spirituality; to sustain its worship, ordinances, discipline, and doctrines.

As Christian Stewards

To contribute cheerfully and regularly to the support of the ministry, the expenses of the church, the relief of the poor, and the spread of the gospel through all nations.

Alone and at Home

We also engage to maintain family and secret devotion; to educate our children religiously; to seek the salvation of our kindred and acquaintances.

Before the World

To walk circumspectly in the world; to be just in our dealings, faithful in our engagements, and exemplary in our deportment; to avoid all tattling, backbiting, and excessive anger; to abstain from the sale and use of intoxicating drinks as a beverage; and to be zealous in our efforts to advance the kingdom of our Saviour.

Toward One Another

We further engage to watch over one another in brotherly love; to remember each other in prayer; to aid each other in sickness and distress; to cultivate Christian sympathy in feeling and courtesy in speech; to be slow to take offense, but always ready for reconciliation and, mindful of the rules of our Saviour, to secure it without delay.

When We Move

We moreover engage that when we remove from this place, we will as soon as possible unite with some other church, where we can carry out the spirit of this covenant and the principles of God's Word.

Some Beliefs We Cherish

1. We believe that the Bible is God's Word to man and that it is the only sufficient authority as the rule of doctrine and practice.

2. We believe in a regenerated church membership and that the conversion experience is a prerequisite to church membership.

3. In the New Testament the candidate was taken to the water, not the water brought to the candidate; the candidate was placed in the water, not the water put on the candidate; so we believe in immersion only as answering Christ's command of baptism and symbolizing the heart of the gospel message —death, burial, resurrection.

4. We believe in the New Testament order of baptism and the Lord's Supper. New Testament Christians were baptized before taking the Lord's Supper.

5. We believe in the right of each member of the church to a voice in its government, plans, and discipline. A Baptist church is a true democracy at work.

6. We believe in the freedom of the individual conscience; in the voluntary principle, not the coercive principle, in religion.

7. We believe in the total independence and separation of church and state. [1]

ARTICLES OF FAITH

Many and varied are the "creeds of Christendom." Some of them possess great historic value; some have been used as instruments of evil.

---

[1] Adapted from First Baptist Church, Austin, Texas.

It is well to bear in mind that original Christianity does not consist of creeds and confessions of faith, nor systematic theologies or philosophies of religion, but is essentially a *relationship*—the relationship of the regenerate believer to God in Christ through the Holy Spirit on the basis of the revealed Word.

What constitutes an irreducible statement of this saving faith has never been fully agreed upon. Perhaps we need little more than Peter's sublimely simple confession: "Thou art the Christ, the Son of the living God" (Matthew 16:16). Any effort to set forth a complete creedal statement to which everyone *must* agree would be abortive and intolerable. English and American Baptists have, from time to time, formulated "confessions of faith," some of which have gained wide currency. The two most popular of these in America are the *New Hampshire Confession,* more familiar to the churches of the North, East, and West, and the *Philadelphia Confession,* popular among the churches of the South and Southwest.

When the Southern Baptist Theological Seminary was organized in 1859, the famous faculty of four—Boyce, Broadus, Manly, Williams—drew up what they were pleased to call an "Abstract of Principles," which became an integral part of the "Charter and Fundamental Articles" of the seminary. Every professor of the school, from that time to the present, has engaged "to teach in accordance with, and not contrary to, the Abstract of Principles hereinafter laid down, a departure from which Principles, on his part, shall be considered ground for his resignation or removal by the trustees." These Articles have been greatly influential with the churches of the Southern Baptist Convention, and are given below as a model of clarity and comprehensiveness, worthy of acceptance as the common ground of faith of any New Testament Church:

I. The Scriptures

The Scriptures of the Old and New Testaments were given by inspiration of God, and are the only sufficient, certain and authoritative rule of all saving knowledge, faith and obedience.

II. God

There is but one God, the Maker, Preserver and Ruler of all things, having in and of himself all perfections, and being infinite in them all; and to Him all creatures owe the highest love, reverence and obedience.

III. The Trinity

God is revealed to us as Father, Son and Holy Spirit, each with distinct personal attributes, but without division of nature, essence or being.

IV. Providence

God from eternity decrees or permits all things that come to pass, and perpetually upholds, directs and governs all creatures and all events; yet so as not in any wise to be the author or approver of sin nor to destroy the free will and responsibility of intelligent creatures.

V. Election

Election is God's eternal choice of some persons unto everlasting life—not because of foreseen merit in them, but of His mere mercy in Christ—in consequence of which choice they are called, justified and glorified.

VI. The Fall Of Man

God originally created man in His own image, and free from sin; but, through the temptation of Satan, he transgressed the command of God, and fell from his original holiness and righteousness; whereby his posterity inherit nature corrupt and wholly opposed to God and His law, are under condemnation, and as soon as they are capable of moral action, become actual transgressors.

VII. The Mediator

Jesus Christ, the only begotten Son of God, is the divinely appointed mediator between God and man. Having taken upon Himself human nature, yet without sin, He perfectly fulfilled the law, suffered and died upon the cross for the salvation of sinners. He was buried, and rose again the third day, and ascended to His Father, at whose right hand He ever liveth to make intercession for His people. He is the only Mediator, the Prophet, Priest and King of the Church, and Sovereign of the Universe.

VIII. Regeneration

Regeneration is a change of heart, wrought by the Holy Spirit, who quickeneth the dead in trespasses and sins, enlightening their minds spiritually and savingly to understand the Word of God, and renewing their whole nature, so that they love and practice holiness. It is a work of God's free and special grace alone.

IX. Repentance

Repentance is an evangelical grace, wherein a person being, by the Holy Spirit, made sensible of the manifold evil of his sin, humbleth himself for it, with godly sorrow, detestation of it, and self-abhorrence, with a purpose and endeavor to walk with God so as to please Him in all things.

X. Faith

Saving faith is the belief, on God's authority, of whatsoever is revealed in His Word concerning Christ; accepting and resting upon Him alone for justification, sanctification and eternal life. It is wrought in the heart by the Holy Spirit, and is accompanied by all other saving graces, and leads to a life of holiness.

XI. Justification

Justification is God's gracious and full acquittal of sinners, who believe in Christ, from all sin, through the satisfaction that Christ has made; not for anything wrought in them or done by them; but on account of the obedience and satisfaction of Christ, they receiving and resting on Him and His righteousness by faith.

XII. Sanctification

Those who have been regenerated are also sanctified, by God's word and Spirit dwelling in them. This sanctification is progressive through the supply of Divine strength, which all saints seek to obtain, pressing after a heavenly life in cordial obedience to all Christ's commands.

XIII. Perseverance of the Saints

Those whom God hath accepted in the Beloved, and sanctified by His Spirit, will never totally nor finally fall away from the state of grace, but shall certainly persevere to the end; and though they may fall, through neglect and temptation, into sin, whereby they grieve the Spirit, impair their graces and comforts, bring reproach on the Church, and temporal judgments on themselves, yet they shall be renewed again unto repentance, and be kept by the power of God through faith unto salvation.

XIV. The Church

The Lord Jesus is the Head of the Church, which is composed of all his true disciples, and in Him is invested supremely all power for its government. According to his commandment, Christians are to associate themselves into particular societies or churches; and to each of these churches he hath given needful authority for administering that order, discipline and worship which he hath appointed. The regular officers of a Church are Bishops or Elders [Pastors], and Deacons.

XV. Baptism

Baptism is an ordinance of the Lord Jesus, obligatory upon every believer, wherein he is immersed in water in the name of the Father, and of the Son, and of the Holy Spirit, as a sign of his fellowship with the death and resurrection of Christ, of remission of sins, and of his giving himself up to God, to live and walk in newness of life. It is prerequisite to church fellowship, and to participation in the Lord's Supper.

XVI. The Lord's Supper

The Lord's Supper is an ordinance of Jesus Christ, to be administered with the elements of bread and wine, and to be observed by his churches till the end of the world. It is in no sense a sacrifice, but is designed to commemorate his death, to confirm the faith and other graces of Christians, and to be a bond,

pledge and renewal of their communion with him, and of their church fellowship.

XVII. The Lord's Day

The Lord's day is a Christian institution for regular observance, and should
be employed in exercises of worship and spiritual devotion, both public and
private, resting from worldly employments and amusements, works of necessity
and mercy only excepted.

XVIII. Liberty of Conscience

God alone is Lord of the conscience; and he hath left it free from the doctrines
and commandments of men, which are in anything contrary to his word, or not
contained in it. Civil magistrates being ordained of God, subjection in all lawful
things commanded by them ought to be yielded by us in the Lord, not only
for wrath, but also for conscience sake.

XIX. The Resurrection

The bodies of men after death return to dust, but their spirits return immediately to God—the righteous to rest with him; the wicked, to be reserved
under darkness to the judgment. At the last day, the bodies of all the dead,
both just and unjust, will be raised.

XX. The Judgment

God hath appointed a day, wherein he will judge the world by Jesus Christ,
when every one shall receive according to his deeds: the wicked shall go away
into everlasting punishment; the righteous, into everlasting life.

SUGGESTED FORM OF CONSTITUTION AND BY-LAWS

A democratic body needs constitution and by-laws for its government
and guidance. There is no form handed down by tradition which is binding on Baptist churches; hence every church may formulate its constitution and by-laws and its covenant and articles of faith as it chooses. Yet,
in this matter, as in many others, we turn to the wisdom of the past for
help.

The form which follows is in the nature of a composite. Many docu-
ments from varied Baptist churches have been examined and excellences
in common lifted out and combined. The resultant statements have been
subjected to classroom criticism and have been more or less tested by use.
Perfection is by no means claimed, nor is the form submitted as having
been "standardized." Perhaps no church would want to adopt it unchanged, and it is submitted as having value primarily for guidance.

It is earnestly recommended that any church not having constitution
and by-laws, together with articles of faith and covenant, appoint a com-

mittee to draft such a document and submit it to the congregation for discussion and adoption. It is likewise suggested that churches having already adopted such a form might do well to appoint a committee to study the document, perhaps comparing it with the form that follows, with a view to possible revision looking toward needed improvement.

Preamble

For the more certain preservation and security of the principles of our faith, and to the end that this body may be governed in an orderly manner consistent with the accepted tenets of the missionary Baptist denomination, and for the purpose of preserving the liberties inherent in each individual member of this church and the freedom of action of this body with respect to its relation to other churches of the same faith, we do declare and establish this constitution.

I. Name

This body shall be known as the _____ Baptist Church of
_____.

II. Articles of Faith

(Some churches may desire to include Articles of Faith in the Constitution.)

III. Church Covenant

(See preceding suggested form)

IV. Character

SECTION 1. *Polity.* The government of this church is vested in the body of believers who compose it. It is subject to the control of no other ecclesiastical body, but it recognizes and sustains the obligations of mutual counsel and co-operation which are common among Baptist churches.

SECTION 2. *Doctrine.* This church receives the Scriptures as its authority in matters of faith and practice. Its understanding of Christian truth as contained therein is in essential accord with the belief of the Baptist churches as indicated in the Articles of Faith herewith.

BY-LAWS

Article I. Membership

SECTION 1. *Qualifications.* The membership of this church shall consist of such persons as confess Jesus Christ to be their Saviour and Lord, and who, (1) after due examination by the church as to their Christian experience, and, if coming from other churches, as to their letters of dismission and recommendations or satisfactory substitutes therefor, (2) have been accepted by vote of the church, and, having been baptized, (3) enter into its covenant.

SECTION 2. *Duties.* Members are expected, first of all, to be faithful in all the duties essential to the Christian life; and also to attend habitually the services of this church, to give regularly for its support and its causes, and to share in its organized work.

SECTION 3. *Rights.* Such members as are in full and regular standing, and do not hold letters of dismission, and such only, may act and vote in the transactions of the church.

SECTION 4. *Quorum.* Five per cent of the active roll of the membership shall constitute a quorum, except that for the election of officers, 10 per cent, and for call of a pastor, 25 per cent shall be necessary.

SECTION 5. *Termination.* The continuance of membership shall be subject to the principles and usages of the Baptist churches, and especially as follows:

(1) Any member in good and regular standing who desires a letter of dismission and recommendation to any other Baptist church is entitled to receive it upon his request. In case of removal to another community, he should promptly make such request. This letter shall be valid as a recommendation for only six months from its date, unless renewed, and this restriction shall be stated in the letter.

(2) If a member in good standing requests to be released from his covenant obligations to this church for reasons which the church may finally deem satisfactory, after it shall have patiently and kindly endeavored to secure his continuance in its fellowship, such requests may be granted, and his membership terminated.

(3) The church may also, after due notice and hearing and kindly effort to make such action unnecessary, terminate the membership of persons for the space of one year nonresident, or for the same space of time not habitually worshiping with the church, or for the same space of time not contributing to its support according to the system prescribed by the church or in some way satisfactory thereto.

(4) Should a member become an offense to the church and to its good name by reason of immoral or unchristian conduct, or by persistent breach of his covenant vows, or nonsupport of the church, the church may terminate his membership, but only after due notice and hearing, and after faithful efforts have been made to bring such member to repentance and amendment.

(5) The membership of no person shall be terminated (except by letter) at the meeting when the recommendation for such action is made.

(6) All requests for termination of membership or action looking thereto shall first be considered by the deacons, who shall make recommendations to the church.

SECTION 6. *Restoration.* Any person whose membership has been terminated for any offense may be restored by vote of the church, upon evidence of his repentance and reformation; or, if on account of continued absence, upon satisfactory explanation.

Article II. Church Officers

The officers of this church shall be as follows:

Pastor

A pastor shall be chosen and called by the church whenever a vacancy occurs. His election shall take place at a meeting called for that purpose, of which at least one week's public notice shall be given. A pulpit committee shall be appointed by the church to seek out a suitable pastor, and their recommendation will constitute a nomination, though any member has the privilege of making other nominations. The committee shall bring to the consideration of the church only one man at a time. Election shall be by ballot, an affirmative vote of three-fourths of those present being necessary to a choice. The pastor, thus elected, shall serve until the relationship is terminated by mutual consent. The pastor shall have in charge the welfare and oversight of the church. He shall preside at all meetings of the church, except as hereinafter provided.

Deacons

SECTION 1. *Number, Election, Terms of Service.*

(1) There may be seven deacons for the first three hundred members whose names are on the church roll, and one additional deacon for each additional one hundred members. It shall be pertinent for the church to promote to honorary life membership any deacon who by reason of age or infirmities shall, after honorable service, be no longer able to render active service.

(2) There being _____ members on the church roll as of this date, the church is therefore entitled to _____ deacons. These shall be elected at a regular business meeting of the church as follows:

Without nomination, secret ballots shall be cast for _____ men as deacons. The _____ receiving the highest number of votes shall be

declared elected for a term of service of three years; the _____ receiving
the next highest number of votes shall be declared elected for a term of
service of two years; the _____ receiving the lowest number of votes
shall be declared elected for a term of service of one year. In case of a tie,
the vote shall be taken over until the tie is broken. After the initial election, the term of office of one-third of the number of deacons shall expire,
and election shall be held to fill the vacancies. In case of death or removal
or incapacity to serve, the church may elect to fill the unexpired term.
There is no obligation to constitute as deacon a brother who comes to the
church from another church where he has served as deacon.

(3) After serving a term of three years, no deacon shall be eligible
for re-election until the lapse of at least one year.

SECTION 2. *Duties.* In accordance with the meaning of the word and
the practice of the New Testament, deacons are to be servants of the
church.

(1) They are to be zealous to guard the unity of the spirit within the
church in the bonds of peace.

(2) They shall serve as a council of advice and conference with the
pastor in all matters pertaining to the welfare and work of the church.
With the pastor they are to consider and formulate plans for the constant
effort and progress of the church in all things pertaining to the saving of
souls, the development of Christians, and the extension and growth of
the kingdom of God.

(3) By proper organization and method among themselves, they are
to establish and maintain personal fraternal relations with, and inspiring
oversight of, all the membership of the church. Especially are they to
seek to know the physical needs and the moral and spiritual struggles of
the brethren and sisters; and to serve the whole church in relieving, encouraging, and developing all who are in need.

(4) In counsel with the pastor, and by such methods as the Holy Spirit
may direct in accordance with the New Testament teachings, they are to
have oversight of the discipline of the church, in administering which
they are to be guided always by the principles set forth in Matthew
18:15–17; 1 Corinthians 5:9–13; 1 Thessalonians 5:12–14. The deacons
shall be free to call upon any member of the church to aid in disciplinary action.

(5) The deacons shall serve as a general pulpit committee. In case
of absence or inability of the pastor, subject to advice from and conference
with him, they will provide for pulpit supplies. In any period when the
church is without a pastor, unless the church shall otherwise provide, the

deacons will arrange the temporary ministry and take counsel with reference to securing a pastor. It is not intended in any wise to prejudice herein the method by which the church shall proceed in securing a pastor.

(6) The deacons shall serve as a general finance committee. They shall organize themselves as they deem best for this part of their work, calling to their assistance other members of the church as they see fit. The duties of this finance committee shall be:

a. To supervise the raising of all money in the church and have supervision over the expenditure of the same, which includes the preparation of the annual budget.

b. No contract for supplies, materials or services, pledging the credit of the church, shall be made except upon approval of the finance committee, unless authorized by direct vote of the church.

c. All expenditures shall be made only upon authorization of the finance committee upon the authority of the church, save that the church may give general authorization to the committee for normal supplies and also for general items.

d. All payments for such supplies, materials, and services shall be made by the church treasurer upon vouchers approved by the chairman of the finance committee, the chairman of the house committee, and the chairman of the deacons, any two of whom may act in case the third is not accessible; and also such as may be authorized any time by direct vote of the church, in which case the voucher is to be signed by the clerk.

e. All money collected by and through the Sunday school, Training Union, Woman's Missionary Union, or any other church organization, shall be duly recorded by said organization and turned in to the church treasurer, or in case of special expenditures reported to the finance committee.

f. The finance committee shall provide for an annual audit of all books and accounts of the church.

Section 3. *Method of Procedure*

(1) The whole body of deacons shall be organized as a unit for the consideration of all larger problems and general policies, and shall meet regularly on Monday evening after the first Sunday in each month. They may organize themselves into such committees as their wisdom may direct for efficiency in service.

(2) They shall apportion the membership of the church among themselves and maintain the Deacon-Led Spiritual Growth Program so as to maintain regular spiritual contact with the entire membership.

(3) Each deacon shall freely confer with the pastor about all matters and cases of discipline which in his judgment would be most wisely and spiritually handled in private.

Moderator

The moderator shall be the pastor. In the absence of the pastor the chairman of the deacons shall preside; or in the absence of both, the clerk shall call the church to order and a moderator pro tem shall be elected.

Clerk

The clerk of the church shall keep in a suitable book a record of all the actions of the church, except as otherwise herein provided. He shall keep a register of the names of members, with dates of admission, dismission, or death, together with a record of baptisms. He shall also notify all officers, members of committees, and delegates of their election or appointment. He shall issue letters of dismission voted by the church, preserve on file all communications and written official reports, and give legal notice of all meetings where such notice is necessary, as indicated in these by-laws. The clerk shall consider it a part of his responsibility to promote loyalty and efficiency in church life.

Treasurer

The church shall elect annually a church treasurer. It shall be the duty of the treasurer to receive, preserve, and pay out, upon receipt of vouchers approved and signed by the budget secretary, all money, or things of value paid or given to the church, keeping at all times an itemized account of all receipts and disbursements. Payment of bills for local work and expenses shall be made promptly by check, and all funds received for denominational or other causes shall be remitted at least monthly by check. It shall be the duty of the treasurer to render to the deacons at each regular monthly meeting an itemized report of receipts and disbursements for the preceding month, and this report shall be read to the church in its regular monthly business meeting. Within thirty days after the end of each fiscal year, the treasurer shall render to the deacons and to the church an annual report showing the total amount of receipts, and an itemized statement of all disbursements. Prior to the rendition of this annual report, upon its completion by the treasurer, the report shall be audited by the auditing committee, and its chairman shall sign the report before it shall be accepted by the church. All books, records, and accounts kept by the treasurer shall be considered the property of the church. The books shall be open to inspection at all times by any member of the church.

Upon rendering the annual account at the end of each fiscal year, and its approval by the auditing committee, and its acceptance and approval by the church, the same shall be delivered by the treasurer to the church clerk, who shall keep and preserve it as a part of the permanent records of the church. The treasurer shall, upon the election of his successor, at the completion of his fiscal report, promptly deliver to the active chairman of the deacons all books, records, and accounts in his hands pertaining or relating to in any manner the duties of the office he is relinquishing. He shall consider it a part of his responsibility to promote in every proper way scriptural giving on the part of the entire membership of the church.

Financial Secretary

The financial secretary shall be elected annually. He shall receive the empty collection envelopes after the money has been removed and counted by the proper persons selected by the deacons to serve in turn; and from these he shall give each donor individual credit as provided in the Church Finance Record System published by Broadman Press and Supplies. He may keep the enevelopes for reference if he so wishes. He will also fill out the sheet for the monthly balance and report found in the record book, which will indicate receipts from envelopes, plate or loose, and miscellaneous or special offerings. He shall also be responsible for preparing and mailing semiannual statements to all contributing members.

The financial secretary has no responsibility for keeping money of the church. He will record in a suitable book all totals received through any channel of the church offering and also credit each object in the accepted budget with its quota or percentage of the receipts. He will draw all vouchers for payment of accounts and see to it that each of the several objects keeps within its allotted amount. A general order may be made by the church directing the financial secretary to draw orders at stated times in favor of persons drawing regular salaries or for payment of mission money paid in or designated benevolences. All bills coming to the church which are not provided for in the general order should go automatically to the secretary for investigation; if he approves and the church votes, he then draws the order; the clerk also signing it, and the treasurer writing a check to pay the bill or bills.

Music Director

The music director shall be charged with responsibility to provide worshipful music for all services and departments of the church, and shall have general oversight and direction of the music. He (or she) is to direct the choir or choirs in practice and public singing, and is to cooperate with the pastor and other leaders in the selection of suitable music and the devising of appropriate musical programs for all occasions where such services are needed.

Chairman of Ushers

The chairman of ushers shall, on the approval of the church, associate with himself a sufficient number of aides to care for the seating and comfort of the congregation, the greeting and introduction of visitors, the prevention of interruptions and distractions, and similar needed services.

Officers of Church Organizations

All organizations of the church shall be under church control, all officers being elected by the church and reporting regularly to the church. It is understood that the pastor is ex-officio head of all the organizations named, and his leadership is to be recognized in them all.

1. Sunday School Officers. Three months before the close of the Sunday school year the general superintendent shall be elected, upon nomination of a committee consisting of pastor and four others named by the church. One month later this committee, supplemented by the general superintendent, will bring to the church nomination of general officers—associate superintendents, department superintendents, secretary, treasurer, librarian, chorister, accompanist, and other needed officers. One month later the committee, enlarged by the addition of these officers, will bring a complete list of nominations of all teachers and department officers. In each case the nominations will call for election on the part of the church at its discretion, with any changes it may decide to make. Following their election a public installation service shall be held. The duties of these officers and teachers shall be those ordinarily designated in the approved denominational standards.

2. Training Union Officers. The Training Union director and other general officers of the Training Union shall be elected annually by the church upon joint nomination by the Training Union and a committee from the church, of which the pastor shall be a member.

Each union shall elect its own leaders semiannually upon recommendation of a nominating committee. The leaders in Junior and Intermediate unions and the presidents of the Young People's and Adult unions shall appoint this nominating committee. Each nominating committee shall consult the Training Union director and pastor before making recommendations. The officers of all unions shall be approved by the church in regular business session. The church shall hold a public installation service for all Training Union officers after their election.

The regular committees of each union shall be appointed by the executive committee of that union.

3. W. M. U. Officers. The general officers of the Woman's Missionary Society, consisting of president, vice-presidents, secretaries, treasurer, circle chairmen, together with leaders of auxiliary organizations (Sunbeam Band, Junior and Intermediate Girls' Auxiliaries, Young Woman's Auxiliary), constituting the graded Woman's Missionary Union, shall be elected annually by the church upon joint nomination by the W. M. U. and a committee from the church, of which the pastor shall be a member. Other officers, leaders, and committees shall be selected by the W. M. U. Executive Committee. The duties of these officers and committees shall be those designated by the approved denominational standards. Following their election, the general officers of the W. M. U. shall be publicly installed.

4. Officers of the Brotherhood. The officers of the Baptist Brotherhood shall consist of president, vice-president, secretary, and treasurer, who shall be elected annually by the church upon joint nomination by the Brotherhood and a committee from the church, of which the pastor shall be a member. The duties of these officers and committees shall be those designated by the approved denominational standards. Following their election, the general officers of the Brotherhood shall be publicly installed.

5. Other necessary officers shall be nominated and elected as indicated above.

6. Employees and Staff Members. Janitor, caretaker, hostess, or similarly employed persons, shall be recommended to the church by deacons (or a committee of the deacons), and approved for employment by church action. Staff members, such as church secretary, assistant or associate pastor, minister of education or of music, business administrator, and the like, shall likewise be nominated to the church by deacons (or committee of deacons) and duly elected by ballot. Employees and staff members shall be under general direction of pastor, aided by committee of deacons specifically designated for this purpose.

Article III. Committees

The following standing committees shall be elected:

1. Committee of trustees, one-third of whom shall be elected at each annual meeting to serve for three years, and, until their successors shall be appointed, will hold in trust the property of the church. They shall

have the actual care of the place of worship, but shall have no power to buy, sell, mortgage, lease or transfer any property without a specific vote of the church authorizing such action.

2. The membership committee shall consist of three members, not more than one of whom shall be a deacon, and one of whom shall be a woman. This committee shall have general charge of the membership rolls, and to it all requests for letters of dismission shall be referred for investigation and recommendation to the church. This committee shall make a detailed quarterly report as to all changes in the membership. The membership committee shall annually examine the membership rolls, making a list of all members who have died, all who are nonresident, all who have during the year failed of attendance and financial support of the church; this list shall be reported to the church, and every reasonable means shall be used to maintain an active membership roll of resident members.

3. The missions committee shall consist of five members, at least two and not more than three of whom shall be women, and shall make report to the monthly business meeting of the church. It shall be the duty of this committee to have the oversight of mission work to be undertaken and conducted by the church. Further, it shall be the duty of this committee to provide ways and means of instructing and enlisting the full membership of the church in the moral and financial support of the whole missionary interest of the kingdom, especially as conducted by the organizations of Southern Baptists. When invited to do so, this committee shall counsel with the finance committee in planning the annual budget of the church.

4. The properties committee shall consist of five members, who shall have general charge of the administration and upkeep of the grounds and buildings.

5. The music committee shall consist of five members. It shall be the duty of this committee to have general charge of all matters in connection with the music of the church. It shall recommend suitable persons for organist and chorister and other such positions as may be authorized.

6. Committees on administration of the ordinances: (1) The baptismal committee shall consist of two men and three women. It shall be the duty of this committee to make all necessary arrangements for the ordinance of baptism and to render such assistance to the pastor and to the candidates as may be necessary. (2) The deacons shall name from their number a committee responsible for preparation and conduct of observance of the Lord's Supper.

7. A committee on nominations shall be appointed annually by the moderator at least three months prior to the annual election of officers,

consisting of pastor (ex-officio) and five others, whose duty it shall be to bring to the church nominations of officers and committees as provided for heretofore. No persons eligible for re-election shall be a member of the nominating committee. This committee shall canvass the church rolls and otherwise seek to discover persons suitable for office-bearing, and tactfully obtain from members expression as to preferences for persons to fill the various offices.

Article IV. Church Finance

SECTION 1. The finance committee, in consultation with the pastor, deacons, and responsible leaders of various organizations, shall prepare and submit to the church for approval at its annual business meeting (or at such other time as may be deemed best by the church) an inclusive budget, indicating by items the amount needed and sought for all local expenses and purposes, and in like manner for all denominational or other approved nonlocal causes.

SECTION 2. Receipts from all sources shall be kept in separate accounts, a local expense account, and a missions and benevolence account. From the former account shall be paid all local expenses as the church may direct; from the latter account, according to the schedule adopted by the church (as suggested by the denomination), shall be remitted at least monthly any and all money received for this purpose, provided always that individuals be permitted to designate the manner in which their gifts may be distributed.

SECTION 3. All funds, for any and all purposes, shall pass through the hands of the treasurer and be properly recorded on the books of the church. The expenses of all organizations, as approved by the church, shall be paid from the local expense fund as heretofore provided.

SECTION 4. Special offerings may be sought by the church or by any of its organizations only upon approval of the church after recommendation of the finance committee. This does not preclude individuals making special offerings to various causes at any time as the Spirit of God may move them.

SECTION 5. It is understood that membership in this church involves financial obligation to support the church and its causes with regular, proportionate gifts. Each new member shall therefore be immediately approached by a representative of the finance committee for a subscription to the church's inclusive budget; and at least annually plans shall be put into operation for securing a worthy subscription from each member of the church. Failing to make any payment for one year, the delinquent member shall be dealt with patiently and lovingly by a committee from the deacons, and if failure is due to no good cause, and future support refused, the member's name shall be placed on an inactive list.

Article V. Meetings

Section 1. *Worship*

(1) Public services shall be held statedly on the Lord's Day and on some regular evening or evenings of each week.

(2) The Lord's Supper shall be celebrated on the first Sunday of each month, or at such other time as the church may determine.

(3) Occasional religious meetings may be appointed by the pastor at his discretion, or by vote of the church.

Section 2. *Business*

(1) At any of the regular meetings for worship, the church may, without special notice, act upon the reception of members or upon the dismissal of members to other churches, and upon the appointment of delegates to councils, but not upon other business.

(2) The pastor may, and shall, when requested by the deacons, trustees, or a standing committee, call from the pulpit special business meetings, the particular object of the meeting being clearly stated in the notice.

Special meetings of the church may also be called by the clerk upon the written application of any five adult members specifying the object thereof, which notice shall be read at the public service on the Lord's Day next preceding the day fixed for such meeting.

(3) The annual meeting of the church shall be held on _____, at which time the annual reports shall be presented and officers elected, and such other business transacted as may be specified in the call or authorized in the by-laws.

(4) At the annual and all special meetings, _____ members shall be necessary to constitute a quorum for the transaction of business.

Article VI. Discipline

Section 1. Should any unhappy differences arise between members, the aggrieved member shall follow, in a tender spirit, the rules given by our Lord in the eighteenth chapter of Matthew.

Section 2. Should any case of gross breach of covenant, or of public scandal, occur, the deacons shall endeavor to remove the offense; and if such effort fail, shall report the case to the church.

Section 3. If the church vote to entertain a complaint, which must be made in writing, it shall appoint a reasonable time and place of hearing and notify the person in question thereof, furnishing him with a copy of the charges.

SECTION 4. At such hearing, the accused member may call to his aid any member of the church as counsel. If he shall not present himself at the time appointed, or give satisfactory reasons for his neglect so to do, the church may proceed in his absence.

SECTION 5. All such proceedings shall be pervaded by a spirit of Christian kindness and forbearance, but should an adverse decision be reached, the church may proceed to admonish the offender or declare him to be no longer in the membership of the church.

SECTION 6. In case of grave difficulty, the church will be ready, if requested, to ask the advice of an acceptable council from neighboring churches.

Article VIII. The Church Council

SECTION 1. The Church Council, upon being established by authorization of the church, shall seek to correlate and co-ordinate the activities and organizations of the church, yet with advisory powers only.

SECTION 2. The Council, unless otherwise determined by vote of the church, shall be composed of pastor, staff members, clerk, treasurer, chorister, one or more representatives of deacons and each of the church organizations (Sunday school, Training Union, Woman's Missionary Union, Brotherhood), and of the congregation at large.

SECTION 3. The Council shall meet monthly or quarterly, as may be desired, or on call of pastor or chairman at any time deemed necessary.

SECTION 4. The functions of the Council may be indicated by the following agenda, subject to change as occasion may require: (1) Scripture reading and prayer; (2) reports of progress since last meeting; (3) calendar of activities and meetings for the month (or quarter) ahead; (4) problems which need joint consideration; (5) needs which should be supplied co-operatively; (6) objectives which call for teamwork; (7) possibilities of friction which should be prevented; (8) spiritual emphases in which all may join; (9) denominational calendar which should be taken into account; (10) season of prayer for special objects.

SECTION 5. All matters agreed upon by the Council, calling for action not already provided for, shall be referred to the church for approval or disapproval.

Article IX. Amendments

This Constitution and accompanying By-Laws may be amended by a two-thirds vote of the members present and voting at any annual meeting of the church, or at a meeting specially called for that purpose, the proposed amendment being inserted in the call; but no change shall be made in "Articles of Faith" and "Covenant" except by a two-thirds vote of all the members of the church present entitled to vote, said proposed change having been laid before the church in writing at a business meeting not less than one month before the time of the proposed action, and read from the pulpit on the Lord's Day next succeeding such proposal.

PURPOSES AND USES OF CHECK LISTS

Pastor and people need to know their church and community. Both church and community have become complex in today's culture. Continuous change calls for continuous restudy of the church in all its relationships and activities and of the community in its ever-varying constituency and needs. As the program of a church is being planned, as the plan is being put into operation, questions should be raised and answered that will concentrate attention on essential matters of fact and opinion that will serve to give safe guidance. The check lists provided throughout this book are for use of pastor, staff, deacons, church officers, responsible leaders and teachers of the several church organizations, committees, and interested members at large as they work together to make the church a vital spiritual factor at home and abroad.

For use of pastor and staff. The check lists may prove well-nigh invaluable to the pastor in the objective study of his field and forces, his needs and opportunities, his assets and liabilities, his purposes and program, his responsibilities and opportunities. As he approaches any phase of his work, the pastor will do well to turn to an appropriate form and check his knowledge and opinion concerning it. Copies of the form may be made, and members of the staff requested to check the questions or statements for comparison. Then key persons may be asked to check the list for further comparison and validation. Values of the results will be many and varied. Preaching will be given direction and enrichment, prayer will be stimulated and guided, conference and counsel will be made more definite and intelligent, discovery and enlistment of fellow workers will be easier and surer, and the pastor's total relation to church and community placed on a firmer and more enduring basis.

For use of deacons and church officers. Next to pastor and staff, deacons and church officers are responsible for the church's welfare. Yet these busy men may have vague ideas as to their offices and duties, and even more indefinite information as to the church's life and work and ways in which it is related to and conditioned by the community. From time to time each deacon and church officer should be given copy of appropriate check list for study and checking, after which the several forms may be tabulated and results brought to the deacons' meeting for joint interpretation and application. In the course of years a new and higher level of efficiency may be attained by these lay office-bearers because of concentration of attention on particulars rather than on generalizations concerning their functions.

For leaders of church organizations. The modern church employs many officers, teachers, leaders, sponsors, and helpers to carry on the work of its several organizations—Sunday school, Training Union, Woman's Missionary Union, Brotherhood, Music Department, etc. The check lists may serve for them several highly useful purposes. As occasion arises, the appropriate form may be reproduced and checked individually and by groups. The organized and tabulated results will then provide a solid basis for procedures looking to improvement. Used in connection with a study course, or clinic, or enlargement campaign, the forms may give point and definiteness of direction to the project which might otherwise become diffused and relatively fruitless. Of high value will be the use of the forms to determine matters of correlation brought to the attention of the church council.

For use in integrating and vitalizing the church program. The tendency of the modern church toward fragmentation may be checked by common knowledge by all departments of one another and of their relation to the church as a whole, and of common concern for the total program. Such community of understanding and responsibility will strengthen the church immeasurably, vitalizing its great central functions of worship, evangelism, nurture, fellowship, stewardship, and service. The check lists will serve to concentrate attention on essentials of the whole church life as distinguished from its constituent parts. Committees may well be named from time to time to survey aspects of church and community, of organizations and leadership, of equipment and materials, of services and functions, of needs and opportunities, of resources and difficulties, of methods and aids, of strength and weakness, bringing their conclusions and suggestions to the church for consideration and action.

The need of adaptation. Obviously no forms could be devised that would suit all situations equally well. Some of the lists may be too elaborate, hence need to have items canceled. Other lists may have omitted items of importance. In some instances the questions or statements should be rephrased. The author urges that the forms be used as *guides* rather than as stereotypes, and the publisher grants gladly full liberty in reproducing the forms with any desired changes.

CHECKING UP ON THE CHURCH'S BEGINNINGS

Items for evaluation	Yes	No	To some extent	Don't know
1. Was the church begun under favorable circumstances?				
2. At its beginning, was it located in a well-defined community?				
3. Was its location in accordance with a larger plan of Christian conquest?				
4. Was there a sense of felt need of the church by the community?				
5. Was the church located with a view to its maximum accessibility?				
6. Has the locale of the church improved with the years?				
7. Have population changes lessened the church's usefulness?				
8. Is the community now overcrowded with churches?				
9. Was the church begun auspiciously with inauguration ceremonies?				
10. Has the church a record of consistent co-operation with the district association?				
11. Has the church magnified its interdependence as well as its independence?				
12. Has the church been positively missionary throughout its history?				
13. Is the "church covenant" recognized and emphasized?				
14. Has the church adopted and emphasized "articles of faith"?				
15. Has the church adopted and publicized a "constitution"?				
16. Is the constitution, if any, adequate for present needs?				
17. Has the church formulated "by-laws" which are known and followed?				
18. Would it be well for the church to restudy its constitution and by-laws?				
19. If there are none, would it be advisable for the				

Items for evaluation	Yes	No	To some extent	Don't know
church to formulate and adopt constitution and by-laws?				
20. Are there items in the constitution and by-laws herewith that by reason of omission should be emphasized in the revision?				
21. Are there items in the constitution and by-laws herewith that are unacceptable?				

A Church Knowing Its Community and Itself

Much popular confusion prevails as to the meaning of "church." Sometimes the church is identified with its building. Again, the word may refer to the stated services of worship. Frequently, "church" means the organization in its official capacity. Often the word is used generically, as "church and state." Sometimes it is used poetically, as "the church of the redeemed." Quite widely "church" is confused with denomination, as "the Roman Catholic Church" or "the Presbyterian Church." In the great majority of cases in the New Testament, "church" refers to a local body of baptized believers.

A CHURCH IS MADE UP OF ITS ORGANIZATIONS

A church is an organism; but all living organisms require organization. For each of the major functions of a church some type of organization is necessary. The services of worship and preaching call for sanctuary, choir, ushers, minister, orderly procedures. The function of teaching demands educational equipment, curriculum materials, faculty and staff, administrative and promotional skills. The function of training requires time and space, leadership and programs, enlistment and enterprise. The business of missions necessitates continuous prayer, publicity, promotion, support. The financing of the church and its causes will not succeed apart from a program of stewardship and tithing that enlists and utilizes the men. Undergirding all is the necessity for vital co-operation of church and home, of the local congregation with the denomination, together with a serious and abiding sense of responsibility for community, national, and international welfare.

The organizations of a church are not ends within themselves but means to several major ends. In the achievement of its purposes a church needs a carefully planned and attractive program of worship and evangelism, an effective church school, a fruitful training department, a vital plan of missionary promotion and support, a dynamic organization for enlistment in service and giving, a worthy program of co-operation with agencies beyond the local church. Yet a church is more than a worship service surrounded by Sunday school, Training Union, Woman's Missionary Union, Brotherhood, Music Ministry, and committees. Nor is a church properly conceived as the sum of its services and organizations. A church is a unity, an organic whole, an undivided body, with Christ as the head, and each group "severally members thereof."

A CHURCH IS MADE UP OF ITS MEMBERS

When Jesus said, "I will build my church," he obviously was not thinking primarily in terms of a building, services, organizations. Evidently to him "church" meant the body of believers who had stood the test of *people* his challenge to their faith and discipleship. We miss the mind of the *first* Founder of the church when we fail to put persons first. Concerning every activity of a church, the crucial question is, To what extent is it transforming and enriching individuals and stimulating and guiding them toward the ideal of the kingdom of God?

The potential and actual constituency of a church consists of four main groups: children, adolescents, young people, and adults. The basic question is not, How can we induce these various groups to take part in the church services and activities? but, rather, What can the church do to lead them toward, to, and into Christ and his service? To this end all who are concerned for the children of the church should come together frequently to discuss the total program of the church on behalf of its children. In like manner, those who teach and lead adolescents, young people, and adults, in each of the organizations and in the church as a whole, should plan and work together with a view to maximum benefits to each group. Thus a high degree of teamwork may be secured, as the primary objective becomes increasingly the salvation and development of persons as persons, not just their significance as numbers added to a roll or their contribution to the success of an organization.

Division of the church's constituency into age groups, sex groups, and interest groups is further evidence of a church's person-mindedness. These groups constitute the cells of the living body, from which come its growth and health. Like the cells of the human organism, these units, departments, divisions, and organizations are not independent but interdependent, not "auxiliaries" but integral parts of a common whole. Thus provision is made for worship, Bible witness, stewardship, service, and fellowship for each individual for whom the church is responsible. The units are not merged, just as the hand or the eye maintains its individuality, but along with separateness is maintained the equally important fact of togetherness, else ill-health and inefficiency are bound to follow. Paul states the aim of this division of function yet unity of purpose: "That there should be no schism in the body; but that the members should have

CHECKING UP ON THE CHURCH'S TOTAL PROGRAM

Items for evaluation	Yes	No	To some extent	Don't know
1. Is there definite sense of the worth of each individual member?				
2. Is there a worthy program of nurture and care for all the children?				
3. Are the services of the church attractive to young people?				
4. Is there a sympathetic and appreciative attitude toward young people?				
5. Are there enough qualified teachers and leaders of young people?				
6. Are the social and recreational needs of the young people met?				
7. Is guidance provided young people in their life choices?				
8. Are the lost of all ages being won to Christ?				
9. Are all age groups being enlisted in Christian service?				
10. Is sufficient recognition being given to the women of the church?				
11. Is too much dependence placed upon the women for church work?				
12. Are the fields of service of women in church and community well defined?				
13. Are the services of the women brought before the church for approval?				
14. Is there appreciative understanding of the junior organizations sponsored by the women?				
15. Is the organized work of the women effectively correlated with other church organizations?				
16. Are the women fully enlisted in the total program of the church?				
17. Are the men of the church given recognition and appreciation?				
18. Is there a spirit of true brotherhood among the men of the church?				
19. Is there a special organization for men?				
20. Do the men accept responsibility for the boys of the church?				

Items for evaluation	Yes	No	To some extent	Don't know
21. Are the men being utilized for missionary and denominational purposes?				
22. Are the men being developed as soul-winners?				
23. Is there a deep sense of unity among the many individuals in the worship services?				
24. Do the worship services sustain the sense of individual responsibility and corporate unity?				

the same care one for another. And whether one member suffer, all the members suffer with it; or one member be honoured, all the members rejoice with it" (1 Corinthians 12:25-26).

GETTING THE CHURCH READY FOR THE STUDY

A church needs to know its community; it also needs to know itself. The typical pastor might be surprised at his own lack of definite information concerning all aspects of the church's life and work. Almost certainly most members would fail on an examination intended to disclose their knowledge of the details of the church enterprise. Even those who constitute the official leadership of a church can scarcely be expected to know all the facts, since the modern church is a complex institution. Confronted with their relative lack of acquaintance with the affairs of their church, pastor and people may be led to make systematic investigation that will yield high values.

As in the case of the community survey, the church survey project should be approved by the church, placed under competent leadership, and conducted in accordance with carefully planned schedules that will yield definite returns. The leadership of a church may well be captivated by the proposal to make thorough analysis of the church in all its aspects, and the membership at large may well develop enthusiastic interest in the undertaking and its significance. The instruments provided below are suggestive and should be revised to meet the needs and circumstances of a given church.

THE COMMUNITY SURVEY

A church represents two worlds—the world of material values and the world of spiritual values. A church could not exist apart from a community of flesh and blood people with their needs and possibilities; nor would it have any reason for being apart from its representation of God and of the things of God. In a real sense the community exists for the church, for without support of the people it would have no chance of life. In just as real sense, the church exists for the community, for unless it contributed to human welfare it would not deserve the people's support.

In many ways the community conditions the life of a church. The ideal church pattern remains constant, having been derived from the New Testament original; but the expression of its life will vary in accordance with the pressures of community demands. In accordance with the law of all living things, a church must adapt itself to its changing environment or perish. It is therefore of utmost importance that a church know and serve its community and establish and preserve vital relationships between itself and its community.

To know its community, a church should devise and follow certain systematic procedures. General information and subjective judgments are not enough. Every community possesses peculiar characteristics. No two villages, no two towns, no two cities are exactly alike. "Community" means more than physical boundaries and vital statistics. Back of the individuality of a community are many factors—the early settlers, the type of civic and religious leaders, the changing mores, the moral standards, the institutions of public welfare, types of industry and the economic level, cultural advantages or disadvantages, the spirit of co-operation or conflict, the homogeneity or the heterogeneity of the population.

If a church is to know its community, and thus to be enabled to establish and maintain constructive relationships, it should study its field according to a carefully devised survey plan. Such a study cannot be made once for all, but should be progressive and continuous. Community changes are like those that take place in the life of a growing person—they occur gradually and almost imperceptibly to the observer, yet in the course of years bring about radical differences. The systematic study of its community is a never-ceasing responsibility of the church through its leadership, with varying aspects receiving special emphasis from year to year.

PREPARING FOR THE COMMUNITY SURVEY

The average church does not have resources for making a community survey comparable to civic, commercial and social agencies. The questions uppermost in a church's study of a community are: What facts are relevant to the religious life of the people? What bearing have these facts on the work of a particular church or of the churches of the community? How are these facts to be secured? How are they to be interpreted and utilized?

The community survey should grow out of a sense of felt need and not be imposed as a "busy activity." Pastor and church leaders, facing problems of the church's functions and future, will doubtless become keenly conscious of their need to know more accurately community conditions which afford the church both its challenge and its opportunity. Granted that certain facts must be known if the church's program is to be planned intelligently, the question arises as to whether the data shall be secured haphazardly or systematically. If the latter, the church should authorize the setting up of the survey project. This will include designation of competent leadership, determination of the general scope and purposes of the survey, provision of sufficient funds for expenses, the setting of time limits for the progressive completion of the undertaking.

COMMUNITY HISTORY AND SPIRIT

Essential Information Needed

When and by whom was the community settled? Who were the early leaders in the life of the community? In what ways did these pioneers shape community attitudes and outlook? Around what centers of interest did the community life develop? When and by whom were established the community's institutions—schools, churches, libraries, fraternal organizations, clubs, etc.? What historic events have occurred in the community? What have been some epochs in the community's growth? What unfortunate circumstances have retarded the community's progress? How summarize the community's spirit today—wholesome or unwholesome, progressive or backward, co-operative or factional, democratic or stratified, generous or self-centered, law-abiding or lawless, well governed or politically corrupt, church-minded or worldly-minded?

SURVEY SCHEDULE AND RESOURCES

Survey items	Survey resources
1. Early settlers	Recollections of oldest inhabitants
2. Beginnings of the community	Newspaper files
3. Leading men and women in the community's history	Books and pamphlets with local references
4. Early institutions	Church minutes
5. Historic events	Interviews with representative citizens
6. Notable community changes	Opinions of religious leaders
7. Constructive and destructive developments	
8. Present attitudes—favorable and unfavorable to religion	

Essential Information Needed

Who goes to church in the community and why? How many persons are church members? Where do these persons hold church membership? How many are members of a Sunday school? Where do they attend? If not in attendance at Sunday school, are they prospects for the Cradle Roll or Extension Department? If not church members, do they have a denominational preference? If denominational preference, do they have a local church preference? Into what age groups may the total population be classified? What would be necessary to attract and hold the unreached? What could be done to win the lost to Christ?

SURVEY SCHEDULE AND RESOURCES

Survey items	Survey resources
1. Separate card for each individual	Division of territory into separate districts
2. Name	
3. Address	Selection of leaders for each district
4. Age	Enlistment and training of leaders
5. Church member? Where?	Securing and instructing census takers
6. Member Sunday school? Where?	Thorough house-to-house census
7. Cradle Roll or Extension Department prospect?	Analysis of returns by age groups
8. Denominational preference?	Enlargement of facilities and organization on basis of discovered prospects
9. Local church preference?	Attractive visitation to enroll all Sunday school prospects
10. How best approached?	
11. Who should follow up contact?	Teaching, preaching, and witnessing to win those enrolled
12. Other vital information?	Enlistment in service of those thus won

OTHER CHURCHES AND RELIGIOUS INSTITUTIONS

Essential Information Needed

How many churches are there in the community? What is the relative size of these churches? In what time order have they been established? Are there too many or too few churches? Are the churches co-operative or non-co-operative? Which churches seem to be aggressive and growing, which appear to be passive and declining? Are there unchurched areas where new churches are needed? Are there neglected spots where missions should be established?

What other institutions are there in the community of a religious nature? How are these institutions promoted and supported? What valuable religious services do they render? Are more such institutions or agencies needed?

SURVEY SCHEDULE AND RESOURCES

Survey items	Survey resources
1. Number of churches in community	Spot map of community showing churches and other religious institutions
2. Number in membership of each church	Lists of churches
3. Value and adequacy of property of each	Annual reports of churches
	United States census statistics
4. Annual budget of each church	City or county welfare studies
5. Average Sunday school enrolment and attendance	Interviews
	Calendars of activities
6. Proximity of church locations	Opinion polls of leading churchmen
7. Too many or too few churches	
8. Need of other churches or missions	
9. Description of nonchurch institutions or agencies	
10. Evaluation of these nonchurch enterprises	

PHYSICAL LIMITATIONS AND OPPORTUNITIES

Essential Information Needed

What constitute the natural boundaries of the church community? Do these natural boundaries constitute too much or too little territory for the church? What percentage of members or prospective members live outside these boundaries? Do transportation facilities make it easy or difficult for the church to be reached by those living within the boundaries? by those living outside the boundaries?

Is the community of the church primarily residential, semiresidential, commercial, industrial? Do the physical characteristics of the community make it favorable or unfavorable for the church? Are there zoning restrictions, and do they affect the church favorably or unfavorably? Can the church look forward to increased or decreased opportunity within the next ten to twenty-five years? How might the church use its influence to improve physical aspects of the community?

SURVEY SCHEDULE AND RESOURCES

Survey items	Survey resources
1. Natural boundaries (streams, hills, ravines, lakes, etc.)	United States census
	Social surveys
2. Artificial boundaries (railroads, highways, industrial properties, trade centers, etc.)	Zoning commission studies
	Topographical maps
	Industrial spot-maps
3. Social boundaries (residences of the highly privileged, of the middle class, of the working people, of the severely underprivileged)	Studies made by city or county planning commission
	Studies made by utility research departments
	Interviews with building inspector
4. Transportation (bus and streetcar lines, automobile highways)	Interviews with city or county engineer
5. Areas of land use (industrial, commercial, residential)	Data gathered by real estate board
6. Residential development (increasing or decreasing number of residences, improvement or deterioration of housing, availability or unavailability of land for residential development, topography and drainage, adequacy or inadequacy of public utilities)	
7. Community outlook (probability of conditions growing more or less favorable for the church as conditioned by physical characteristics)	

POPULATION FACTS AND FIGURES

Essential Information Needed

How many people live within the boundaries of the church community? How many should be added for the church's "marginal community"? What percentage of the total are (1) native white stock, (2) foreign-born or children of foreign-born, (3) Negro, (4) Asiatic? What proportion of the population consists of (1) children (birth to 12); (2) adolescents (13–16); (3) young people (17–24); (4) adult women; (5) adult men? Has the population been increasing or decreasing during the past decade? Do conditions indicate further increase or decrease during the next decade? What decided population shifts, if any, have occurred within the church community?

Has the ratio between native whites and other racial groups changed materially? Approximately what percentage of the population may be classified religiously as (1) Protestant, (2) Catholic, (3) Jewish, (4) unclassified, (5) unaffiliated? Are some racial groups legally segregated from other racial groups? Are there clear lines of demarcation between social groups? Are there marked divisions among industrial groups? Do population differences produce noticeable tensions? Is the population of the church community more heterogeneous than homogeneous? What problems and challenges do population facts and figures present to the church?

SURVEY SCHEDULE AND RESOURCES

Survey items	Survey resources
1. Population of county	United States census
2. Population of city, town, or community area	Social surveys
	Population statistics from city hall and
3. Population of church community	county courthouse
4. Percentage of population belonging to several racial groups	Public school enrolment
	School surveys
5. Percentage of population in each of several age groups	Church membership lists
	Interviews with city and county officials
6. Graph showing population variations within past decade	
	Analysis of religious census
7. Map showing population shifts within past decade	Interviews with leaders of racial groups
8. Percentage of population in each of the major religious bodies of community	Interviews with Chamber of Commerce officials
	Interviews with union labor leaders
9. Legal requirements of racial segregation	Study of population spot-maps
10. Map showing distribution of racial groups	
11. Evidences of tensions or divisions within community	

SOCIAL AND FAMILY CONDITIONS

Essential Information Needed

Is the community characterized by an attitude of neighborliness? Do families move frequently or infrequently? Do the majority of families own or rent their residences? Would family life in the community be characterized as stable or unstable? Are there areas within the community which may be thought of as "neighborhoods"? Are some of these neighborhoods isolated from others?

Has the community been disturbed by neighborhood feuds? Do racial differences create social problems? Is there high, low, or medium incidence of crime? Would juvenile delinquency be rated as high, low, medium? Are the breeding places of crime and delinquency many, few, none? Are recreation facilities to be rated as excellent, fair, poor? Does family disorganization through divorce, desertion, separation, strife, present a problem? Are church-going families in the majority or minority? What might the church do to improve social and family conditions?

SURVEY SCHEDULE AND RESOURCES

Survey items	Survey resources
1. Percentage of families who own and rent homes	Studies of population changes by decades
2. Frequency with which families move in and out of community	Studies of crime statistics
3. Records of family or community feuds	Studies of juvenile delinquency statistics
4. Records of racial disturbances	Interviews with real estate dealers
5. Records of recent criminal court cases	Information from family service organization
6. Court records of juvenile delinquency	Information from public school officials and teachers
7. Principal services required of social welfare agencies	Information from child welfare organization
8. Records of divorces, desertions, broken homes	Interviews with leaders of parent-teacher organizations
9. Comparison of wholesome with unwholesome places of amusement and recreation	Interviews with pastors, priests, rabbis
	Inquiries from representative parents
	House-to-house survey
10. Comparison of church-going with nonchurch-going families	Use of books describing and interpreting social change and the family
11. Percentage of unchurched persons in community	
12. Evidences of social concern of the churches	

ECONOMIC FACTORS

Essential Information Needed

In what principal ways do the people of the church community earn their living? Is there a wide variety of occupations, or is income derived from limited sources? What percentage of incomes is estimated to come within (1) the upper brackets, (2) middle brackets, (3) lower brackets? Is poverty an acute problem? Is there high or low incidence of unemployment? Is income for the majority stable or unstable? Is labor strongly or loosely organized? Are there frequent or occasional clashes between organized labor and management?

SURVEY SCHEDULE AND RESOURCES

Survey items	Survey resources
1. Number and variety of occupations	City and county tax offices
2. Principal industries	State and federal income bureaus
3. Analysis of income brackets	Payrolls of principal industries
4. Employment and unemployment statistics	Unemployment office
5. Dependent families or individuals and reasons for dependency	Veterans' Administration office
6. Status of organized labor	Interviews with organized labor leaders
7. Status of farmers' or producers' co-operatives	Interviews with heads of co-operatives
8. Labor-management relationships	Reports of Community Chest or similar welfare agencies
9. Vocational opportunities for youth	Interviews with newspaper manager and editor
10. Outlook of free enterprise	Study of relation of church income to members' economic level
11. Politics as help or hindrance to business and industry	Listing of economic needs which might be met or influenced by the church
12. Relation of economic level to church enterprise	
13. Opportunities of the church to promote economic welfare	
14. The church as an example of Christian business dealing	

Is the political setup conducive to economic welfare? Is considerable income derived from antisocial business—liquor, gambling, prostitution, lawlessness? Are leading professional and businessmen public-spirited? Do farmers' or producers' co-operatives operate successfully? Are vocational education and guidance provided for the youth of the community? Does the community tend to hold or to lose its most capable young people? What service might the church render in the interest of the economic welfare of the community? In general, what is the effect on the church of economic conditions in the community?

CONSTRUCTIVE AND DESTRUCTIVE FORCES

Essential Information Needed

Besides churches, what other constructive institutions and agencies are there in the community? Are public schools adequate for present needs? Are there private or church-related schools, and are they of high quality? Are the schools of the community an asset or a liability to religion? Is there a well-managed public library? Are there well-operated health clinics? Is there an effective program of public health? Are hospital facilities available for all who need them? Are there sufficient wholesome recreation facilities? Are there moral hazards created by places of amusement and commercialized evils? Is there evidence that such evils receive police protection?

Has the church an offsetting program of wholesome amusements and recreation? What might the church do to encourage the wholesome and eliminate the unwholesome agencies and influences of the community?

PRESENTING AND APPLYING THE COMMUNITY SURVEY DATA

Wise leadership in the making of a community survey will avoid ex-hausting the interests and energies of the people by undertaking too much at a given time. A community is a living, growing, changing thing, hence its study is a never-ending necessity. During a given period one aspect of the community may be studied, then another and another. Of little use will be any study, however, unless the findings are carefully analyzed, interpreted, applied.

Relevant facts and authoritative opinions should be presented and interpreted to the church or to appropriate church groups. Mere "dry statistics" will arouse little interest and provoke little action.

There are many attractive ways of presenting the results of a community survey. Significant comparisons may be made by means of graphs. Some of the facts may be presented visually, by means of the filmstrip or the motion picture. Some truths may be presented in the form of a pageant or play. Some of the findings may be made subjects of sermons, addresses, discussions. Many of the facts disclosed will call for definite and earnest prayer. Some conditions will demand immediate, direct action, where other remedies may be sought more indirectly through other agencies. Changes in the church's program may be indicated by some of the findings.

At every point the questions should be raised: What is the will of God? What comes within the province of the church? What changes are needed? How may Christian concern be aroused and expressed? How may informed public opinion be mobilized? How may the level of public welfare be lifted? How may Christ and his cause be exalted? How may souls be won and lives reclaimed? How may the community be made a better place for little children, for young people, for fathers and mothers, for men and women in all the walks of life?

SURVEY SCHEDULE AND RESOURCES

Survey items	Survey resources
1. Names and locations of churches	Survey of constructive nonchurch agencies
2. Names and locations of other constructive agencies	Printed reports of these agencies
3. Relationship of churches and constructive nonchurch agencies	Spot-map showing location of these agencies
4. Principal activities or services of nonchurch agencies	Interviews with heads of these agencies
5. List of influences or agencies inimical to child welfare	Schedule showing Sunday activities and events
6. List of Sunday commercialized events and activities	Spot-map showing location of theaters and motion picture houses
7. List of all commercialized amusements	First-hand analysis of offerings of theaters and picture shows
8. Analysis of all commercialized amusements, to determine whether wholesome, unwholesome, or borderline	Spot-map showing location of all places where alcoholic beverages are sold
9. Evaluation of reading materials on sale at newsstands	Police records showing actual results of liquor business
10. List of immoral and lawless enterprises	Spot-map showing location of gambling places and other illegal activities
11. Study of police responsibility for social evils	Interviews with police officers
12. Study of community attitudes toward social evils	Examination of newsstands for salacious literature
13. Study of church's social program	Inquiry into social-recreational program of churches
14. Study of church's opportunity and obligation in this field	Inquiry as to what church might do to provide worthy social and recreational activities

THE CHURCH SURVEY

Jesus recognized that his followers, constituting his church, must live in the society of which they are a part; yet he prayed that they might not be "of the world," identified with its purposes and partaking of its spirit.

Paul pleaded with those to whom he wrote at Rome that they "be not fashioned according to this world," but that they be transformed by the renewing of their mind, thus making proof of the will of God (Romans 12:2).

It is always a question as to which will change the other more, the community or the church. The community inevitably affects the church. The problem is how to prevent the church from being conformed to the world-spirit of the community while still being in many ways identified with it. The ever-present challenge is that the church change the community into a society that is increasingly Christian and in widening circles to bring about such change from its center to the circumference of the world.

The members of the church may know the community better than they know the church. They probably know community assets and liabilities better than they know the church's assets and liabilities. Even the minister and the church leaders may have only general ideas as to strength and weakness of the church in its attack on unbelief, indifference, unenlistment, unenlightenment, injustice, immorality. Taking the facts concerning the church for granted, pastor and people may never have instituted systematic inquiry into origins, history, trends, constituency, prospects, leadership, program, activities, building, equipment, finances, opportunities, difficulties, and the like.

Such an analysis may be made best by means of the church survey. As the community can be understood and served more intelligently in the light of the facts concerning its life, so a church can function more fruitfully when it has a clear understanding of the circumstances and conditions according to which it serves and is served. A pastor may learn what he needs to know about his church by the trial and error method, but obviously this is a wasteful procedure. The leaders of the church may understand it as a whole, but the chances are that their picture of the church will be fragmentary, each viewing the church from his or her perspective of special interest and responsibility. Rarely will the members of a church see it as a unitary entity, nor will they comprehend it in its relationships. The detailed study of a church in all its workings is a continuous and fascinating project. Every year should bring some new aspect up for study, as a result of which the church's program will be kept ever fresh and new.

ADMINISTRATIVE EFFICIENCY

Essential Information Needed

Compared with a well-managed business institution, would the church's administration rate high, medium, low? Does the pastor look upon himself as the chief administrative officer of the church? Is he provided with enough competent office help? Is the church office well-equipped? Do his aides, staff, deacons, and church officers take their administrative responsibilities seriously? Is there careful division of labor? Does each head of department fully understand his or her duties? Are needed training and supervision given to all church workers? Are responsible leaders and workers chosen with sufficient care? Are meetings and activities properly routinized?

Is the membership file up-to-date and accurate? Is there an adequate system for financial accounting? Are records of the church organizations (Sunday school, Training Union, Woman's Missionary Union, Brotherhood, etc.) kept accurately and used faithfully? What improvements are needed in order to lift the level of the church's administrative efficiency?

SURVEY SCHEDULE AND RESOURCES

Survey items	Survey resources
1. Attitude of pastor toward administrative efficiency	Statement of administrative ideals by pastor
2. Attitude of lay leadership toward administrative efficiency	Conferences with deacons and church officers
3. Office assistance needed	Inventory of church office equipment
4. Office equipment needed	Interviews with heads of several departments
5. Division of labor and responsibility	
6. Training and supervision of all church workers	Examination of several systems of records
7. Methods of selection of leaders and workers	Comparison of present systems with recommended standard systems
8. Kind and adequacy of recording systems (membership, financial, Sunday school, Training Union, Music Ministry, etc.)	Rating of present officers and workers
	Discussion of better ways of securing officers, teachers, leaders, etc.
9. Analysis of administrative improvements	Services of experienced administrator to discover and recommend needed changes

MEMBERSHIP AND CONSTITUENCY

Essential Information Needed

How many names are on the church roll? How many of these are unaccounted for? How many rarely if ever attend? How many constitute the enlisted, active, dependable membership? What could be done to make the reported membership correspond more nearly with the actual membership? What is the proportion of girls and women to boys and men on the church roll? Is the church predominantly male or female in attendance and leadership? What percentage of the membership is represented by the several age and sex groups? Is any group notably unreached or neglected?

What estimated number of nonmembers belong to member families? What are the unreached "possibilities" of the church? How are these unreached persons divided as between unaffiliated and unsaved? What proportion of nonmembers attend (1) the worship services, (2) the Sunday school? What is being done (1) to enlist inactive church members, (2) to reach unaffiliated church members, (3) to win the unsaved?

SURVEY SCHEDULE AND RESOURCES

Survey items	Survey resources
1. Total number of members on roll	Total names and addresses in membership file
2. Total number unaccounted for	
3. Total number inactive	List of members unaccounted for
4. Number males by age groups (under 12, 13–16, 17–24, 25–40, above 40)	List of inactive members
	Analysis of membership according to age and sex groupings
5. Number females by age groups (under 12, 13–16, 17–24, 25–40, above 40)	Preaching attendance records
	Prayer meeting attendance records
	Attendance records of Sunday school, Training Union, Woman's Missionary Union, Brotherhood
6. Proportion of males to females	
7. Age or sex group least reached	
8. Sources of new members (unaffiliated and unsaved)	Interviews with pastor and heads of organizations
9. Plans for reaching the unreached	Interviews with church clerk and church secretary
10. Comparative attendance on various services and organizations	Spot-map indicating by colored pins (1) members, (2) unaffiliated (3) nonmember attendants
	Census returns and visitors' cards
	Names of newcomers obtained from utilities and other sources

EMPLOYED AND VOLUNTEER LEADERSHIP

Essential Information Needed

What is the church's budget for "salaries"? What proportion of the total budget is this item? How was amount of pastor's salary determined? Is his salary adequate to the needs of himself and family? Is the matter of pastor's salary regularly reviewed with a view to necessary adjustments? What other persons receive compensation from the church for services? Are these services paid for on a level with similar services elsewhere? Does the church need more or fewer paid workers? If increased staff is needed, what stands in the way? If some paid services are unsatisfactory, what should be done about it?

How are volunteer leaders and workers secured? Are important officers (superintendents, directors, teachers, leaders, sponsors, etc.) elected or appointed? In what areas of the church's life is lay leadership strongest? weakest? How might the level of lay leadership and service be lifted? How might the church's concern be increased for more and better leaders and workers? From what sources would they best be obtained?

SURVEY SCHEDULE AND RESOURCES

Survey items	Survey resources
1. Breakdown of church budget under "salaries" item	Church budget
	Interview with budget committee
2. Tactful inquiry as to adequacy of pastor's salary	Interview with pastor
	Interviews with other paid workers
3. Study of other paid workers to evaluate suitability and efficiency	Job analysis of all church employees
	Survey of needs and opportunities requiring paid workers
4. Inquiry to determine if salary levels are in line with compensation for similar services	Analyzed lists of all volunteer leaders and workers
	Interviews with key leaders and workers
5. Study of needs of church for more or fewer paid workers	Study of records of several departments
6. Study of church's plan to secure volunteer leaders and workers	Canvass of church rolls to discover potential leaders and workers
7. Study of procedures by which higher level of leadership and workmanship might be obtained and maintained	

ORGANIZATIONS AND COMMITTEES

Essential Information Needed

Is the church organization-minded? Does it appear to be overorganized, underorganized, or well-organized? Could the church get along as well without one or more of the organizations? Does there seem to be too much competition of the organizations with one another? Do any of the organizations lack vital relation to the church? Does any organization give evidence of being a liability to the church? In what specific ways is each organization an asset to the church? Should any new organization be added?

Has each organization (Sunday school, Training Union, Woman's Missionary Union, Brotherhood) its full quota of departments or junior organizations or committees? Has each organization or unit the required officers and leaders? Measured by the several standards, what are the strong and the weak points of each organization? Does the church council operate successfully to correlate and co-ordinate the several organizations? What improvements are most obviously needed in order to secure maximum functioning of each organization?

SURVEY SCHEDULE AND RESOURCES

Survey items	Survey resources
1. Conspectus of all church organizations, showing relationships to one another and to church as a whole	List of all church organizations
	Names of leaders and workers of all organizations
2. Detailed analysis of each of the organizations as to functions and objectives	Membership rolls of all organizations
	Records of attendance of all organizations
3. Detailed analysis of each organization as to enrolment and average attendance	Interviews with heads of all organizations
4. Detailed analysis of each organization as to leaders and workers	Studies of achievement records of all organizations
5. Analysis of enlargement possibilities of each organization	Evidences of loyalty of organizations to church as a whole
6. Analysis of building and equipment	The several organizational standards
7. Points of strength and weakness disclosed by checking each organization against its appropriate standard or standards	Interviews with deacons
	Observation of functioning of church council
8. Immediate improvements thus indicated	
9. Long range improvements to be ultimately provided	

BUILDING AND EQUIPMENT

Essential Information Needed

Is the building well located? Is it in good repair? Is it attractive to passers-by? Is there a sign giving the church's name? Has it an attractive outdoor bulletin board? Is the sanctuary large enough? Is the interior attractively decorated, well lighted and ventilated, comfortably heated or cooled, with chancel and pews well arranged? Is there adequate provision for fully graded teaching and training services? Is there adequate provision for social, fellowship, recreational, and other activities? Are there ample administrative facilities? Is there a well-equipped nursery? Is there provision for library, audio-visual aids, music, graded worship? Has the church enough property for expansion? Is the property well cared for? What changes, if any, should be made immediately in building and equipment? What long-range program of improvement should be projected?

SURVEY SCHEDULE AND RESOURCES

Survey items	Survey resources
1. Study of church locale—environment, accessibility, location assets and liabilities	Pictures of building from several angles
2. Checkup on needed repairs	Pastor's opinion of adequacy or inadequacy of sanctuary
3. Detailed study of adequacy and attractiveness of sanctuary	Opinion poll of selected members as to needed changes in sanctuary
4. Detailed study of educational provisions	Comparison of sanctuary with other places of worship
5. Detailed study of building and equipment needs for maximum usefulness socially and culturally	Services of competent architect, decorator, lighting and ventilation experts to consider desirable changes
6. Listing of immediate building and equipment	Floor plans showing present educational and other provisions
7. Forecasting of long-range needs	Building and equipment score card
8. Plans proposed for meeting present and future needs	Interview with trustees and church properties committee
9. Fire insurance underwriter's check of building for fire hazards	Blueprints and specifications of proposed changes
	Conferences as to how changes may be financed

BUSINESS AND FINANCE

Essential Information Needed

Is the church treasurer bonded? Is the credit of the church rated high, medium, low? If the church has a debt, how was it contracted? What is the plan of liquidation? Is it being paid off as rapidly as practicable? Does the church operate on the budget plan? Does the budget represent the ability and devotion of the membership? Is the Christian doctrine of stewardship-tithing preached and practiced? How nearly is the ideal of every-member giving attained? How is every-member support of the church sought? What has been the total of gifts for all causes each year for the past ten years? What division of receipts has been made during the decade between local expenses and missionary and benevolent causes?

What is the record of per capita giving (total divided by members) during the decade? What percentage of resident members give (1) the tithe or above, (2) regularly but less than the tithe, (3) irregularly, (4) nothing of record? What proportion of total gifts come through (1) weekly offering envelopes, (2) monthly offering envelopes, (3) semi-annual or annual payments, (4) occasional gifts? Has the church any income from other sources than direct gifts? How might the dependable income of the church be increased? How might its gifts to missionary and benevolent objects be increased?

SURVEY SCHEDULE AND RESOURCES

Survey items	Survey resources
1. The church's bank connection	Bank records
2. Bank balances over a period of years	Interview with banker
3. Deficits, if any—why incurred and how met	History of church's debt-making and debt-paying
4. History of indebtedness and its liquidation	Treasurer's books
	Pastor's stewardship sermons
5. Present indebtedness and plan of liquidation	Educational promotion of steward-ship-tithing
6. Plan of stressing stewardship-tithing	Analysis of budget
	Analysis of gifts ($1 or less per week, $1–$2, $2–$3, $3–$4, $4–$5, $5–$10, etc.)
7. The budget—how and by whom determined	
8. Method of getting budget sub-scribed	Reports to denomination (associa-tional letter, etc.)
9. Analysis of giving—number of givers, categories of gifts, per capita average, sources of fi-nancial support	Interview with treasurer and financial secretary
	Comparison of financial record with other churches
	Interview with finance committee
10. Unrealized potentialities of church support	Inquiries directed to representative members
11. Strength and weakness of present financial plan	Materials on "Forward Program of Church Finance"
12. Possibilities of placing church fi-nances on better basis	

SURVEY SCHEDULE AND RESOURCES

Survey items	Survey resources
1. Community agencies and influences opposed to the church	Reference to community survey
2. Unfortunate incidents in the church's history	Interviews with discreet older members
3. Evidences of factionalism now in the church	Comparison of church attendance with attendance on places of worldly amusements
4. Evidences of lack of devotion on the part of some members	Comparison of time given to church work with time devoted to secular enterprises
5. Indications of indefiniteness of objectives	Comparison of church gifts with luxury spending
6. Present preaching attendance and goal for next year	Comparison of definiteness of business goals with indefiniteness of church goals
7. Present prayer meeting attendance and goal for next year	Enrolment and attendance records of morning and evening preaching services, prayer meeting, Sunday
8. Present Sunday school attendance and goal for next year	school, Training Union, Woman's Missionary Union, Brotherhood, as
9. Present Training Union attendance and goal for next year	basis of projected goals for each during the year ahead
10. Present W. M. U. attendance (all organizations) and goal for next year	Statistical records of other phases of the church life and work as basis for projected goals for next year
11. Present Brotherhood, active membership, and goal for next year	Conferences with pastor, deacons, church council, and representative
12. Total gifts, local expenses, and goal for next year	members as to how obstacles may be overcome and suggested goals
13. Total gifts, Cooperative Program, etc., and goal for next year	attained
14. Vacation Bible school attendance and goal for next year	
15. Total additions to the church and goal for next year	
16. Study course awards and goal for next year	
17. Items of personal service and goal for next year	
18. Study of ways and means to attain these goals	

OBSTACLES AND OBJECTIVES

Essential Information Needed

What difficulties inside the church impede its progress? What external enemies threaten its welfare or existence? Has the church been hindered by too short pastorates? Has the church been set back by unfortunate leadership? Has the church been troubled by divisions or factions? Have there been at times lack of missionary and evangelistic devotion and fruitage? Compared with present attendance, what should be set as some of the church's major goals? How would these goals best be determined? How could they be so presented to the church as to become functional? What elements would have to be present if obstacles were overcome and objectives achieved?

CHANGES INDICATED BY CHURCH SURVEY DATA

Uppermost questions raised by the survey are the following: What difference should it make? What is revealed as right, quite satisfactory as matters now stand, therefore needing no change? What is revealed as fairly satisfactory, needing no radical change but requiring some improvement? What is revealed as definitely wrong, clearly unsatisfactory, calling for radical change? On the basis of these answers, the church's strategy would be to capitalize on its strong points, strengthen its weak points, and seek intelligently to revolutionize its points of failure.

In all of this, the congregation should be fully informed and led rather than driven to accept change. The most eloquent argument for change is not made in persuasive words but in the quiet facing of indisputable facts. Herein lies one of the chief values of the church survey: it replaces argument with fact, it dispels prejudice by knowledge, it supersedes chance with certainty. Should it be objected that this process is not sufficiently spiritual, the reply is found in the example of constructive Christian leaders, the practice of Jesus and the apostles, and the nature of God, all characterized by orderliness and law.

A Church and Its Pastor

A more signal mark of God's approval rarely comes to a church than when one of its number is called to full-time Christian service. The Old Testament abounds with examples of God's call to men—and occasionally to a woman—to special service. The prophets were forth-tellers, spokesmen for God. Jesus chose a select group of men whom he "ordained" or "appointed" to be his special representatives. When Paul and Barnabas ordained or appointed for the churches elders or pastors (Acts 14:23), the Greek word used signifies "to elect by stretching out the hand," thus indicating that ordination was a function of the local congregation.

ORDINATION TO THE GOSPEL MINISTRY

Ordination, in the New Testament view, confers no status, no ecclesiastical power, no special rights of office not possessed by any other devout and trusted member of a church by its authorization. Ordination is simply recognition and confirmation by a church of one of its member's evident call of God to the gospel ministry. It further represents the judgment of competent brethren of the candidate's fitness to undertake the duties of the Christian ministry, a partnership with him in his future ministry, and a commendation of him to the sisterhood of churches. Ordination meets certain legal requirements in the performance of wedding ceremonies, in service as chaplain, and the like.

Since ordination involves other churches and the denomination as a whole, it places upon the ordaining church heavy obligation not to lay hands lightly on any man. Request for ordination having come from one of its members, the church by vote should proceed to call an examining council, usually made up of ordained men from its own ranks and from neighboring churches. Prayerful and sympathetic but searching inquiry should be made into the candidate's experience of grace, the soundness of his conversion, the certainty of his call, the adequacy of his preparation, the quality of his character, the vitality of his faith, the worthiness of his concept of his calling, the steadfastness of his loyalty to the Christian body whose representative he becomes, the determination which he discloses as to his future life of sacrificial devotion and continuous advancement toward the ideal of "a good minister of Jesus Christ." In most cases, "licensure," the liberating of the candidate to exercise his spiritual gifts, should have preceded ordination. As a rule, ordination should not take place until a man is called to a definite field of labor. There should ordinarily be a sufficient lapse of time between examination and ordination that no embarrassment will be felt should the candidate's request be denied or postponed.

The ordination service usually takes the following form:

1. An ordination sermon.

2. A charge to the candidate like that of Paul to Timothy in 2 Timothy 4:1–5. This may be accompanied by a charge to the church which he is to serve in case representatives of that church are present. It may be closed very fittingly by presentation of a Bible as a memorial of the occasion.

3. An ordaining prayer. Ministers, deacons, and others appointed by the church to represent it encircle the candidate in view of the congregation, the presiding officer offers an explanation concerning the laying on of hands which is to follow, as to its symbolic nature and reliance upon the Holy Spirit solely to give it meaning. The remaining parts of the service may then be allowed to follow this prayer without further announcement.

4. Laying on of hands according to the custom mentioned in 1 Timothy 4:14.

5. Extension of the hand of fellowship by the congregation. If circumstances are not propitious for the coming of the whole congregation, invitation may be extended to those who will to do so for special reasons, either at this time or after the benediction.

6. Benediction. It is appropriate for the church to ask the newly ordained minister to pronounce this benediction.

ESTABLISHING RIGHT RELATIONSHIPS

"And he gave some to be . . . pastors." Thus Paul crowns the list of gifts which Christ gave to men when he ascended on high. The office of *pastor* has long been considered by Christians as "the highest office." Deeply imbedded in Christian belief and tradition is the conviction that the pastor or minister is first called of God and then received by the people. In democratic church bodies the pastor is elected or approved by the local congregation. In any event, his usefulness is largely conditioned by his acceptableness to the church's membership.

It is of great importance that right relationships be established and maintained between pastor and people. The progress of a church will be gravely retarded if the minister is a misfit, if he develops wrong attitudes toward the church or the church toward him, if conditions are such as to make his ministry unfruitful, or if he moves on before he has had time to achieve worth-while results. Almost without exception churches that have consistently grown and prospered have maintained relatively long pastorates.

At scarcely any point in its history does a church need guidance more than when it selects a pastor; and the choosing and changing of fields is a major crisis in the life of the minister and his family. Always there are two elements in the situation—the divine and the human. Neither can be ignored without the risk of disaster. First of all, God's will should be sought. But God does not ordinarily reveal his will miraculously. He calls on a church to exercise its corporate wisdom as it interprets facts and circumstances relating to the man whom it calls to be its leader; and likewise God through his Holy Spirit would make known to his minister the divine guidance needed in considering a call through faithful and prayerful study of the human elements involved. Similarly, pastor and church should be divinely led through interpretation of circumstances in maintaining happy relationships in the eventual termination of these relations.

THE PASTOR-CHURCH RELATIONSHIP

Few human relationships are more intimate and sacred than that of pastor and people. If this relationship is not established on a sound and enduring basis at the beginning, many difficulties may ensue. Some pastors and many church members are not clear concerning the ties that bind them together. There are certain questions which pastor, deacons, and representative church leaders and members might well be called upon to discuss occasionally, even when there is no immediate necessity for considering the matter, to the end that misconceptions may clear up and right ideas prevail. For instance:

By what titles are Christian ministers properly known? What is the significance of the title "Reverend," and when is it properly and improperly used? What are the chief duties of the pastor or minister? How does one become a minister-pastor? What are his most important qualifications? What are some of his rights and privileges? What has the individual church member the right to expect of him? What constitutes success or failure for the minister? What may he properly expect of the church and individual members of the church? Why do many ministers move quite often? Are relatively long pastorates desirable, and, if so, how may they be made possible? What is expected of the pastor's wife? of the pastor's family? How is the pastor called from one church to another? What steps should a church take when it becomes pastorless? Why should the office of pastor be held in highest regard?

HOW A CHURCH "CALLS" A PASTOR

In a democracy the leader should be the choice of the majority of the members. In a church-democracy the expression of choice should be based on more than mere human considerations. Back of the vote of the church should be the discovered will of God. The assumption may well be made that the Holy Spirit has in mind the right man for the spiritual leadership of every true church. Yet the Holy Spirit's guidance must be found and followed by fallible human beings who are not always sensitive to his leading. The divine will must therefore be made known through circumstances and instrumentalities that are humanly recognizable. The calling of a pastor by a church will involve, therefore, consideration of such questions as these:

Has prayer for guidance been sincerely made? Is the church willing to be led of the Holy Spirit in its choice? Has prayerful selection been made of a dependable committee to represent the congregation in their search for the right man? Has this committee first considered the qualifications of the man best suited to the needs of the field? Have they renounced all selfish motives? Have they determined to have under consideration only one man at a time? Have they sought counsel from dependable Christian leaders living elsewhere? Have they listened thoughtfully to suggestions within the membership? Have they narrowed the list of possibilities down to a few worthy and desirable men? Have they studied the previous records of these men? Have they been attracted to one man toward whom they feel divinely led? Have they canvassed properly his availability and suitability? Have they taken into account their moral responsibility to the church of which he is at present pastor? Have they had personal contact with him, preferably on his own field? Are they ready now to open correspondence with him, perhaps inviting him to the church for conference and acquaintance with the people, yet avoiding all appearance of making him a "candidate"? Unless hindrances develop, would they be willing to recommend his call by the church?

ETHICAL PRINCIPLES OF THE RELATIONSHIP

Stated in business language, the pastor becomes the employee of the church; in political language, he becomes the elected servant of the people. Even in business and politics there are ethical principles involved in the relation of employer to employee, of the citizen to the officeholder. It would ordinarily be assumed that the relation between the church and its pastor would be on the highest ethical plane, yet this is not always true. Too often there is strange disregard for elementary principles of right and wrong in the dealings of a church with its minister. This ethical carelessness, which may become downright cruelty and injustice, might be avoided by the asking and answering of such questions as the following:

Have the needs of the pastor been carefully considered? Does the support proposed by the church adequately meet these needs? Is it fair to require the pastor to pay his moving expenses? Has provision been made for office expense and the upkeep of the automobile used by the pastor in his service of the church? If a home must be rented, has rent allowance been added to the salary? If a home is furnished by the church, will its upkeep be the responsibility of the church? Will wholehearted support be given to the pastor, or does he come to a divided church? Will the pastor be regarded as a "hired man" or as a spiritual leader? Will deacons and other officers take their share of the work of the church, or will they unload on the pastor burdens too great for him to bear? Will he be protected from unjust criticism? Will the members be as faithful in their attendance on the pastor's preaching as they expect him to be faithful in preparation and delivery of his sermons?

Continuing this self-examination, the questions may be raised: Is the church sincerely committed to follow the pastor's leadership as he follows Christ? Will the pastor be given a sense of security so that he may project a long-range program, or is he subject to an "annual call"? In the event that dissatisfaction arises from any quarter, will the pastor be given sympathy and help to overcome the difficulty? Should the time come for the severing of the relationship, will the pastor be dealt with on the high plane of his holy office, rather than as an unsatisfactory employee to be discharged?

Has due consideration been given, in the proposed call of the pastor, to the interests and welfare of the church from which he is being called? Should a church ruthlessly seek to take away the pastor of a sister church? Should a church ever place a minister in the position of being a "candidate" for the office, or in competition with one or more fellow ministers? Is it ethical ever to have more than one man at a time under consideration? Should there be any concealment of facts, pleasant or unpleasant, from the pastor being sought?

DETERMINING THE PASTOR'S SUITABILITY

Common sense would indicate that not every minister is equally suitable for every situation. A man may succeed in one field, yet fail in others. The demands made by churches vary greatly. Ministers vary just as greatly in preparation, previous experience, and personality. It is not enough to say that the call of a church is the call of God. God's will in the matter may not have been sufficiently sought and found. The Holy Spirit does not ordinarily guide a church to the right pastor through a supernatural disclosure. More often divine guidance is given through the available channels of prayer, investigation, conference and discussion, reasoning, conclusions based on sound judgment, confirmation by vote of a praying people.

When a committee of a church sets about to find a suitable pastor, they will, of course, be called upon to consider a number of men. The impression made by a "candidate" who preaches a "trial sermon" is quite likely misleading. The visit of the prospective pastor should be the climax of inquiry and correspondence, culminating in face-to-face conference leading to a satisfying decision.

The minister's preaching ability is highly important, but this is just one of the factors in a successful ministry. As well have him make a round of "trial" calls, or conduct a "trial funeral," or perform a "trial wedding ceremony," or hold a "trial revival meeting" as to base judgment as to his fitness for the pastorate on the "trial sermon!" Some of the important matters concerning the pastor under consideration might thus be shaped by the committee:

Were you reared in a rural or urban environment? Was yours a Christian home? At what age were you converted? When did you yield to the call to the ministry? What educational preparation have you had? What experience have you had? What length of time have you served in each pastorate? In each case what has been your principal reason for moving? Do you think that your best work can be done in a relatively short or a relatively long pastorate?

What do you consider, in the order of their importance, your chief duties as minister? Under normal conditions, how would you divide your time between your duties as preacher and your duties as pastor? Have you a fairly adequate library? Do you seek to make thorough and consistent preparation of sermons and addresses? What is your policy as regards pastoral visitation? Have you given attention to the art of counseling those who are in trouble? What is your policy in performing wedding ceremonies? Do you feel yourself well equipped to deal with the sick and suffering? What are your convictions and policy concerning evangelism? How often would you like to be away in evangelistic meetings elsewhere? To what extent do you promote and practice personal soul-winning? What is your position concerning missions?

What leadership would you expect to give to the organizations of the church—Sunday school, Training Union, Woman's Missionary Union, Brotherhood, etc.? Do you feel that you have an adequate knowledge of these organizations, their functions and relationships? What would be your purpose concerning the enlistment of inactive church members? Are you prepared to give loyal support to the denominational program? Do you feel that you are in line doctrinally with the basic beliefs of Baptists? Should you find yourself out of line with these beliefs and committed to a doctrinal position contrary to that of the church, what would you do? In the event of a division in the church, what would be your general attitude so far as you can forecast it?

CONSUMMATING THE CALL

The committee, having made careful and prayerful inquiry concerning the prospective pastor and having been reasonably convinced of his suitability, may then extend invitation to him to consider the possibility of a call. The minister in turn has both the right and the duty to make certain inquiries concerning the church. This may be done by examination of the church's record as revealed in minutes of the association, church bulletins, etc. The inquiry may be pursued by correspondence and eventually in personal conference. Here are some of the questions which the minister may well raise:

Why has the church turned to him as prospective pastor? Has careful inquiry been made by the church as to his suitability? What occasioned the resignation of the former pastor? How many pastors has the church had during a given period, say twenty-five years? If there has been a rapid succession, how account for it? Does the church favor short or long pastorates?

What are significant facts about the church—its history, its location, its building and equipment, its record of growth in membership, its organizations and their enrolment and attendance, average attendance on the preaching service, attendance on the midweek prayer service, financial record over a period of years, division of budget between local expenditures and Cooperative Program, evidences of missionary-mindedness? What are the prospects of the church for growth, enlargement of building and equipment, evangelistic opportunity, increased giving, increased attendance, increased missionary activity?

Is the church harmonious or divided? If there have been divisions, are they in process of being healed? Has the church reasonably dependable and adequate lay leadership? Will it respond to a vigorous program of leadership training? As indicated by the past, does the church give its pastor loyal support? What are the chief hindrances to success? What hardships will the pastor be called upon to share with his people? What would be most liable to bring about his relative failure? Will the salary be sufficient to prevent undue worry and the misfortune of debt? Will the church furnish a residence, or must it be rented? What provision is there for the pastor's necessary expenses of the work—office expenses, office help, stationery and stamps, upkeep of automobile, etc.?

Will there be unusual demands made on the pastor? May he count on co-operation and assistance from deacons, officers, leaders? Will he be sent to meetings of associations and conventions? Will he be given annual vacation, and on what terms? Does the church participate in the Relief and Annuity Retirement plan? In the event of severance of relationship, whether on initiative of church or pastor, what would be the normal procedure?

Of course the minister would not condition his acceptance of the call on a favorable reply to all these questions. Many replies might be unfavorable, yet the call appeal to the minister as being of the Lord. The important matter is *not* that he be secure, well paid, with success and happiness assured. It is highly important, however, that he know in advance the circumstances of his ministry and thus be prepared to make whatever adjustments are necessary in order to serve as "a good minister of Jesus Christ."

After careful and prayerful study of all the factors involved, the prospective pastor may indicate his willingness to consider the call. The church, duly called together for the purpose, will hear recommendation of the committee, upon which it will act favorably or unfavorably. If favorably, the call of the church will be formally extended in a letter covering major items which have been agreed upon in previous correspondence and conference. Led of God to make reply, the minister may accept or reject the call. If it is accepted, he in turn will write the church, specifying in his letter those matters which are of uppermost concern in the forming of this new relationship.

INSTALLING THE MINISTER

The coming of the new minister should mark an epoch in the life of the church. A propitious beginning is of much value. Inauguration ceremonies lend dignity to the taking of office by officials of state and society. The President of the United States, the governor of a state, the mayor of a city, the president of an educational institution, the newly-elected head of a corporation are thought worthy of a service of installation. Should not the pastor of a church be given the benefit of this good beginning? Frequently neighboring churches will dismiss their services in order to participate in the inaugural of a new pastor, thus giving him opportunity for wider acquaintance immediately.

Call to Worship: "I myself will be the shepherd of my sheep, and I will cause them to lie down, saith the Lord Jehovah. I will seek that which was lost, and will bring back that which was driven away, and will bind up that which was broken, and will strengthen that which was sick; but the fat and the strong I will destroy; I will feed them in justice" (Ezekiel 34:15-16 ASV).

Doxology. Invocation. Gloria
Hymn: "Saviour, Like a Shepherd Lead Us"
Scripture Reading: 1 Timothy 6:11-21
Prayer and Offertory
Introduction of pastor to the church, by senior deacon or other appointed leader
Pledges of people and pastor received and given: (Congregation standing)

Leader: Having called this man of God to be your minister, do you now solemnly pledge to him your prayerful interest, your sympathetic understanding, your faithful support?

Congregation: We do.

Leader: Do you promise to hear attentively his preaching of the Word, to participate reverently in the services of worship, to share with him in the responsibilities of teaching and learning, to assume your proportionate part of the church's benevolent ministries, to receive him into your hearts and homes, to counsel with him concerning the welfare of the church and the winning of souls, to encourage him in his stand for the right, to forgive him when he makes mistakes, and to follow his leadership as he follows Christ?

Congregation: We do.

Leader: Let us together reaffirm our high resolution and devotion. To the preaching of the good tidings of salvation:

People: We consecrate our gifts.

Leader: To the teaching of Jesus' way of life:

People: We consecrate our time.

Leader: To the healing of broken bodies and the soothing of troubled minds:

People: We consecrate our service.

Leader: To the leading of children and youth to the knowledge of the love of Christ:

People: We consecrate our talents.

Leader: To the caring of helpless age and the relief of all who look to us for help:

People: We consecrate our strength.

Leader: To the evangelization of the community and the worldwide extension of the kingdom of God:

People: We consecrate our wealth, our efforts, and our lives.

Leader (addressing the pastor, who stands beside him): Having been called to be the pastor of this church, do you take this people to be your people, this field of labor to be your field, without reservation of mind or heart?

Pastor: I do.

Leader: Do you promise to give yourself faithfully to the ministry of the Word and to prayer, to be the good shepherd of this flock of God, to minister to the needs of all alike, to be the friend of all who will permit you, to seek the salvation of souls and the nurture of the saved, to put the service of Christ and his kingdom above all else, if wronged to forgive as you expect to be forgiven, to seek always to keep yourself mentally alert and physically fit, as much as in you lies to be at peace with all men, and to lead this church in the ways of Christ as the Holy Spirit may give you wisdom and strength?

Pastor: I do.

Leader: May you now enter with us into these purposes and resolutions. For the high privilege of being followers of Christ and co-workers with his people:

Pastor: I give thee thanks, O God, and ask thy favor upon us.

Leader: For the eternal truth of God's Word, which you are called upon to interpret in our daily lives:

Pastor: I give thee thanks, O God, and pray that it may ever be a lamp unto our feet, a light unto our path.

Leader: For the high visions and noble ideals which we gain through our comradeship and which make life fruitfully happy:

Pastor: I offer grateful praise, O Lord, and pray that the vision may never dim nor the ideals lose their power to inspire and strengthen us.

Leader: For the church of Christ which is our spiritual home on earth, and which prepares us for the Church triumphant:

Pastor: I bless thy name, O God, and pray that we may be diligent to uphold her honor and advance her ministry.

Leader: For the acceptance of our lives in service, in the knowledge that we can do all things through Him who strengthens us:

Pastor: I give thee thanks, O God, and pray that we may be kept teachable by thy Spirit, unto the day of our promotion into the eternal King-

THE MINISTER'S SELF-RATING AS ADMINISTRATOR [1]

Items for evaluation	Yes	No	To some extent	Don't know
1. Possesses requisite dignity of bearing				
2. Accepts good suggestions from others				
3. Has excellent physical endurance				
4. Maintains superior self-command under stress				
5. Seeks competent advice when conditions warrant				
6. Accepts full responsibility for his own work				
7. Speaks and acts with assurance				
8. Can plan and execute work on his own initiative				
9. Adapts himself easily and quickly to changes in conditions of his work				
10. Uses calm judgment in the performance of his duties				
11. Has the confidence and respect of his associates				
12. Possesses a sense of humor				
13. Gives clear and concise instructions to aides				
14. Appearance creates a distinctly favorable impression				
15. Inspires and maintains a high degree of morale under trying conditions				
16. Realizes the value of making needful concessions				
17. Grasps the essentials of a situation quickly				
18. Opinions are logical and well considered				
19. Subordinates personal interests to demands of his office				
20. Remains level-headed under pressure				
21. Accurate in reporting facts about a situation				
22. Can make quick and firm decision when necessary				
23. Anticipates problems that are his responsibility				
24. Is logical in presenting his ideas				
25. Takes denials of his requests with good grace				
26. Is aware of the limits of his authority				
27. Inspires confidence in the soundness of his judgment				
28. Gives a situation sufficient consideration before acting				
29. Accepts adverse decisions without quibbling				

[1] Adapted from Rating Scale for Candidates for Officer Training.

Items for evaluation	Yes	No	To some extent	Don't know
30. Shows persistent energy on the job				
31. Finishes work he begins				
32. Has ability to translate knowledge into actual execution				
33. Carries a hard job through in spite of changes in plans				
34. Exhibits exceptional ability to direct others				
35. Leads people to co-operate with him and with one another				
36. Personal habits are above reproach				

dom of thy love and light, where we shall dwell with thee in the land of perfect day.

Prayer led by the pastor.

Reception of pastor and family into the church.

The hand of fellowship extended by members of the congregation and visitors, in pledge of loyalty and welcome.

Dismissal by the leader.

A Church and Its Officers and Staff

By its very nature, a church requires leadership beyond that of its pastor. Indeed, the New Testament makes no sharp distinction between clerical and lay leadership. The difference is largely one of degree rather than of kind.

The selection of its lay leadership is one of the gravest responsibilities of a church. It is imperative that the right persons in the right places should be given training for their duties. The work of officers and committees should be clearly defined. Mistakes in the selection and election of its lay leadership may bring tragic results in the life of a church. A consistent policy of discovery, election, and training of its general officers, the officers and teachers and leaders of its several organizations, and the personnel of its committees will go far toward avoiding mistakes and guaranteeing the future.

In mapping a policy concerning its inner circle leadership, and in implementing this policy practically, a church needs to provide guidance somewhat as follows in (1) establishing the New Testament ideal of leadership; (2) defining the church officers needed; (3) determining the qualifications of church officers and leaders; (4) discovering and selecting the right persons; (5) inducting into office those selected; (6) continuing certain officers for a term of service; (7) retiring officers from active service; (8) the relation of officers to pastor and staff; (9) the relation of officers to the congregation and the denomination.

THE NEW TESTAMENT CONCEPT OF OFFICE-BEARING

The New Testament knows nothing of "orders of the ministry." This is all the more striking in view of the world into which Jesus came, with its complex priestcraft both in Judaism and in paganism. Jesus swept away the whole involved system of lawyers, rabbis, scribes, and priests, and instead called about him a band of disciples wholly equal in status and privilege. These men came from the ranks of working men and were not scholars or professional religionists. Mark records that the twelve were appointed "that they might be with him, and that he might send them forth to preach, and to have authority to cast out demons" (Mark 3:14–15 ASV). Later Jesus "appointed seventy others, and sent them two by two before his face into every city and place, whither he himself was about to come" (Luke 10:1 ASV). Following Pentecost "there arose a murmuring of the Grecian Jews against the Hebrews because their widows were neglected in the daily ministrations." As a result, seven "brethren, . . . of good report, full of the Spirit and of wisdom," were appointed to look after "this business" that the apostles might "continue steadfastly in prayer, and in the ministry of the word" (Acts 6:3-4 ASV).

"Deacons" as officers of the church are first specifically mentioned by Paul in the salutation of the letter addressed to "the saints in Christ Jesus" with the bishops (overseers or pastors) and deacons (ministrants or servants) in the pastoral epistles (1 and 2 Timothy, and Titus). The qualifications and duties are set forth alongside bishops or pastors, with very little distinction between the two. In Ephesians, Paul lists "apostles . . . prophets . . . evangelists . . . pastors and teachers" (Ephesians 4:11), though the list does not seem to connote separate church officials so much as the varied functions of those whom Christ gave to the churches as his ministers and witnesses. Paul speaks of certain women as his fellow workers, and specifically mentions and commends "Phoebe our sister, who is a servant of the church that is at Cenchreæ" (Romans 16:1 ASV). The term, "servant of the church," is properly translated *deaconess*. Clearly a church has the right to designate whom it will as its servants, to fill positions of responsibility according to need and fitness. Ordination has been historically confined to pastors and deacons in the practice of most Baptist churches. Ceremonies of induction into office of others may well be held in recognition of the church's appointment and to give dignity to these positions of responsibility and honor.

THE SELECTION OF CHURCH OFFICERS

There are right and wrong ways of discovering and electing the officers of a church. Wrong ways include haphazard nomination from the floor; "candidating" for an office as if it were a political plum; election to office as an honor or to curry the favor of an individual or family; routine reelection of those already in office; appointment to office by pastor or other official or group; continuance in office as a matter of course.

The right way would involve prayerful study and discussion of the significance of office-bearing in a church; the setting up by the church of a simple list of essential qualifications such as church member in good standing, vital Christian experience, availability, willingness to serve, dependability, co-operativeness, attractive personality, native ability and common sense, friendliness, doctrinal soundness, faithfulness to obligations, good reputation; thorough canvass of entire church membership to discover men and women who possess these qualifications in reasonable measure; study of this list to determine special interests and abilities;

tactful approach to secure commitment to serve if needed; nomination by committee if the way is clear; election by the church.

No hard-and-fast list of officers may be given, since the needs of churches vary widely. A rather complete list will show the following:

Deacons, servants and representatives of the church, helpers to the pastor.

Clerk, responsible for the church's records.

Treasurer, responsible to receive and disburse the church's money.

Financial secretary, responsible with the treasurer for church funds, especially the detailed financial records.

Head usher, responsible for order and comfort in worship services.

Chorister and musician, in charge of the music program of the church.

Sunday school superintendent, chief administrative officer of the teaching department.

Training Union director, chief administrative officer of the training department.

W. M. U. president, head of the organized women's work.

Brotherhood president, head of the organized men's work.

Trustees, responsible for the church's property.

Janitor, responsible for cleanliness and upkeep of the property.

Minister of education (salaried), supervisor and director of the church's total educational program.

Minister of music (salaried), supervisor and director of all the music of the church.

Age-group specialists.

To these (and perhaps other) major offices will be added all departmental superintendents, secretaries, and teachers in the Sunday school; all heads of unions or departments of the Training Unions; all officers and leaders of Woman's Missionary Union; all officers and leaders of the Brotherhood; all officers and leaders of Music Ministry.

Checking the list of officers, teachers, leaders in service at present against the list given above, what is indicated as to the adequacy or inadequacy of the church's leadership? Are too many positions held by the same person? Would it be possible to inaugurate and maintain the general rule, "one major office to a person"? What needs to be done to increase the number and improve the quality of the church's official leadership?

THE OFFICE OF DEACON

Deacons are *servants* of the church. Only within recent years has the body of deacons been referred to as the "board." The objection to this designation is that it may somehow imply that deacons are managers rather than ministrants. Deacons are not to give orders to the church; they are to receive instructions from the church. Deacons are not to decide for the church, they are to carry out the decisions of the church. To them will come many matters calling for deliberation and recommendation, and on their own initiative they will be watchful over the welfare of the church. They should never arrogate to themselves any authority for running the church. Their greatest service to the church will usually be found in their assistance to the pastor. To them he will bring the problems, the needs, the plans, the purposes, the opportunities, the difficulties, the embarrassing situations, the material and spiritual concerns of the church. In closest confidence, with combined wisdom, in much prayer for guidance, pastor and deacons will seek to conserve the interests of the church and the kingdom and to project the work and influence of congregation and denomination "from Jerusalem . . . unto the uttermost part." Certain questions arise:

How are deacons selected? First, men should be sought who have the right qualifications. Paul, having stated the qualifications of the bishop or pastor, proceeds to a description of the sort of men needed as deacons. "Deacons in like manner," he writes, "must be grave, not double-tongued, not given to much wine, not greedy of filthy lucre, holding the mystery of the faith in a pure conscience. And let these also first be proved; then let them serve as deacons if they be blameless." Undoubtedly recognizing immediately the place of women as "servants of the church," or "deaconesses," Paul states their qualifications: "Women [deaconesses] in like manner must be grave, not slanderers, temperate, faithful in all things." Returning to the men servants of the church (deacons) Paul continues: "Let deacons be husbands of one wife, ruling their children and their own houses well. For they that have served well as deacons gain to themselves a great standing, and great boldness in the faith which is in Christ Jesus" (1 Timothy 3:8–13 ASV).

Dr. P. E. Burroughs once suggested that these qualifications be organized under four heads: (1) *Spiritual requirements,* "full of the Holy Spirit," "full of wisdom," "full of faith." (2) *Moral qualifications,* "gravity . . . the deacon should be a man who counts," "right in regard to speech . . . straight speakers, not speaking double," "right in regard to strong drink . . . no church can hesitate or occupy middle ground on this question," "right on the money question . . . entrusted with the management of church money, they are to inspire and challenge believers in their giving of money." (3) *Doctrinal qualifications,* deacons ought to know and understand the doctrines of Christ's gospel," "they should understand the distinctive teachings of their own denomination." (4) *Personal qualifications*, "the husband of one wife . . . the deacon shall, if he is a married man, be the husband of but one wife," "ruling well his own children and his own home . . . the man who as the head of a family conducts an exemplary household . . . is by so much to be trusted to serve wisely and helpfully in the church family." The reference to "wives" of deacons (King James Version) "women" in general (American Standard Version), "deaconesses" can scarcely be interpreted as describing officers of a church and so constituting a part of the diaconate. That the reference applies specifically rather than to women in general would seem obvious. Women may and do hold positions of responsibility and leadership for which they are selected by the church. Such women are in fact deaconesses, "servants of the church," but that they should be "ordained" and form an official group was quite evidently not the practice of the early churches, nor apparently the intention of the Scriptures. Indeed, the word "official body" is not New Testament language, whether applied to the men or the women, and should have a strange sound to Baptist ears.

How shall deacons be chosen? When the need arose in the Jerusalem church for helpers to the apostles, that they might not be overburdened with details of administration, the twelve called the church together and said: "Look ye out therefore, brethren, from among you seven men of good report, full of the Spirit and of wisdom, whom we may appoint over this business . . . And the saying pleased the whole multitude: and they chose [certain men] whom they set before the apostles: and when they had prayed, they laid their hands upon them" (Acts 6:3–6 ASV). Just how these men were chosen we are not told. It is interesting to note that they all bore Greek names.

Scriptural precedent and long established tradition would indicate the following steps in the choice of deacons: (1) earnest prayer for guidance; (2) clear exposition of basic requirements and duties; (3) determination of the number of deacons needed (not necessarily seven); (4) nomination by a competent committee of certain men who seem to be qualified and who are available, usually more than the number to be elected so as to permit a choice; (5) other nominations by any members who so desire; (6) ballots cast by members to determine their choice; (7) election declared on the basis of returns; (8) ordination and induction into office. This procedure may, of course, be varied. Some churches dispense with the nominating committee and proceed with balloting, any man of the church in good standing being eligible. From those receiving the highest votes, twice the number to be elected will be presented for a second balloting, the required number to be elected then being taken from those receiving the most votes. Whatever the procedure, the election should be a deeply spiritual experience and result in the choice of men who are best qualified for the office.

How long shall deacons serve? A deacon, duly elected and ordained, is obviously a deacon for life, unless his deaconship should be voided by the church. But this does not mean that he is to be in active, uninterrupted service as deacon for the whole of life. In a given church there may be several ordained ministers who hold membership, yet only one of them serve as active pastor. Likewise there may be a number of ordained deacons in a church, but only those of them in active service whom the church designates.

The plan of rotating deacons in service has grown in favor among the churches. This plan provides that a deacon shall be elected to serve for a limited time. In beginning the plan, a church usually designates one-third of the deacons to serve for one year, one-third to serve two years, one-third to serve three years. The order of service may be determined by priority of original election. At the end of the designated term of service, the deacon is usually ineligible for re-election until the lapse of a year. After the plan has been put into operation, since one-third of the number of deacons will retire each year, they must be replaced by church election. Men who are already deacons may be selected, or new names may be added. In the latter event, of course, the newly elected deacons will need to be ordained.

Advantages of the rotation system may be thus stated: [1]

First, the deacon elected by this method realizes that he has a limited term and that his hope of re-election depends upon his faithfulness; he is ambitious to have the vindication of another term and is thereby stimulated to more zealous activity in the discharge of his duties. The deacon elected for life realizes that he has a permanent job and is less likely to be aggressive.

It is claimed by the advocates of the life plan that the church suffers loss by the retirement of efficient men for even one year. They insist that such a policy is unjust both to the deacons and to the church. The friends of the rotation method think, however, that the one year in the capacity of a private member will serve as a vacation for the faithful deacon and afford him the opportunity to study the office from a new angle. He is returned to his office at the expiration of the year with new vigor, a broader conception of his duty, and with a stronger purpose to make good. It should also be borne in mind that the counsel of this efficient deacon may be secured in a quiet way and that he

---

[1] J. T. Henderson, *The Office of Deacon* (Kingsport, Tennessee: The Kingsport Press), pp. 59–61.

also will find many avenues of usefulness during the period of his retirement from office.

This plan enables the church to retire inefficient deacons with less shock and disappointment to them, to their families and to their friends. It also affords the opportunity to call into service as deacons some choice young men who will honor the position and impart new life to the board. If men have the position for life, they are likely to decline in spirit of aggressiveness and at the same time they shut out a number of strong and consecrated men who would bring new vitality to this important office.

Why and how should deacons be ordained? Little is said in the New Testament about ordination. Certainly it was never considered a ceremony conferring any priestly authority or bestowing any special grace or imprinting any special character. It was simply a beautiful ceremonial service of recognition of fitness, approval of selection, and expression of benediction. About all we know is that the ceremony included "prayer and the laying on of hands," the latter a "God bless you" on the part of those representing the church in the ceremony. Deacons, thus set apart, are the recognized servants of the church, assigned responsibilities which they share alongside the pastor.

The ordination service should be carefully planned and should be a memorable experience, especially in the lives of those ordained. The order of service may be somewhat as follows:

Reading of minutes, showing the action of the church in election of the deacon or deacons.

Prayer of thanksgiving and for guidance.

Scripture reading: Acts 6:1–7; 1 Timothy 3:1–13.

Inquiry (led by pastor or other appointed minister): Briefly and informally the deacon or deacons to be ordained may tell of their conversion experience, their activities in the church since becoming members, their conception of the office of deacon, particularly the deacon's relation to the pastor, the deacon's spiritual responsibilities, the deacon's example before the people, the deacon's doctrinal convictions, the deacon's practical duties. (This is not a critical "examination," but a simple inquiry eliciting heartfelt testimonies, for which there may have been brief preparation in advance.)

Charge to the deacons: Brief address of exposition and exhortation directed to those being ordained by someone appointed for this service.

Charge to the church: Similar words of explanation of the significance of what the church is doing, the church's responsibility to pray for and cooperate with the deacons, and how together they may aid the pastor, promote the church's well-being, and carry out Christ's commission.

Laying on of hands: Ministers and deacons who themselves have been ordained will pass by the kneeling men, placing their hands on their heads, reverently and affectionately breathing a benediction.

Ordaining prayer: For divine approval, blessing, guidance, protection, that those thus set apart may be worthy of the honor and fruitful in lives of Christian service.

Hand of fellowship: Extended by all present in token of fellowship, appreciation, co-operation, while "Blest Be the Tie" is sung.

GENERAL CHURCH OFFICERS

1. *Church Clerk*

What are the qualifications and duties of the church clerk? The person selected for this office should know how to write, how to keep accurate records, how to present these records economically and attractively. He should be regular in attendance, interested in every phase of the church's life, quick to perceive the difference between essentials and nonessentials, reliable and trustworthy. The efficient church clerk is more than a recorder of minutes of business meetings. The clerk, if he magnifies his office, is the church's historian. He records interestingly all significant events as they transpire—the services Sunday by Sunday, special occasions and meetings, deaths and funerals, marriages and births, building projects and local missions, progress of the several organizations, election of officers and change of pastors, participation of the church in denominational or other meetings and enterprises, special honors that come to the church or its members. The clerk may on occasion bring these significant records to the attention of the church in attractive fashion.

Of course the clerk will keep careful minutes of all church meetings, reading them for correction and approval when called for. The clerk will bring to the church's attention requests for letters of dismissal and will report receipt of letters from other churches. The clerk will report those received for baptism and baptized, and will call attention to changes in the membership by reason of death or removal. The clerk will use every endeavor to keep the church membership roll in good order, making it easy to ascertain the number of resident and nonresident members, those who are active and inactive, those who hold office or other positions of responsibility, those who need to be dealt with because of apparent lapses. The church clerk should be prompt in writing for letters requested from other churches and equally prompt in requesting and forwarding letters of dismissal to other churches. The letter of dismissal (rarely issued to an individual but rather to the sister church) should be honest and informative. A form of letter of dismission such as this will be found useful:

LETTER OF DISMISSION

To the _____ Church, _____

This letter will certify that M___ _____ united

with this church on _____ 19__ and at _____ request is

now dismissed from our fellowship to unite with you.

To help you enlist this new member in the life of your church the following record of _____ work with us is appended.

Attended: Morning worship__ Evening worship__ Prayer meeting__

Member: S.S.__ T.U.__ W.M.U.__ Brotherhood__

Contributor: __ Tither__ Regularly__ Irregularly__ Not at all as of record__

Special service rendered_____Offices held_____

By order of the church _____ 19__

2. Church Treasurer and Financial Secretary

What are the qualifications and duties of the church treasurer and financial secretary? In a small church a treasurer alone may be needed, but in the larger church two officers are imperatively needed. The treasurer may well be thought of as the church's chief steward. He should understand and be committed to the New Testament principle of stewardship. That he should be a tither goes without saying. He should, of course, be a man of unquestioned integrity, thoroughly acquainted with good business procedures, skilled in bookkeeping and accountancy, accurate and dependable in all his work. For his own protection and that of the church, he should usually be bonded. He should have an approved set of books in which to keep his records, and these books should be audited annually. He should make monthly reports to the church of all receipts and expenditures for the church's information and approval. He should make all payments by check, upon proper authorization, and each check signed by him should be countersigned by the financial secretary, or someone appointed by the church. Not because of any distrust of him, but that he may be relieved of all possible criticism and maintain utmost confidence of the entire membership, every safeguard should be placed about his office that would apply to the treasurer of a business corporation.

The treasurer is one of the most important spiritual officers of a church. He should realize keenly that giving is symptomatic. Those members who give systematically and worthily are almost certain to be in spiritual health; those who give spasmodically or not at all are almost certain to be spiritually sick. The treasurer, more than any other person in the church, is in position to observe the direct relationship between giving and worship, between giving and service, between giving and good churchmanship. His concern therefore will not simply be to take note of those who give, but even more importantly to consider lovingly and prayerfully those whose record of giving is unworthy.

The treasurer's best opportunity to enlist in giving is when the new member joins the church. Immediately the new member should be presented with a carton of envelopes, a copy of the church budget, a good tract on stewardship-tithing, and a pledge card. Perhaps the treasurer will need a committee to help to make this approach, lest the task become too burdensome. Yet the treasurer should find this enlistment of new members one of his most joyous opportunities.

The treasurer will seek to implement the ideal of every-member giving. This calls for an effective approach to each member of the church annually, with detailed statement of the church's needs and proposed budget, and personal effort to secure every-member support. Variations of the every-member canvass may be employed. So long as there is one member unaccounted for in the church's giving program, the treasurer should be dissatisfied. He should stimulate and direct a campaign of education to indoctrinate the entire church membership in the Christian principles of stewardship-giving and to keep the membership informed concerning the causes to which they give through the church.

The financial secretary is the treasurer's associate. Assisting the treasurer (and deacons who in rotation may be appointed to help), the financial secretary will share in counting the money and recording each individual gift. The financial secretary will keep detailed accounts of all receipts and expenditures, guarding carefully against any irregularities or unnecessary expenses. The financial secretary will promote unity of giving throughout the church and its organizations, and will undertake to keep each item of the budget in balance. The financial secretary will usually see to it that statements of their giving are sent to all members at stated intervals. The records of the financial secretary should be easy of access and open to inspection at any time.

3. Church Ushers

What are the qualifications and duties of ushers? The head usher is an important church officer. He should be a man of dignity, poise, friendliness, possessing unusual ability to meet and greet people. He is not just a "professional hand-shaker," nor is his responsibility merely that of seeing that the people are comfortably seated at the church services. He should gather about him a group of men having something of the same qualifications that he himself possesses and instill into them the high ideals which should characterize their service.

Some of the principles and rules which should govern in the functioning of church ushers may be thus briefly summarized:

1. The ushers of the church are its public relations representatives; they should therefore at all times be friendly, courteous, considerate.

2. The ushers are especially the guardians of the worship services; hence they should study conditions of lighting, heating, ventilation, and seek to prevent anything that would bring discomfort or distraction.

3. Ushers are the pastor's assistants in the worship services no less than the choir; they should therefore seat the people so as to enhance the pastor's preaching and the choir's singing, not merely following the line of least resistance and leaving an insulating space of empty pews at the front.

4. Much of the value of the worship service may be lost through carelessness; the ushers should accordingly seat late comers only at appropriate points in the service.

5. Every attendant is an honored guest, and should be treated accordingly; the usher should accompany the worshiper to the desired seat, assist in being seated as may be needful, always avoiding any possible embarrassment.

6. Thoughtless persons may disturb the service; ushers should be on guard to seat children or young people so that they will not be tempted to irreverence.

7. To be known as a friendly church is to possess a great asset; ushers should be near the exits at the close of the service especially to greet strangers and to introduce them to members or to the pastor.

8. The ultimate objective of every service is to add to the church those that are saved; ushers crown their services by personal soul-winning followed by effective invitation to church membership. In all these ways church ushers under the skilful guidance of the head usher may render notable service to Christ and the church.

MAKING DEFINITE THE RESPONSIBILITIES OF THE CHURCH STAFF

Many of the larger churches are finding necessary a "multiple ministry." This is not something new but goes back to the New Testament. Churches of the New Testament seem usually to have had more than one minister. The "seven helpers" appointed by the Jerusalem church, as indicated in the sixth chapter of Acts, illustrate the principle of division of labor and responsibility.

Usually the pastor-preacher is looked upon as the "chief of staff" in the church. His position would ordinarily make this desirable, if not necessary. However, he should always think of himself as "first among equals." Difficulties and tensions inevitably arise if the pastor seeks to lord it over other members of the staff or even to assume that he is in authority and others must implicitly obey his will. The ideal is that of Christian teamwork. Obviously, it is highly important that each member of the church staff understand his or her responsibilities and fields of labor. Naturally, there will be overlappings, but it is to the advantage of all if each member of the staff knows definitely what is his or her primary duties.

1. *The Minister of Education*

What are the qualifications and duties of the *educational director* or *minister of education?* This relatively new vocation has developed because of the increasing demands for a specialist in religious education who will give full time to this supremely important aspect of the church's life and work. In many churches this office has become almost as well established as that of pastor. The man or woman who occupies it must have educational preparation that falls scarcely short of that of the pastor. Little distinction will be made between this called and consecrated servant of the church and that of its chief servant, the pastor, as to qualities of dedication, devotion, conviction, resolution, education. This director or minister should know modern educational theory and practice, should be thoroughly acquainted with the plans and purposes of each of the organizations, and should be possessed of a high order of administrative ability.

Among the most important duties of this office are the following: (1) to co-operate with the pastor, loyally and efficiently; (2) to work harmoniously with all the officers, teachers, and leaders of the several organizations; (3) to discover and recruit, according to the church's plan, needed workers for all the departments; (4) to maintain and supervise a comprehensive program of leadership training; (5) to give help wherever needed in the prevention of failure; (6) to give guidance to plans for increased enrolment and attendance of all the organizations; (7) to give oversight to the selection and use of appropriate materials and methods; (8) to install and operate an adequate system of records, with the assistance of well-trained secretaries; (9) to give guidance to executive and planning groups, such as Sunday school workers' conference and officers and teachers' meetings, Training Union Council meetings, W.M.U. Executive Committee meetings, Brotherhood planning meetings, and committees of various kinds; (10) to direct weekday and vacation Bible school education; (11) to relate the organizations happily to one another and to the church; (12) to give stimulation and leadership to personal evangelism; (13) to harness the powers of all the organizations to the denominational program of world service.

The minister or director of education should be called by the church in much the same way as the pastor. He should of course be acceptable to the pastor, and his success is largely determined by the happy relationship which exists between him and the pastor, but he is not the pastor's "hired man," and he should not be expected to resign when the pastor leaves. Gladly should the minister or director of education accept the pastor's priority of leadership, but he should not be made to feel that his position is secondary or subordinate. In some respects his responsibilities and opportunities are even greater than those of the pastor, just as the pastor's are in many respects greater than his. The two are fellow workers in an enterprise whose burdens are too heavy for either to bear alone and whose success depends largely on their mutual confidence and reinforcement. The compensation of the educational minister or director should reflect the church's appreciation of the high importance and value of the position as associate to the pastor.

2. The Minister of Music

The minister of music stands alongside the minister of education as an elected staff member and officer of the church. To his recognized qualifications as musician should be added full dedication to the service of Christ and the church. He will co-operate with the pastor in planning and conducting the stated services of worship; he will seek approval by the church of those who in official capacity are to assist him in the Music Ministry; he will organize and train those who constitute the choir or choirs; he will offer his services to the several church organizations with a view to raising the standards of music and worship; he will recognize the relation of music to all other aspects of the church's life and carry out the policy of the church in all matters pertaining to his leadership.

3. Leaders of Age Groups and Special Activities

A church may elect to its staff age-group specialists, such as Director of Children's Work, Director of Youth Work, Director of Adult Work, etc. A church may also obtain the services of a Director of Recreation, Hostess, an Engineer in Charge of Buildings and Grounds, etc. For the sake of efficiency and to avoid misunderstandings, a careful job description should be furnished each employed worker. A personnel committee of the church may well assist the pastor in giving general direction to such staff members.

4. *Church Secretary* [2]

Many a minister has been sorely tempted during the first harassing months of his new pastorate to send an S.O.S. for his former secretary. Many a minister has thus solved the problem, but in so doing he placed his successor under a handicap. Why should not a church secretary who knows the affairs of one church stay on to help the incoming pastor, rather than trying to seek employment elsewhere?

Any woman who works on a church staff must be possessed with a boundless amount of patience, tact, and understanding, as well as the ability to keep confidences. As in any job, a pleasing telephone voice is a necessity and a telephone memory an asset. The secretary should have an enthusiasm for her work which will carry her through storm and turmoil, late hours and rushing schedules.

If the church is able to provide two or more secretaries, the division of work should be as complete as possible. No two of the women should work in the same office, not only that they might hinder each other by engaging in small talk, but that any office visitor would interrupt both employees. Whether the office visitor comes seeking someone to whom she can pour out her woes or to make a reservation for the dining room, the conversation should include only the one person addressed.

The division of labor will almost automatically give secretary number one the position of minister's secretary and to other secretaries responsibilities as division of labor demands.

The minister's secretary can best dispatch her numerous duties if she is taken into the minister's confidence and told his attitudes and policies. The secretary who knows that the minister has an unbreakable rule that he will marry no couple unless he is able to have at least an hour's premarital counseling period with them will never calendar a ceremony without first inquiring if the two are willing to give the time for such a counseling session. Thus she is able to save valuable time for the head of the staff.

The ability to see all, know all, and tell nothing should apply in the case of the minister's secretary. Much that goes across the minister's desk would make interesting conversation outside the office, but the strictest confidence must be maintained. Many a secretary knows family secrets

---

[2] Adapted from article by Roberta White, "How to Organize Church Secretarial Work," *Church Management*, July, 1946.

which have been bared in a church office. Like the physician's assistant, confidences die with the individual who has shared them.

One of the problems confronting the secretarial staff of a church is the meeting of outside demands. Too many church secretaries are harried by requests from youth fellowships, women's groups, the finance committee, and other interchurch bodies for work these groups could usually do for themselves. From these outside demands the church staff must be protected.

The secretary should have a definite pride in her work, believing that it demands her best, and that no work goes out from the office as an ambassador of the church unless it is her very best. And that means, among other things, letters without erasures, envelopes with the stamps placed straight (and no lipstick smears on the flaps), letter-perfect printed materials, and neat mimeographing which has been slip-sheeted.

One final consideration is the relationship between the minister and the members of his staff. Each member must have a chance to grow. They are not created some slave and some free. All should have a chance to plan, create, suggest, and carry out their ideas. Between the minister and the staff members there must be a feeling of mutuality and common concern in their tasks. The duties of all must be clearly defined, responsibilities listed, and as there must be no overlappings, so also there must be no infringing.

The church secretary has a place all her own, and by her own initiative she can make it a most enjoyable and happy position. She can find satisfaction, pleasure, humor, pathos, and live close to the public. She will associate with the great and near great, the rich and the poor, the weak and the strong. Given the right combination of attributes, surroundings, and associates, she will come forth feeling she has one job in a million. She is a church secretary, and she is glad she is.

5. The Associate Minister [3]

The associate minister or minister of church activities is the pastor's first assistant and will, in the pastor's absence, exercise pastoral privileges and responsibilities. He will be responsible to the pastor. He will give supervision and leadership to all educational activities.

During the pastor's absence the associate minister will be responsible for and give direction to the full staff, excepting the pastor's secretary, who will at all times be under the pastor's directions. It is understood that the pastor's secretary is without authority in any and all matters, and

---

[3] Adapted from regulations of First Baptist Church, Oklahoma City.

will, in the pastor's absence, refer all pastoral and administrative matters to the associate minister.

Ordinarily the associate minister will be responsible for the church council program and the supper meetings on Wednesday evenings. He may well be responsible for the publication of the bulletin and church paper. He will do general pastoral and enlistment visitation.

Under the direction of the pastor, he will be responsible for all worship services during the pastor's absence. He will give supervision and leadership to mission stations of the church. He will be subject to special assignments, such as assistance with the every-member canvass, evangelistic meetings, installation of special records, making study of housing facilities for the work of the church, and other tasks that appear needful.

It is not the prerogative of the associate minister to select and install personnel, either for the staff or organizations of the church, without the knowledge and consent of the pastor and without church authorization. He should refer all matters of policy and general programs to the pastor and the church for confirmation. When the pastor is available, the associate minister will refer all funerals and weddings to him. The associate may perform these services in the pastor's absence or upon his request.

These are the general duties and responsibilities of the minister of church activities. No effort is made to detail the work of this assistant. Freedom to exercise good judgment and aggressive leadership is left to him. Details in promoting the general program outlined above are also left to him. We might sum up the privileges and responsibilities of the office by saying again: The minister of church activities is the pastor's first assistant. The pastor is to be respected as the head of the church and all of its auxiliaries and work, but he considers the minister of church activities his partner in all things.

6. *The Church Administrator*

The church administrator will have complete charge of the bookkeeping; the bookkeeper will be under his supervision; he shall determine the system of bookkeeping; he will call on the bookkeeper for any reports, assistance, or make any requirements.

The church administrator will approve every bill that is paid; request every check that is drawn; check literature orders; take over all storage rooms; supervise engineer and janitors; co-operate with hostess in all expenses incidental to meals, etc.; be responsible for upkeep of all church property, including the missions; visit or cause to be visited the new members of the church with reference to the financial program; improve efficiency of offices wherever possible; take charge of the benevolent fund.

A Church Conserving Its Membership

The study of a typical church membership roll is often a disillusioning experience. Many names of persons will be found in the list who are unaccounted for, the church having no knowledge of their whereabouts. The addresses of a large number of other members may be known, but their record of attendance and support would indicate no vital connection with the church. Another group will be found who have a loose relationship, attending and giving occasionally, but apparently feeling little or no responsibility for the church's welfare. A few members may be found who are bitter toward the church, having some grievance which they are nursing and frankly confessing their attitude of antagonism and estrangement. Some may be discovered to be living in open sin, their lives a contradiction of their Christian profession, their example a stumblingblock to unbelievers. Over against all these, of course, are the faithful and loyal members, the "salt of the earth" and "the light of the world."

It is not enough to deplore the facts of absentee membership, indifference and inactivity, backsliding and bad spirit. Every name on a church membership roll represents a "brother (or sister) for whose sake Christ died" (1 Corinthians 8:11 ASV). Nor may we sit in judgment on these unworthy church members, condemning them for their weakness and sin, if we have the spirit of Christ. Will not judgment upon the church be even more severe if it complacently permits these members of the "household of faith" to be lost from the family circle without concern for their recovery? If every case could be traced from the time of baptism to the time of loss of usefulness to the church, often there would be uncovered a tragic story of human weakness, of hard circumstances, of gradual yielding to temptation, of repeated defeat in the Christian struggle.

Every church needs a definite plan for the conserving of its members. The great majority of those considered "dead timber" might have been saved to usefulness and happiness in their church relationships had they been given the right start after baptism and then nurtured from Christian infancy to maturity in the faith and fellowship of their church. An aggressive program of membership-conservation is therefore urgently needed.

A CHURCH'S RESPONSIBILITY FOR MEMBERSHIP CONSERVATION

The lost sheep in the parable had once been a member of the fold. "How think ye," Jesus searchingly asks, "if any man have a hundred sheep, and one of them be gone astray, doth he not leave the ninety and nine, and go unto the mountains, and seek that which goeth astray? And if so be that he find it, verily I say unto you, he rejoiceth over it more than the ninety and nine which have not gone astray" (Matthew 18:12–13 ASV). According to Jesus, it is more important to seek and find and bring back one straying church member than to minister to the ninety-nine who are safe in the fold.

Churches generally have refused to take Jesus seriously in this teaching concerning their responsibility for their lost, strayed, sometimes stolen members. The attitude of many churches is that of almost complete indifference concerning the members who never attend the services, who give nothing to the church's support, who are engaged in none of the church-sponsored activities, who belong to none of the church's organizations, and who bear no testimony to their faith.

Indeed, a church may be callously indifferent to members who are living in open sin, as in the case of the church at Corinth, to whom Paul wrote: "It is actually reported that there is fornication among you, and such fornication as is not even among the Gentiles, that one of you hath his father's wife. And ye are puffed up and did not rather mourn, that he that had done this deed might be taken away from among you . . . Your glorying is not good. Know ye not that a little leaven leaveneth the whole lump? Purge out the old leaven, that ye may be a new lump, even as ye are unleavened" (1 Corinthians 5:1–2, 6–7 ASV). Clearly the leaven that needed purging was not only the shameful sin of a guilty member, but the equally shameful neglect of the church to do something about it. The reclamation of this erring member Paul put first in this church's obligations. One of the greatest revivals that could come to our churches today would be a revival of deep and compassionate concern for its weak, wayward, careless, indifferent, worldly, useless church members.

DISCOVERING AND INTERPRETING THE FACTS

The first step in a constructive program of conservation is to make careful analysis of the church membership rolls. Often the membership records are inaccurate and confused. Names may still be carried of those who are dead or long since removed from the community, or changed because of marriage, or wholly unaccounted for. Information concerning each member may be quite incomplete, the only notation often being date and manner of reception into the church. No note may be taken of service

CHECKING UP ON THE CHURCH'S MEMBERSHIP RECORDS

Items for evaluation	Yes	No	To some extent	Don't know
1. Has the church a modern, efficient system of membership records?				
2. Has attention been given recently to these records?				
3. Is there need of a better system of membership records?				
4. Would a card system with permanent book for transfer be practicable and acceptable?				
5. Has separate list been made of all nonresident members?				
6. Has persistent effort been made to induce nonresident members to transfer membership?				
7. Has every effort been made to locate those whose addresses are unknown?				
8. Has an "unknown" roll been set up for those unaccounted for?				
9. Has a "nonresident" roll been set up for those removed but addresses known?				
10. Has an "inactive" roll been set up for resident members who are nonattendants and noncontributors?				
11. Has the church a plan for restoring if possible these inactive members?				
12. Should greater concern be shown for their restoration?				
13. Does the church seek to enlist immediately all new members?				
14. Are new members given formal instruction as to their duties and privileges?				
15. Has the church any plan for dealing with members overcome by temptation?				
16. Does the church take seriously its responsibility for preventive discipline?				
17. Does the church sometimes find it necessary to exercise corrective discipline?				
18. Is the New Testament ideal of a regenerate church membership positively upheld?				

as officer or leader, activity in church organizations, participation in special service, support of the church financially. No distinction may be made between those who are active, inactive, unaccounted for. Unless the church's records are in good shape, a strong committee should be appointed to work with pastor and clerk to revise the rolls and install a more adequate system. Even if the records are in good condition, they should be analyzed annually and the church made acquainted with the facts and their interpretation.

As a result of this analysis, pastor and people should confront seriously and intelligently the following questions:

What needs to be done to make our membership recording system efficient and adequate?

What should be done with the names of those who are unlocatable?

What should be done with the names of members who have removed to other communities but whose addresses are still known?

What policy should the church adopt concerning those who, for a considerable period of time, have been nonattendants and noncontributors?

What plan should the church adopt in dealing with members known to be living in sin?

How may new members be so inducted into the life of the church as to insure their conservation?

A PRACTICAL PLAN OF MEMBERSHIP ACCOUNTING

When a person becomes a customer of a modern, well-managed store, name and address are carefully entered on the company's books. If the customer opens a charge account, much more information is secured and recorded—age, marital status, occupation, amount and stability of income, bank connection, property ownership, promptness in paying bills elsewhere. If the customer then makes application for employment by the firm, still more information is sought and recorded—educational advantages, previous experience, special abilities, interests and aptitudes, personality traits, opinion of former employers, citizenship loyalty, honesty and integrity of character, prospects of promotion, willingness and ability to learn. Customers and employees would probably be surprised at the amount and variety of data concerning themselves to be found on the books of a first-class department store.

Contrast such human accounting on the part of a business concern with the membership records of a typical church. Usually only the barest facts are given—name and address of member, how received and date, when and for what cause name removed. In many cases names of persons are carried who have been lost track of for many years. Sometimes notice has not been taken of the death of a member. Women who have married may still be listed by their maiden names. Even when such corrections have been made through occasional revision of the membership rolls, nothing may be recorded beyond barest statistics.

A church member is more than a name on a book, a number on a carton of envelopes, a "cash customer" who gives when he attends, a customer with a "charge account" whose contributions are recorded on the treasurer's books. A church member is even more than an employee. *A church member is a member of the firm.* Each person received into the church becomes a "member of the body of Christ," with every privilege and responsibility of any other member.

What, then, would constitute a reasonably adequate human accounting system for a church? It should not be too elaborate, yet it should represent something of the value which Christ and his church place upon the individual.

Whether in loose-leaf book or on cards kept in filing case, as much of this information as may be available and practicable should be continuously recorded by a church that takes seriously its duty to demonstrate the primary Christian doctrine of the supreme value of the individual. If the objection be made that this involves too much bookkeeping, the ready reply is that no amount of bookkeeping would be too much if it resulted in saving precious lives to usefulness that are now being lost through carelessness. Of course, the mere process of accounting will not of itself produce the result, but it will go far toward concentrating attention of pastor, deacons, church officers, teachers, and leaders on the *persons* for whom they are responsible, the growth and development of each of whom constitutes the church's high obligation and the loss of any one of whom represents its accountability in the judgment.

A form for the church's human accounting would, when printed, be somewhat as follows:

A CHURCH HUMAN-ACCOUNTING SYSTEM

For Personal File of Pastor and Staff

Name _____

Residence _____ Tel. _____

Business Address _____ Tel. _____

Birthday _____ Other Anniversaries _____

When and how received _____

A CHURCH HUMAN-ACCOUNTING SYSTEM—(*Continued*)

Family Connections

Place in family:
Other members of family:
Religious status of other members:

Church Relationship

Previous to membership:
When and by whom baptized:
Tither_____Reg. Contrib._____Noncontrib._____
Attends worship: Regularly_____Irreg._____Never_____
Enrolled in: S.S._____T.U._____W.M.U._____Bro._____
Especially interested in:
Special abilities:
Responsive to service calls: Yes_____No_____

Personal Inventory

Occupation:
Educational status:
Financial status:
Prefers what church activity: Evangelistic_____Missionary_____Teaching_____
    Training_____Music_____Other_____
Extent of enlistment:
Happy and useful Christian:
In need of counsel:

Christian Growth and Developments

Age when received into membership:
Promotions:
Progress in enlistment:
Office or special service:
Changes in family status:
Accidents or illnesses:
Other personal or family crises:
Away from home:
Removal to other community:

Unenlistment and Loss

Unresponsive and inactive from beginning:
Invitation to enlistment neglected:
First began to be inactive:
Circumstances accounting for inactivity:
Evidences of spiritual backsliding:
Evidences of personal or family difficulties:

Effort of church to reclaim:
Response to efforts to reclaim:
Removal to another community:
Efforts to secure transfer of letter:
Record of transfer of membership:
Death and funeral of member:

PREVENTIVE AND REMEDIAL DISCIPLINE

Originally, *discipline* meant the instruction or training given to a disciple or learner. Its primary meaning remains "the cultivation of the mind and formation of the manners." A derived meaning of discipline is "rule of government, method of regulating principles and practice." Because rules and regulations, to be effective, must be enforced, discipline has the further derived meaning of "punishment inflicted by way of correction and training . . . especially on a delinquent."

Popularly the last-named meaning has become attached to "church discipline," a significance carried over from the Catholic practice of inflicting chastisement or mortification on the transgressor as penance or as penalty. The extreme Catholic penalty was excommunication. Protestants generally abandoned this harsh term for the softer "turning out of the church," or "withdrawal of fellowship." "Penance" was restored to its more scriptural "penitence," which found expression in confession and plea for forgiveness, accompanied by promises of amendment or restitution.

In Baptist circles breaches of faith and morals were often presented at the "church conference," the establishment of guilt with failure to make amends resulting in exclusion from membership. Not many churches follow this practice today. Yet there is scriptural warrant as well as practical need for some form of church discipline. Granting that the Catholic concept of punitive discipline, enforced if necessary by the civil arm, is unchristian, and that the former Protestant or Baptist concept of "church trial" and withdrawal of fellowship is impracticable and inadequate, what course may worthily be followed? Types of difficulty may first be noted, and then procedures suggested for dealing with delinquents and offenders, both preventively and remedially.

1. *Broken fellowship.* Jesus himself dealt specifically with this situation. He provided in advance for the eventuality of broken fellowship by binding together his disciples with strong bonds of common faith, common purpose, common loyalty, common love of himself and of one another. Then when the break came, as he must have known it inevitably would

come, he gave explicit directions as to how the difficulty should be dealt with. The person wronged, he directed, should first go to the one who had wronged him and seek privately to bring about reconciliation. Should this fail, the aggrieved brother should take with him one or two more, that they might together heal the breach. All these efforts having failed, the matter should then be brought to the church. If the combined intercession and mediation of the church failed, there is but one conclusion— such unforgiveness is *prima facie* evidence of unregeneracy, hence the hard-hearted and obdurate person is to be classed with the unsaved gentile and publican. His fellowship with the Christian body having thus been nullified, the self-declared lost man is to be won to Christ as any other sinner. It is significant that Jesus dealt thus in detail with the most important single aspect of church discipline—the restoration of broken fellowship.

2. *False faith.* Jesus dealt gently and patiently with ignorance, honest doubt, slow understanding. He was severe and uncompromising, however, toward "false prophets," "blind guides," "hypocrites." To him the great sins were sins against love, light, truth. Those deliberately guilty of such sins ruled themselves outside the circle of his purpose and discipleship. In unmistakable language he declared that counterfeit disciples would be revealed by the final judgment, to whom he would say, "Depart from me, ye cursed, into the eternal fire which is prepared for the devil and his angels" (Matthew 25:41 ASV).

Jesus gave no specific instructions as to how false teachers and disciples are to be dealt with by the church. He clearly anticipated them and warned against them. When actual situations arose, his inspired interpreters dealt with them according to the mind and in the spirit of their Master. The first overt threat to Christianity from false teachers came through the Judaizers—those who taught that Gentiles must first become Jews before they could be accepted in the church as Christians. This controversy led to the calling of the Jerusalem conference. Notwithstanding the seriousness of the Judaizers' false doctrine, the "orthodox" did not move to unseat as messengers those who represented the opposition, but discussed the problem freely and in orderly fashion until agreement was reached that satisfied both groups.

Judaizers and gnostics continued to plague Paul and other faithful followers of Christ and the gospel. Paul wrote gently but firmly concerning those who were causing divisions and occasions of stumbling contrary to sound doctrine, saying simply, "Turn away from them" (Romans 16:17). In stronger language he warned against those who have made "shipwreck concerning the faith," mentioning Hymeneus and Alexander particularly, "whom I delivered unto Satan," Paul explains, "that they might be taught not to blaspheme" (1 Timothy 1:19-20 ASV). Describing vividly as "puffed up, knowing nothing, but doting about questionings and disputes ⸜f words," Paul sets the heretical teacher over against the man of God who is to "follow after righteousness, godliness, faith, love, meekness" (1 Timothy 6:3-5, 11-12 ASV).

In dealing with false teachers and disciples, error is to be met with truth, darkness is to be driven out by light, agreement is to be reached through open discussion, divisive trouble-makers are to be turned away from, blasphemers are to be recognized as belonging to Satan, those who believe and teach false doctrines are to be matched by those who follow after righteousness.

3. *Immoral character and conduct.* Jesus established high ethical standards for his followers. Good character and conduct, though not a means of salvation, he clearly made a proof of salvation. "By their fruits ye shall know them," was the test which he applied both to men and to institutions. A Christian who continues to live in unrepented sin is a contradiction in terms. Baptism and church membership cannot take the place of "fruits that befit repentance." The doctrine of a regenerate church membership becomes a mockery when members of the church continue to live in known sin unnoticed and unrebuked.

Ananias and Sapphira constitute the first example of the drastic consequences of deliberate sin within the church. The shock of their public exposure was not only too much for the guilty couple, it also brought holy fear to the whole church and to all who heard of it. Another case in point is the situation which Paul faced at Corinth. Shameful immorality and indecent conduct had invaded the Corinthian church. Flagrant sin went unrebuked, indecorum characterized its worship, divisions weakened its witness. Paul called for a house cleaning. He commanded the church to "purge out the old leaven," and to "put away the wicked man from among yourselves" (1 Corinthians 5:7-13 ASV). He pled for Christian living worthy of their calling. He exalted the rule of love rather than of law, pointing out that all they say or do would be as nothing without love. Clearly a church wrongs Christ, itself, the sinning member within, and the lost without when it permits immorality in character and conduct to go unchallenged.

4. *Indifference and neglect.* The claims of Christ admit no neutrality. "He that is not with me is against me," Jesus plainly declared; "and he that gathereth not with me scattereth" (Matthew 12:30 ASV). He asserted the clear-cut principle: "Not every one that saith unto me, Lord, Lord, shall enter into the kingdom of heaven; but he that doeth the will of my

Father who is in heaven" (Matthew 7:21 ASV). Emphatically he asserted that the halfhearted, vacillating man could not be his disciple, stating the rule: "No man, having put his hand to the plow, and looking back, is fit for the kingdom of God" (Luke 9:62). Throughout the New Testament faithfulness is exalted as an essential Christian virtue and made a necessary mark of discipleship. Paul thus states the necessity: "Here, moreover, it is required in stewards, that a man be found faithful" (1 Corinthians 4:2 ASV).

Responsibility for faithfulness to church obligations is twofold. First, the member himself is obligated to fulfil the vows taken in baptism and in assent to the church covenant. Assuredly the very commitment of himself to Christ and the church in the witness of baptism involves as minimum duties attendance on the services of worship, participation in the church's program of teaching and training, financial support of the church and its causes, and the bearing of a faithful Christian witness. If at any of these points the member signally fails, obligation is upon the church to discover reasons for the delinquency and to seek its remedy. Merely to drop the name of the inactive member from the roll or to put it on an "inactive list" is a confession of tragic failure on the part of the church. A positive program of reclamation of indifferent and negligent members is a church's sacred obligation second only to that of winning the lost.

PROCEDURES IN MAKING DISCIPLINE EFFECTIVE

Mistakes of the past do not justify present neglect of preventive and remedial church discipline. The teachings of the New Testament are clear, and the results of their violation are apparent. The life and witness of the churches today are marred and enfeebled by broken fellowship, false teaching and belief, immoral character and conduct, indifference and neglect. There are steps which any church, under the leadership of pastor and deacons and with the Holy Spirit's guidance, may successfully take.

1. *The purpose of discipline established.* Prevention is better than cure. Jesus made fruit-bearing the test of discipleship; he also revealed the secret of fruit-bearing: "He that abideth in me, and I in him, the same beareth much fruit" (John 15:5). A fruitless Christian needs first of all to be reunited with Christ. This restoration of the love relationship between the disciple and Christ usually requires human mediation. With deep insight Jesus continues to say: "This is my commandment, that ye love one another, even as I have loved you" (John 15:12 ASV). Paul interprets the mind of Christ when he admonishes, "Brethren, even if a man be overtaken in any trespass, ye who are spiritual, restore such a

one in a spirit of gentleness; looking to thyself, lest thou also be tempted. Bear ye one another's burdens, and so fulfil the law of Christ" (Galatians 6:1-2). Notwithstanding Paul's firmness of demand that those who "walk disorderly" be marked and at least temporarily isolated from fellowship, he yet points out with equal firmness that the purpose of the discipline is to be constructive and not destructive, restorative rather than punitive. Withdrawal from the company of the offending brother is to the end "that he may be ashamed," but Paul immediately adds: "Admonish him as a brother" (2 Thessalonians 3:15).

2. *The need of discipline canvassed.* What causes lie back of the various forms of backsliding of which church members are guilty? A church is in a sense a spiritual hospital for sick and hurt members. Before prescription and treatment comes diagnosis. How account for cases of broken fellowship? Why are church members misled by false doctrines? Why do they yield to temptations of the flesh? What brings about their indifference and neglect of duty? For every specific case there is an underlying cause, and the remedy cannot be intelligently applied until the cause is known. Since every case presents an individual problem, diagnosis demands personal interview, sympathetic listening, prayerful consideration of difficult circumstances, review and analysis of factors entering into decline of faith and loss of Christian usefulness.

Year by year the membership committee of the church should canvass the church rolls, noting each one whose church fellowship seems to be growing cold or has become lifeless. Resources of Sunday school, Training Union, Woman's Missionary Union, and Brotherhood should immediately be mobilized to reach and enlist those who give evidence of drifting from their moorings. Every effort should be made to bring them back into fellowship and service. Utmost care should then be taken to reclaim those who have broken their church connections. They should be placed in one of the groups suggested above—broken fellowship, false faith, immorality, indifference—so far as ascertainable. Pastor and committee should then place each name of these estranged members in the hands of certain trusted and tactful "inner circle" workers, who, after much prayer and thought, will join in a quiet program of reclamation visitation.

3. *The process of discipline instituted.* Visitors who call upon estranged or backsliden or drifting church members will do well to follow the tested procedures of the trained counselor. Principles of method in such counseling may be thus summarized: (1) the development of *rapport* —cultivation of acquaintance leading to attitudes of friendliness and confidence; (2) tactful inquiry that gets the matter of broken church relations out into the open; (3) selective listening that draws out the whole story,

the listener neither condoning nor sitting in judgment; (4) questioning to discover what the erring church member thinks could and should be done about it; (5) positive suggestions of alternatives looking to the best possible solution of the problem; (6) prayer together that a course may be taken which will please God, honor Christ, and be best for all concerned; (7) decision and committal resulting in immediate action.

Should all this fail, then what? A final question remains: "Are you a Christian? Do you consider that you are saved?" If the answer is in the affirmative, then the course is clear—the church must continue its unceasing efforts to reclaim and restore this "lost sheep of the house of Israel." If the answer is negative, the person being dealt with declaring sincerely that he does not count himself to be a regenerate believer, the course is equally clear—he should be requested to ask that his name be removed from the church membership roll where it has never really belonged. In the former case, the church should be called to intercessory prayer that its straying child may yet be recovered. In the latter case, the church should be challenged to prevailing prayer that the one whose name is being removed as having never been saved may be brought to true repentance and redeeming faith.

The testimony of the reclaimed Christian to his unreclaimed brother possesses twofold power—the power to reach the heart and change the course of the erring one, and the reflex power to sustain the erstwhile backslider in his recovered faith. A wise pastor, utilizing this principle of chain-reaction, has at his command a never-failing strategy for the conservation of the fruitage of discipline.

No other institution that takes itself seriously would receive members into its body as carelessly as some churches receive members into their fellowship. The assumption is not well-founded that a person presenting himself for baptism and thus coming into church membership understands sufficiently the experience he has undergone, the faith he now shares, the privileges and duties which are his, and the fellowship to which he now belongs.

Preceding baptism there should be careful inquiry into the candidate's fitness for church membership. The New Testament knows nothing of church membership until there shall have been a saving experience. No more tragic condition can be imagined than that of an unsaved person in the church, lulled into a false sense of security. Since the saving experience is essentially subjective, little objective evidence can be demanded. To set up conditions of "probation" or "trial membership" would be to run the risk of making salvation a condition of good works and moral character. Reasonable care having been exercised to safeguard against ignorance, impulse, emotion, misunderstanding or false motive, a church can scarcely do other than receive one who presents himself in good faith as having truly repented and believed and as desiring church membership following baptism. The church's obligation is very great, however, to see that every member is given a good start.

THE NEW MEMBERS' CLASS

The "confirmation class" is an age-old device for insuring minimum fitness for church membership. In the Catholic theory, the baptized infant is saved sacramentally; instruction leading to confirmation is required to the end that faith and practice may be established. Pedobaptists who reject the sacramental efficacy of baptism consider the child who has been "christened" to be "an heir of the covenant," or a member of the "household of faith"; instruction is then given in a "communicants' class" or "pastor's class," or "confirmation class," leading to acceptance by the church into full membership. The fundamental weakness in these viewpoints and procedures is apparent—baptism and church membership are too closely identified with salvation. Instruction leading *toward* Christ is needed, but the saving experience, according to the New Testament, comes, not from knowing *about* Christ and the Gospel, but from knowing *him* in a personal experience that remakes life. Instruction following this experience is needed for the nurture and direction of the new life and is the church's lifelong responsibility for every member.

Obviously there is great advantage in immediate intensification of instruction in churchmanship following entrance into church membership. Such instruction is needed not only for the newly baptized member but also for one who has come by transfer of letter from another church. Churches of the same faith and order differ in many respects, and reorientation into the fellowship of the church being joined is by no means a waste of time. The "new members' class" is becoming established in an increasing number of churches as standard practice.

The "new members' class" operates very simply. Class attendance is of course not compulsory, but the values are so obvious that the tradition soon becomes established. The new member is simply notified that he is expected to meet the class for a given period of time at a specified hour and place, in order that he may be aided to a better understanding of the experience undergone, of the faith which he now shares, of the privileges and duties which are now assumed, and of the fellowship which has been entered.

The class may be conducted by the pastor as a unit of the Training Union. It may continue for some four or more meetings. The preferred time of meeting is at the Training Union hour. Care should be taken to make the class attractive, informal, worthwhile. In some instances the class may be conducted annually, following the ingathering incident to the "revival" or special evangelistic effort. Better still, the class may be organized and conducted at regular intervals, as often as there are enough new members to justify it. Most desirable of all is the continuous class, beginning again with a new group each month, or attended by new members as rapidly as they are received, additions to the class coming in at whatever point the discussion may have reached without regard to chronology of the lessons. The last named plan would of course anticipate perennial evangelism with new members being received Sunday by Sunday throughout the year.

CURRICULUM AND CONDUCT OF THE NEW MEMBERS' CLASS

The new members' class may be conducted very much as a regular Training Union unit. It succeeds best when not looked upon as a study course or a series of lectures but rather as a sharing of experiences, convictions, interests, needs, privileges, purposes. For this reason the class need not be closely graded—children, young people, and adults may well share the experience together to mutual profit. Mature members will guide the discussion, seeking participation of the new members. The new members' interest and participation may be challenged by these successive emphases, constituting a four to six weeks' program of study and discussion:

1. *The new life into which the new member has entered.* What it means to be a Christian; the New Testament meaning of repentance and faith; the new relationship which the Christian has to God through Jesus Christ; the work of the Holy Spirit in conversion; the importance and necessity of public confession; the significance and duty of the ordinance of baptism; the symbolism of the Lord's Supper; the duties and privileges of worship and service; the obligations to others involved in church membership.

Some basic Scripture passages: Luke 3:3–14; Matthew 3:13–17; John 3:22–23; Matthew 9:35–38; 28:19–20; Acts 2:41–42; John 15:1–16; Acts 1:6–8; 8:4.

2. *The faith which the new member shares.* What it means to be a member of the body of Christ; a church as an organized body of baptized believers; a church's relationship to other bodies of baptized believers; a church as a family; the individual member's duties and privileges as a member of the church family; what the member has the right to expect of the church and the church of the member; values which the new mem-

ber inherits; responsibilities which the new member assumes; the broader significance of citizenship in the kingdom of God; requirements of the good citizen of the kingdom; the obligation to share privileges of membership in the church and in the kingdom; the tragic possibilities of loss due to carelessness, negligence, selfishness, worldliness.

Some basic Scripture passages: Matthew 16:13–19, 24–25; John 15:12–17; 1 Corinthians 12:1–14; John 4:31–38; John 10:11–15, 27–29; Romans 8:31–37; 1 Corinthians 3:21–23; Matthew 3:1–2; 4:23; 6:33; 18:1–4; 24:14; Romans 14:17; 2 Thessalonians 3:5; Revelation 11:15; Luke 6:30–38; 1 Corinthians 13; 1 John 3:13–18.

3. *Opportunities and responsibilities of the new member.* The privilege and duty of daily Bible reading; the privilege and duty of prayer; the responsibility of regular attendance on and participation in the services of worship and prayer; the privilege and obligation to take active part in the organizations of the church—Sunday school, Training Union, Woman's Missionary Union, Brotherhood, choirs, etc.; the responsibility of preparation for efficient service through leadership and membership training; the opportunity and responsibility of witnessing; the commission to serve and the requirements of service.

Some basic Scripture passages: Psalm 119:9–16; Psalm 19; Isaiah 55:8–11; Mark 4:10–20; John 15:7–11; Psalm 92:1–5; Psalm 122; Isaiah 6:1–8; Matthew 18:18–20; Hebrews 10:24–25; Matthew 28:19–20; Luke 24:44–49; Acts 1:8–11; 26:12–20; Micah 6:6–8; Matthew 7:24–27; 25:14–30; Romans 12:1–8.

4. *The organized body of which the new member is a part.* What is meant by "joining the church"; the major activities of the functioning church; the need of full-rounded enlistment in the church's program of worship, teaching, training, giving, serving, witnessing; the imperative demand that every member be missionary; the inescapable responsibility of every member to be evangelistic; the responsibility of every member for financial support; the scriptural teachings as to stewardship and tithing; the essentials of happy and fruitful church membership; the church covenant into which the new member freely enters.

Some basic Scripture passages: Matthew 23:8–10; John 15:1–8; Ephesians 1:10–23; 2:20–22; Matthew 16:13–26; Acts 6:1–6; 1 Corinthians 12; 3 John 9:10; Matthew 18:15–18; Acts 2:41–47; John 17:11–23.

When the work of the class shall have been finished, a written statement of each member's decisions and resolutions might well be called for, to be copied by the church clerk or secretary onto the membership record. This statement might well include enlistment in Sunday school, Training Union, and other appropriate organizations; and statement of

intention of worship service attendance and of tithing or systematic giving. A service of special recognition should be held for those complet-
ing the class, at which time they may be congratulated on their achievement and perhaps given brief opportunity for testimony. Such a service
held at the prayer meeting hour, or at one of the Sunday worship services,
will impress new members and old alike with the church's seriousness of
concern for each addition to its family. The total influence of class meetings and church recognition will be far-reaching as an effective means
of conserving the church's fruitage of evangelism and enlistment.

A Church Teaching the Bible

A church, unless Bible-centered, becomes corrupted. It would have no authoritative guidebook, no positive message, no certain pattern of organization and activity, no rule of faith and practice—indeed, no worth-while reason for being.

A church exists to make the Bible—and the God of the Bible as revealed in Christ—known, loved, obeyed. The Sunday school, as the school of the church, has become the chief agency of evangelical churches (certainly in America) for the teaching of the Bible. Take this agency away, and many churches would collapse. By the Bible they have been made, and without the Bible they would be unmade.

More and more we have come to realize that Bible teaching and Bible preaching are two halves of a common whole. No sharp distinction is made between the church's promotion and support of its teaching and its preaching services. Considered together, with the Sunday school central as the church's agency for reaching the people and bringing them under the influence of both teaching and preaching, this essential function of a church may thus be analyzed and emphasized:

THE CHURCH AS A TEACHING INSTITUTION

The church began as a school. Jesus was recognized by friend and foe, by believer and doubter, as *rabbi, master,* that is, *teacher.* Those who gathered about him were best known as *disciples,* that is, *learners.* It was following an oral examination of the twelve, which they passed to his satisfaction, that he said, "I will build my church." The functions of a church, as indicated in the Gospels, Acts, and the Epistles, are more nearly described in terms of the functions of a school than any other analogous institution.

The early Christian churches were essentially schools wherein believers were taught the meaning of their faith, the application of the principles and example of Christ to personal and social living, and the propagation of the gospel by intelligent witnessing. The decline of Christianity in later centuries parallels the decline of the teaching functions of the churches. The recovery of New Testament Christianity has always been occasioned and accompanied by the recovery of teaching.

No sharp distinction is made between teaching and preaching. All effective gospel preaching has in it a large element of teaching, and all fruitful Christian teaching has in it an element of preaching. The minister or preacher is the chief teacher in the church. About him are gathered others—deacons, officers, classroom instructors, leaders of groups, specialized workers. The worth-whileness of every one of these helpers in the church must be measured ultimately in terms of teaching and learning outcomes. If an individual or an agency or an activity in a church does not contribute to educational fruitage, directly or indirectly, the right to a place in the church's program should be challenged immedi. ately.

A church needs an organized plan for the teaching of its supreme textbook, the Bible. Historically, in American Christianity, that agency has been the Sunday school. The name has become something of an anomaly, since the school of a church can no longer be thought of properly as confining its activities to the meeting on Sunday. Sometimes it is referred to as "Bible school," yet that is something of a misnomer, since its activities extend beyond the teaching of the Bible content as such. In some quarters it is known as the "church school," but again this is somewhat inaccurate since a church functions as a school through other organizations. Perhaps we would as well continue to designate it the "Sunday school," realizing that its greatest single opportunity is on Sunday, and that from this center it extends its influence into every day of the week.

In checking on the adequacy of a given Sunday school, the form on page 97 may be used.

THE ADMINISTRATION OF THE SUNDAY SCHOOL

Sunday school administration is both an art and a science. As an art it calls for men and women possessed of true artistry—insight, imagination, foresight, originality. As a science it calls for leadership on the part of those who know their work thoroughly, who are accurate in details, who are practical and factual in their attitudes, who are willing to experiment with new ideas and plans, who can stick to a proved policy until they get results, who can generalize their findings and project them successfully. Certainly administrative officers in the field of education should know education, they should keep up with the best books and methods, they should never be satisfied with mediocrity but should strive without ceasing for improvement. They should keep clearly before them end results and thus avoid the error of mistaking means for ends. They should be broad of interest and co-operative of spirit, never narrowly

CHECKING UP ON THE SCHOOL OF THE CHURCH

Items for evaluation	Yes	No	To some extent	Don't know
1. Is the Sunday school an integral part of the church?				
2. Does the church secure the best possible officers and teachers?				
3. Is sufficient and well-adapted literature provided?				
4. Is there a well-planned workers' library?				
5. Is the building well-suited to teaching purposes?				
6. Are departments and classes well-equipped?				
7. Is there an effective plan of officer-teacher training?				
8. Are records maintained and utilized from the church office?				
9. Is the Sunday school represented in the church cabinet council?				
10. Are regular reports made to and approved by the church?				
11. Are the regular expenses of the Sunday school provided for in the church budget?				
12. Does the Sunday school co-operate fully with the church?				
13. Does the Sunday school take constructive interest in the other organizations?				
14. Do Sunday school attendants remain for the preaching service?				
15. Does the Sunday school welcome and follow the pastor's leadership?				
16. Is the educational director functioning efficiently?				
17. If there is no educational director, is one needed?				
18. Is the Sunday school reaching its possibilities?				
19. Is the Sunday school vitally evangelistic?				
20. Does the Sunday school stress missions and denominational loyalty?				

or selfishly devoted to the aspect of the church's work for which they are especially responsible. They should submit themselves and their procedures to rigid criticism, making use of some such instruments as the following:

CHECKING UP ON OFFICERS OF THE SUNDAY SCHOOL

Items for evaluation	Yes	No	To some extent	Don't know
1. Are there enough general officers to do the work well?				
2. Have these general officers been selected with care and elected by the church?				
3. Are these officers taking appropriate training courses?				
4. Do these officers attend faithfully workers' conference, weekly officers and teachers' meeting?				
5. Do they attend faithfully the services of worship?				
6. Do they attend the midweek prayer service?				
7. Do they set a good example of stewardship in their giving?				
8. Are they interested in personal soul-winning?				
9. Are they dependable in the discharge of their duties?				
10. Are they prompt and accurate in their work?				
11. Are they furnished needed equipment by the church?				
12. Do they know specifically the duties of their office?				
13. Do they work together harmoniously?				
14. Do they strive to promote better teaching?				
15. Do they seek to discover and enlist new workers?				
16. Do they promote vigorously a continuous program of enlargement?				
17. Do they make maximum use of records and standards?				
18. Do they support the pastor as chief administrative officer?				
19. Do they work together to maintain an orderly schedule?				
20. Do they take an active work in other organizations of the church?				
21. Do they zealously promote evangelism and missions?				

THE TEACHING EFFICIENCY OF THE SUNDAY SCHOOL

The primary purpose of a *school* is that teachers may teach and learners may learn. All else is contributory to this main purpose. Teaching is not to be thought of narrowly as just that which goes on in the classroom, nor is learning to be confined to information gained in a period of classroom instruction. Teaching and learning are continuous processes. Everything about a Sunday school has value or disvalue for teaching and learning. Yet the heart of the matter is in that precious hour, more or less, when teacher and class are together for the avowed purpose of coming to close grips with the facts and truths and meanings of the Bible. Next to the minister, the most important and destiny-determining persons in a church are the teachers. It is therefore of paramount importance that they be wisely chosen, elected by the church, suitably assigned, encouraged and inspired, provided with the best possible quarters and facilities, and given every assistance to prevent their failure and guarantee their success. On page 100 is a suggested instrument for the sympathetic and appreciative review of the Sunday school's teaching personnel.

METHODS AND MATERIALS

Not only *what* Sunday school officers and teachers do, but *how* they do it is of great importance. Obviously there are right and wrong ways of working and teaching in the Sunday school. So life-giving is the Bible and so dynamic the situation in which it is taught by earnest people that much good may be accomplished with poor methods. It stands to reason, however, that much more good would be accomplished through good methods. There is danger of such overemphasis on method as to take away spontaneity and to hinder the work of the Spirit, but personality and the Spirit have better opportunity to make their impact where conditions are favorable rather than unfavorable. There are no hard and fast methods, no one *best* method of teaching or handling situations, but there are fairly well-defined ways of working which may be variously combined to meet changed and changing needs.

Materials are inseparably related to methods. Superintendents, secretaries, musicians, and other officers cannot do their best work without appropriate materials for their use. Teachers who have no adequate helps for their preparation and teaching are under intolerable handicaps. Members of classes will learn far less than they might unless they are supplied with attractive materials of study which they are induced to use. The Bible, of course, is the essential textbook of every class, yet the Scriptures must be "divided aright." Much of the Bible, read directly to little children, would be almost meaningless to them. The Bible without

CHECKING UP ON THE TEACHERS AND THE TEACHING OF THE SUNDAY SCHOOL

Items for evaluation	Yes	No	To some extent	Don't know
1. Are all classes supplied with teachers?				
2. Are teachers regular in attendance?				
3. Are teachers usually present ahead of time?				
4. Do teachers attend worship services regularly?				
5. Do teachers visit in the homes of class members?				
6. Are teachers concerned to build up their classes through visitation?				
7. Do teachers take active interest in department and school?				
8. Are teachers consistently taking training courses?				
9. Do teachers read books helpful to their work?				
10. Do teachers attend associational meetings?				
11. Do teachers make careful preparation to teach?				
12. Are teachers supplied with adequate helps for their work?				
13. Do teachers take weekday interest in their classes?				
14. Are teachers active personal soul-winners?				
15. Are teachers faithful supporters of the total church program?				
16. Are teachers missionary-minded?				

explanations or guidance as the textbook for older children would be too difficult for them. Even young people and adults, as a rule, find the Bible strange and hard to understand without expositions that help to open up its meaning. Aids to the understanding and use of the Bible must therefore be provided, adapted to the capacities and interests of the several age groups. These aids should never take the place of the Bible itself, but should make the Bible more attractive, more easily understood, more readily applied and obeyed. Materials purchased for officers, teachers, pupils may be sadly wasted. Much profit will come from occasional analysis of methods and materials with the instrument on the next page.

TESTING AND MEASURING RESULTS

Administration and teaching, however effective, are not ends in themselves. "By their fruits ye shall know them," is the test of Jesus which must be applied to persons and trees. Testing and measuring may be

CHECKING UP ON METHODS AND MATERIALS

Items for evaluation	Yes	No	To some extent	Don't know
1. Is the general superintendent a student of methods?				
2. Do department superintendents keep abreast of best methods?				
3. Are there books on methods available for officers and teachers?				
4. Have teachers had the "methods" books in the training course?				
5. Is use made of a variety of methods?				
6. Is the general assembly or departmental assembly a help to teaching?				
7. Is there time enough for teaching of the lesson?				
8. Is participation stimulated and guided?				
9. Are Bibles used freely and effectively?				
10. Do teachers take too much of the time?				
11. Is use made of objects, maps, etc.?				
12. Do teachers and officers confer about problems of improvement?				
13. Are records used to secure better teaching?				
14. Is use made by teachers of pupils' helps?				
15. Is stress consistently laid on home study of the lessons?				
16. Is classroom use made of pupils' preparation?				
17. Are the best available materials provided for pupils' use?				
18. Is checkup made to discover whether materials are being used?				
19. Is reading encouraged beyond the quarterly?				
20. Are class members learning to use their Bibles freely and intelligently?				

either subjective or objective. Objectively, results may be evaluated statistically, as increase or decrease in enrolment, fluctuations in attendance, number on time or tardy, number Bibles brought, number making offerings and the total, number who have studied the lesson, number who attend the preaching services. These items are *factual,* and their analysis will constitute a highly valuable measurement of the individual, the class, department, the school as a whole.

Subjectively, tests and measurements may take the form of intelligent opinion. Qualified observers have the right to reach conclusions concerning matters which cannot ordinarily be reduced to statistics—the personal qualifications of officers and teachers, the quality of teaching and learning, changes that are being wrought in human lives, the influencing of attitudes and choices, the deepening of devotion and loyalty, the carry-over of teaching into conduct and character. These intangible values, ultimately, are more important than the things that can be seen and counted, and need even more to be subjected to careful evaluation. Results may not be as accurately stated as those which can be mathematically calculated, but consensus of informed opinion is trustworthy and may furnish guidance to an understanding of the strength and weakness of the church's teaching program.

THE SUNDAY SCHOOL'S DISTINCTIVE NATURE AND MISSION

The demand has grown through the years that the Sunday school be a school, with the distinguishing marks of an educational enterprise. Numbers may be added and equipment may be furnished and still the Sunday school may not measure up to its highest and best as a *school*. What distinctive principles and ideals should be maintained for the school of the church? If the Sunday school is a school and is to attain its end primarily through instruction in the Bible, does it not follow that it ought to have a definite curriculum, adapted to the pupil's stage of development? If the Sunday school is really an educational institution, can it be carried on by untrained teachers, and, if not, what is the nature of the training required, and what are the necessary qualifications, intellectual and moral, to be demanded of teachers?

If the Sunday school is a part of the distinctively educational work of the church, it needs as its leaders men and women trained for educational work, and specifically for the teaching of the Bible. Can we ever have trained teachers until we have at the head of the school a man educated in the Bible and in pedagogical method? And does not this in turn call for a new type of minister, the teaching minister alongside the preaching minister? Finally, if instruction is the central function, and yet not the only function, of the Sunday school, what are the other legitimate aspects of its work, and how are these related to the teaching work and to one another?

DEVELOPING TEAMWORK AND EFFICIENCY

The best teaching cannot be done in isolation. The teacher's task becomes lonely and discouraging when it is done apart from fellowship

A CHECKUP ON THE SUNDAY SCHOOL'S FRUITAGE

Items for evaluation	Yes	No	To some extent	Don't know
1. Has census been taken to determine enrolment possibilities?				
2. Has there been consistent increase in enrolment?				
3. Is present enrolment equal to number of resident church members?				
4. Is there an active Cradle Roll department?				
5. Is there an active Extension department?				
6. Are Cradle Roll and Extension departments reaching their possibilities?				
7. Is the "point system" used in the keeping of records?				
8. On the six points (Juniors and above) is the average at least 70%?				
9. On the four points and two points (Primaries, Beginners, Nursery) is the average at least 70%?				
10. Are aims in assembly program clearly defined?				
11. Are aims in teaching clearly defined?				
12. Are the several "standards" used for guidance?				
13. Are their requirements being met?				
14. Are pupils acquiring definite Bible knowledge?				
15. Are definite changes in attitudes observable?				
16. Are life choices being positively influenced?				
17. Is spiritual growth evidenced by systematic and proportionate giving?				
18. Is willingness to serve in evidence throughout the school?				
19. Are the teachings of the Bible being carried over into business and social life?				
20. Is devotion to world missions being cultivated and expressed?				
21. Is there strong and intelligent denominational loyalty?				
22. Is some form of missionary activity being carried on in the community?				
23. Are persons being led toward and to Christ throughout the school?				
24. Is the pastor being given faithful support?				
25. Is there a consistent plan for testing and measuring results?				

with others. Teachers have many needs, but none greater than that of feeling a sense of divine call and mission, a spirit of sustained zeal and enthusiasm. Administrative officers need many things, but nothing more than appreciation of the spiritual importance of their work, of sympathetic co-operation on the part of the pastor, fellow officers, and teachers. A Sunday school may get along without a great many things, but it will never reach its richest fruitage without some plan for bringing together in fellowship and study those who are responsible for its conduct.

There are two main ways by which teamwork and efficiency may be developed in a Sunday school. One of these is through the monthly workers' conference; the other is through the weekly officers and teachers' meeting. They are not alternatives, nor should one be substituted for the other. The monthly workers' conference brings together pastor, general superintendent, general secretary, department superintendents, teachers, director of music and such representatives from classes and departments as may be needed. Their procedure will be somewhat as follows:

1. Records reviewed—averages for the preceding month, strong and weak points, need for special emphases.

2. Departmental reports—matters of general interest from each of the departments.

3. Needs presented—statements of needs of the school as a whole and the several departments and classes; discussion of ways to meet these needs.

4. Special problems—unusual difficulties which may have developed since the last meeting, especially in the matter of personnel replacements or classroom situations.

5. Enrolment and losses—names of new members indicated, classification problems discussed, names dropped for adequate cause.

6. Activities or new projects previewed—calendar of events studied, correlation and proper spacing effected, pastor's plans noted, new undertakings approved.

7. Recommendations—to the teachers, to departments of the school as a whole, to the church.

8. A season of prayer—for the unsaved, for the sick or distressed, for special objects, for spiritual guidance, for worthy fruitage.

The weekly officers and teachers' meetings is the key to the highest attainments of the Sunday school. One of its primary purposes is the improvement of teaching and the outcomes of teaching. Often a meal served at the early evening hour will make possible the attendance of many who could not otherwise come. The first consideration is that of closer acquaintanceship and finer fellowship on the part of all the workers. Matters of administration and promotion should of course have regular attention. Definite prayer should be offered for specific objects. Pastor and general superintendent will certainly have an important word for the group. Records will be analyzed and interpreted. Impetus will be given to visitation of absentees and prospects. Special concern will be manifested for the unsaved. The meeting itself may follow this schedule:

1. Fellowship meal—a half hour of breaking bread together that will intensify the sense of togetherness.

2. The secretary's report—brief analysis and interpretation of records.

3. The pastor's word—special emphasis on those matters which are uppermost in the pastor's concern.

4. Superintendent's period—projection of promotional plans, matters of general interest, helpful suggestions to meet specific needs.

5. Open discussion—opportunity for brief statement or statements from the floor on the part of those who have some important question or statement.

6. Prayer—for special objects that will be brought to the attention of the group.

7. Preparation for next Sunday—study of the lesson, preferably by age divisions with a view to effective and fruitful teaching.

8. Adjournment to prayer meeting.

THE PASTOR'S PART IN THE SUNDAY SCHOOL'S SUCCESS

The pastor, as chief officer of the Sunday school, is more responsible for its success than any other man in the church. The minister of education stands alongside the pastor, the two sharing together responsibilities which neither by himself could fully discharge. Since, however, only a relatively few churches are blessed with the services of full-time ministers of education, the burden of the Sunday school's well-being rests for the most part on the pastor's shoulders. We may thus summarize the pastor's part in the success of the Sunday school as its chief officer and leader:

1. To accept his commission as teacher and to follow the example of Jesus, "who went about teaching . . ."

2. To conceive the church as a school in Christian living with himself as pastor-teacher

3. To recognize the Sunday school as an integral part of the church and to identify himself with it

4. To give himself wholeheartedly to the task of discovering, enlisting, and training the best possible officers and teachers for the Sunday school

5. To counsel with the Sunday school officers and teachers, seeking through sympathetic and skilful supervision and counseling to give help where it is most needed

6. To utilize the Sunday school's resources for the achievement of all the church's major purposes, especially seeking to make inseparable the teaching and the preaching services

7. To keep himself thoroughly informed and equipped in Sunday school work, to the end that his leadership may be maximally effective in his own church, in the churches of his association, and in the state and Convention-wide plans and enterprises.

The pastor is the key, and his leadership alone will unlock the door to the treasures of the great new era which is opening up for us as we follow Christ in his program of teaching, preaching, healing for a lost world that awaits redemption.

AN INSTALLATION SERVICE FOR SUNDAY SCHOOL OFFICERS AND TEACHERS

Leader (addressing officers and teachers): "Go ye therefore, and make disciples, . . . teaching them to observe all things whatsoever I commanded you. . . ." This ancient summons from our Master has been heard by countless Christian teachers through the ages. It is heard and heeded by you today—you who are the officers and teachers of this church school—and it is fitting therefore that in beginning this new year, we should reaffirm our faith and rededicate ourselves to the high task that is before us.

Affirmation of the Teacher's Faith [1]

Leader: The Christian teacher believes in the power of truth. He finds the most important truth in Christ, in whom was the life that is the light of men. Falsehood may win battles, but only divine truth can assure ultimate triumph. The Master himself has said:

Congregation: "Ye shall know the truth, and the truth shall make you free."

Leader: The Christian teacher believes in the possibilities of growing life. His task is to call forth the slumbering talents in unfolding lives, and to nurture in youth the hope of bringing to pass what happened to the Youth of Nazareth:

Congregation: "And Jesus advanced in wisdom and stature, and in favor with God and man."

Leader: The Christian teacher believes that, through his precept and example, he can be used of God to communicate help and hope, light and good will to those entrusted to his care, and to lead them into an experience of growing, joyous discipleship to Christ. Like many before him, he would be found faithful in following this tested instruction:

Congregation: "Give diligence to show thyself approved unto God, a workman that needeth not to be ashamed, handling aright the word of truth."

---

[1] Adapted from "The High Task Before Us," by Rolland W. Schloerb, *International Journal of Religious Education*, September, 1945.

Service of Dedication

Leader: O God, who hast made us a part of the enduring fellowship of the church, and who hast given us the high vocation of making the mind of Christ known in the earth, before thee we reaffirm our purpose as we take up the work of this new year.

Officers and Teachers: It is our purpose as officers and teachers of this Sunday school:

to keep before us the needs of those whom we serve,

to strive for ability to do our work well,

to cultivate patience and understanding of those under our care,

to remember always that we are all learners at the feet of our common Lord,

to seek no reward but the approval of him who is the great Leader, and

to keep ever before us our goal of helping young and old to accept Jesus as their saving Lord, and to commit themselves wholeheartedly to his purpose and will for the world.

Congregation: It is our purpose as parents and members of this congregation:

to co-operate gratefully with all who instruct us and our youth,

to strengthen their hands by giving them the resources needed for good teaching, and

to make our homes proving grounds for the practice of Christian living.

Leader: And may the God of truth—the Father of him who said, "I am the way, the truth, and the life"—make you strong to perform his will, and to know that your labor in not in vain in the Lord.

A Church Training in Service

"We study that we may serve" has long been the slogan of the training department of Southern Baptist churches. Jesus said, "I am among you as he that serveth" (Luke 22:27); again, he reaffirmed Moses, saying "Thou shalt worship the Lord thy God, and him only shalt thou serve" (Matthew 4:10). The Lord of the church made service the test of greatness: "Whosoever would become great among you shall be your minister; and whosoever would be first among you shall be your servant; even as the Son of man came not to be ministered unto, but to minister, and to give his life a ransom for many" (Matthew 20:26–28 ASV). He made the basis of distinction between true and false disciples, in the final judgment, their service to others in need or their lack of service (Matthew 25:31–46).

A church, therefore, lives to serve, not to be served. If it is true to the ideal of its founder, a church does not call upon the people to give their service *to* it, but *through* it. A church that would save its life will lose it; a church that will lose its life in sacrificial service for Christ's sake will save it. Churches that do not understand this principle and are not deeply committed to it often wonder why they are relatively powerless and fruitless.

Even though agreed in principle on this primacy of service, the members of a church may have no adequate ways of channeling their service. Skill in service requires training no less than skill in Bible study and in worship. A full-rounded program of training in service would call for plans and procedures as hereafter described.

THE NEED FOR A DEPARTMENT OF TRAINING

No argument is needed for the church's teaching ministry. There has been less conviction as to a church's training ministry. If a church has a sound teaching program, and if it has an effective plan for leadership training, why should it multiply demands by the operation of a training department?

Assuredly there is no sharp distinction between teaching and training. Teaching places its chief emphasis upon instruction, the communication of ideas from teacher to class, the learning by the class of that which is presented by the teacher. Training reverses the emphasis. In the training process, self-activity takes precedence over instruction, the one being trained learns by doing, the leader is needed for guidance and supervision, but the individual is at the forefront with the leader in the background. Obviously teaching and training should never be sharply separated.

If time permitted, the teaching and training processes might be carried on simultaneously. Time limits being as they are, the morning hour in the Sunday church service would better be devoted to teaching. Yet clearly, for the average church member, effectiveness as a working Christian will not be attained unless teaching is supplemented with training. Because this truth has not been sufficiently recognized, multitudes of Christians are part-time church members, content to receive instruction but lacking in ability to translate learning into practice. A training program for its members therefore becomes an imperative necessity for every church that would fulfil its mission.

The concept of a training program for the total membership of the church has gradually evolved. Its origin was in the young people's society, which proposed to give to the youth of a church an active rather than a passive part. The young people's organizations (Young People's Society for Christian Endeavor, Epworth League, Baptist Young People's Union, Westminster League, etc.) attracted the younger boys and girls, who were designated "Juniors." When distinction was made in the Sunday school between Juniors (9–12) and Intermediates (13–16), in Baptist churches separate units of the Young People's Union were formed for these two age groups. Demand for inclusion of adults led to the formation of the Adult union, and because there was needed a place for the children who accompanied their parents, the "Story Hour" was instituted. Now Baptist Training Union is graded on an age basis corresponding exactly to the Sunday school. Gradually this total organization has come to be recognized as a church's most adequate plan for the training of all its people in church membership.

Many churches have caught the vision of a training service on Sunday evening, prior to the evening preaching service, comparable in many ways to the teaching service prior to the morning hour of worship. The possibilities of such a program of training are very great. Impression is given outlet in expression, silent Christians become vocal, church members are led to realize their significance, opportunities for practical Christian service are developed, hidden talents and abilities are brought to light, doctrinal convictions and devotional attitudes are deepened, missionary interests and denominational loyalties are broadened, the joy of witnessing for Christ is discovered, participation in the evening preaching service is made habitual. If these potentialities do not become actualities, it may be due to lack of leadership, to narrow vision, to prejudice and misunderstanding, to carelessness and superficiality in the use of plans and materials. Any church anywhere can carry on some form of membership training that is willing to pay the price. Constructive imagination will often be needed in order to adapt plans and programs to local conditions, but in the very process of adaptation a form of excellent training will be experienced.

Analysis of the church's training program, actual and potential, should frequently be made. Instruments for such an analysis and evaluation are needed.

REALIZING THE NEED OF TRAINING

Many Christians, on coming into the church, have very vague notions of their obligations and privileges. They have accepted Christ as Saviour and have been baptized in obedience to his command, but they can scarcely be expected to know how to live the Christian life and to become efficient church members unaided. The wastage of life opportunities represented by the multitudes of useless Christians whose names are on church rolls is tragic beyond measure. Conceivably every one of these inactive and often backslidden church members might have been a fruit-bearing disciple if he or she had only received the right training.

AS MATTERS NOW STAND

According to the records, a distressing number of the churches of the Southern Baptist Convention have no formal program of membership training. The training program offered by many of the churches is quite inadequate. Enrolment in the training program of almost all the churches is far below possibilities. Great progress has been made, but still greater progress needs to be made. Many churches do not know exactly what is going on in the field of membership training. A careful study of the facts would doubtless be both revealing and disturbing.

AS MATTERS MIGHT BE

That a churchwide training program might be inaugurated and sustained is no longer a fanciful dream. Churches are beginning to turn what was once deemed fantasy into fact. No longer is the emphasis on "joining the Training Union" as if it were some auxiliary organization of the church; rather, insistence is on every member receiving needed training in church membership and service as a part of his or her fundamental Christian obligation. "Save Sunday evening for the soul" is a slogan

CHECKING UP ON THE PRESENT MEMBERSHIP TRAINING PROGRAM

Items for evaluation	Yes	No	To some extent	Don't know
1. Has a study of the membership rolls been made to ascertain those who are available for training?				
2. Has a picture of the present training program (or lack of it) been brought forcefully to the church's attention?				
3. Is the church fairly well satisfied with the present training program?				
4. Are graded departments being provided for the little children?				
5. Does the Training Union enrolment of Juniors compare favorably with that of the Sunday school?				
6. Does the Training Union enrolment of Intermediates compare favorably with that of the Sunday school?				
7. Does the Training Union enrolment of young people compare favorably with that of the Sunday school?				
8. Does the Training Union enrolment of adults compare favorably with that of the Sunday school?				
9. Are there enough officers, leaders, sponsors and counselors to give the Training Union efficient leadership?				
10. Is the Training Union given active support by pastor, deacons, leading laymen and women?				
11. Are Training Union expenses provided for worthily in the budget?				
12. Are there attractive meeting places for the Training Union?				
13. Are study courses held and well attended in the interest of Training Union improvement?				
14. Is the Training Union provided ample equipment and helps?				
15. Are the Training Union meetings vital and attractive?				
16. Are the outcomes of the Training Union worthy and gratifying?				

worthy to become a battle cry. What could be more reasonable than to expect Christian families to come as groups to the church on Sunday evenings, where they will devote an hour to Bible reading review, discussion, testimony, expressional activity, preparation for service, enrichment of mind and soul in the happiest fellowship on earth? The hour of training will then be followed by the hour of worship, in which families and friends will sit together, sing together, pray together, listen together to the sermon, and strive together for the winning of the lost. Possibilities may be thus investigated:

CHECKING UP ON POSSIBILITIES OF THE TRAINING SERVICE

Items for evaluation	Yes	No	To some extent	Don't know
1. Has a survey been made to discover what the church members do with their Sunday evenings?				
2. Have church members been challenged to keep their Sunday evenings for spiritual things?				
3. Do many church members have wrong conceptions of the Training Union?				
4. Would it be practicable to reorganize the Training Union on the basis of total available possibilities?				
5. Would members respond to the call of the church if they were placed in appropriate units and requested to attend?				
6. Could leadership be discovered sufficient to provide for this greatly enlarged enrolment?				
7. Could essential outlines in the quarterlies be followed, yet originality employed in adapting the materials to local needs?				
8. Could the Training Union be made actually to produce competent members to fill church jobs?				
9. Could the evening preaching service be greatly reinforced by enlarged Training Union attendance?				
10. Would intelligent participation in the full Training Union program produce fruits of Christian living and character?				

STANDARDIZED GUIDES FOR A GRADED TRAINING PROGRAM

The training department of a church should not be haphazardly organized and conducted. Large liberty is, of course, permitted, since churches will vary widely in their needs and resources. Long experience has demonstrated, however, that certain forms of organization are essential, that meetings can be most profitably conducted according to a tested pattern, that activities are most fruitful if they follow specifications and calendars that have been agreed upon. In the course of years, "Standards of Excellence" have been devised for the Training Union as a whole and for each

CHECKING UP ON THE TRAINING UNION STANDARDS

Items for evaluation	Yes	No	To some extent	Don't know
1. Has the general Training Union Standard been clearly presented?				
2. Is this Standard emphasized continuously and attractively?				
3. Is the function of the Standard as a *guide* made clear?				
4. Are the administrative requirements of the Standard met?				
5. Is the Training Union accepted as the *training department* of the whole church?				
6. Are there enough unit organizations to meet the training needs of the whole church?				
7. Are there enough officers, leaders, sponsors and counselors to meet the needs?				
8. Are the weekly meetings interesting and worthwhile?				
9. Is daily Bible reading effectively promoted?				
10. Are study courses offered regularly?				
11. Are the study courses sufficiently well attended?				
12. Does the officers' planning council function effectively?				
13. Is the prayer calendar generally observed?				
14. Is the calendar of activities faithfully followed?				
15. Are the several department Standards studied and taken seriously?				
16. Could the training work of the church be improved by faithful use of the Standards?				

of the age-group departments. That these "standards" or "guides" are suggestive and not authoritative cannot be emphasized too strongly. Experience proves that where they are used intelligently as instruments of measurement, and as guides to efficiency and balance, results are more gratifying. The several standards give a comprehensive view of a well-ordered, functioning training department.

A CHURCH TRAINING ITS OFFICERS AND LEADERS

Success in church work depends on more than good intentions. Ability in other fields does not necessarily transfer into the field of lay office-holding. A man may be an excellent member of a board of directors of a corporation but a poor deacon or church trustee. A woman may be highly efficient as a housekeeper or club member but a very inefficient leader in the missionary society. A young man may be dependable and ambitious in his occupation or profession but careless and indifferent in his Christian youth organization.

Efficiency in church leadership demands a reasonable amount of specific training. It is not enough to have sporadic "training courses" in which books about the duties and privileges of leadership are hurriedly discussed. A church, conceived as a school, should have a unified, cumulative program of leadership training according to which those placed in positions of responsibility would be measurably insured against failure and developed in understanding and skills to the point of satisfying and rewarding competency.

In the making of such a program of church-centered leadership training, certain demands must be met, calling for guidance somewhat as follows:

A POLICY OF LEADERSHIP TRAINING

The Sunday school introduced leadership training into present-day churches. The Sunday school began as a lay movement, but gradually gained favor and was adopted in America as the chief teaching agency of the churches. With the rapid increase of Sunday schools and Sunday school enrolment, the demand for competent officers and teachers far exceeded the supply. A similar situation was confronted by the public schools. Teachers whose qualifications were little more than willingness to serve were pressed into service. "Normal schools" were provided for public schoolteachers, where in brief summer terms of instruction they were given some elementary knowledge of principles and methods of teaching.

Books describing "laws of learning" and "steps in teaching" undertook to establish "norms" or standards according to which teachers would be enabled to transmit textbook information to pupils more or less successfully. This idea of equipping Sunday school teachers and officers for their work by means of brief and intensive study of "manuals" was early adopted, and has remained one of the principal plans of leadership training. That it was well adapted to the needs of the church school, with its volunteer teachers and its loosely organized curriculum, is evidenced by the tremendous growth of American Sunday schools.

The public school system outgrew and abandoned the "normal school" plan and advanced to the establishment of teachers' colleges where teaching and school administration are recognized as a profession calling for full-rounded equipment comparable to that demanded in other professional circles. The evolution of the leadership training program in the churches has been slower and of course much less elaborate. The occasional "training school" or "study course" held on five evenings with some two hours of study each evening is standard practice. The city-wide or associational leadership training school is still being promoted, but there is more and more emphasis upon the study course for a group of neighboring churches or for one church.

Study by departmental groups is likewise being emphasized, as also individual home study. The weekly officers and teachers' meeting, when properly conducted, is one of the most effective means of training officers and teachers. Bible teaching clinics, where concentrated attention is given to meeting actual needs, to demonstration of better methods, to the sharing of ideas and problems, and to actual application of principles in the books to local needs, have become a popular variation. Enlargement campaigns afford opportunity to put into practice principles advocated in the textbooks on administration. The school of missions has shown the possibility of missionary study by graded groups.

After much study and experimentation the Sunday School Board developed the "Church Study Course for Teaching and Training" and began promoting it in October, 1959. It was described as "a merger of three study courses previously promoted by the Sunday School Board—the Sunday School Training Course, the Graded Training Union Study Course, and the Church Music Training Course." Effective October 1, 1961, the name was changed to "Church Study Course" when Woman's Missionary Union became a part of it. Book awards earned in the other courses may be transferred to the new course.

The course is comprehensive, with books grouped into twenty categories. The purpose of the course is to (1) help Christians grow in knowledge and conviction; (2) help them to grow toward maturity in

Christian character and competence for service; (3) encourage them to participate worthily as workers in their churches; and (4) develop leaders for all phases of church life and work.

The course is fully graded. Books for Adults and Young People are listed in all categories. Special books which are focused on the peculiar interests and needs of Young People are offered in ten categories. Books for Intermediates and Juniors are placed in proper categories. Provision is made for noncredit courses for Primary, Beginner, and Nursery children. The system of awards provides a series of five diplomas of twenty books each for Adults or Young People, two diplomas of five books each for Intermediates, and two diplomas of five books each for Junior boys and girls.

Further developments of the Church Study Course will probably be along these lines: (1) A program of training adopted by the church with successive steps and gradation of difficulty of subject matter, looking toward the progressive equipment of each worker to ever-increasing competency. (2) Emphasis placed on clinical training for leadership, with more carry-over of actual efficiency in the performance of church duties. (3) Greater care in the selection of those who teach study courses, with requirement of certain minimum preparation, and higher standards for the bestowal of awards.

INTENSIVE TRAINING FOR NEW MEMBERS

The loss of church members through indifference and inactivity should be stopped at its source. As matters stand, for every person who becomes an enlisted and participating member of the average church, there is one who loses interest, drops out of attendance, and receives and contributes nothing or next to nothing. Without passing judgment on the genuineness of the conversion of "backslidden" members, may we not seriously consider the blameworthiness of the church that permits such tragic loss without serious and determined effort to prevent it?

We have assumed that ample provision has been made for the new members through the church's program of worship, Bible study, training, giving, service, and fellowship. But if this provision proves adequate for only one out of two members, may we not seriously question the assumption? Obviously there is need of concentration of concern for each new member as soon as received, whether he is received, by letter, by baptism, or by statement.

The Training Union is the logical agency of the church to provide, under the pastor's guidance, a class for orientation and intensive training leading to clear understanding of the privileges and obligations involved

CHECKING UP ON THE CHURCH'S STUDY COURSE PROGRAM

Items for evaluation	Yes	No	To some extent	Don't know
1. Has the church a well-defined policy of leadership training?				
2. Is the leadership training plan primarily that of special "study course weeks"?				
3. Is emphasis given to individual study of standard study course books?				
4. Are there other plans of study course work besides special weeks and individual study?				
5. Are study courses sometimes given in connection with weekly officers and teachers' meetings?				
6. Are better methods sometimes given demonstration?				
7. Has the Church Study Course been presented and adopted?				
8. Should more emphasis be placed on development of special abilities in the training services?				
9. Is sufficient care given to selection of textbooks for training course purposes?				
10. Has the church a step-by-step plan of guidance for those enrolling in study course work?				
11. Are those enlisted as officers, teachers, leaders, enrolled immediately in a cumulative program of training?				
12. Are careful records kept of all study course awards?				
13. Is recognition given publicly by the church of study course achievements?				
14. Does the church constantly try to enlist promising persons for leadership training?				

in becoming a member of a particular church and to definite committal to specific responsibility for participation in the life and work of the church. To this end the Training Union should regularly organize and conduct a brief course for all new members, using guidance materials supplied for this purpose from Training Union headquarters. The Training Union Department of the Baptist Sunday School Board has provided a book entitled *Your Life and Your Church,* to be used for this purpose. It is available in the Baptist Book Store. In the section of this book dealing with the conservation of church members (Section VI), additional suggestions are given for the conduct of such a course, with outline of topics and basic Scriptures to be used.

The ideal of Sunday school and Training Union as correlative agencies of the church needs to be made increasingly real. The Sunday school cannot provide a complete educational program for the church. Its specialty is Bible study and teaching. Loss rather than gain would be suffered should it depart from this central function and offer "elective" courses in other subjects, no matter how greatly needed. The Sunday school needs the supplement which is provided in the program of the Training Union. In turn, the Training Union should be looked upon as a source from which the Sunday school will ordinarily draw its supply of trained officers and teachers.

It follows, therefore, that the Sunday school should accept definite responsibility for recruiting members of the Training Union, seeking to enlist all church members who attend its classes in the several Training Union departments. No Sunday school can be at its best that is not supplementing its Bible teaching with training in church membership. Since Training Union is the training department of the church, what more natural than that it should undertake to discover and develop teachers and leaders for the Sunday school, Woman's Missionary Union, Brotherhood, music department, and other specialized groups?

The Training Union's department of specialized training proposes to serve this highly practical purpose. First, a survey will be made to discover available persons in the church membership who have leadership qualifications but who are not now enlisted in service. Study should be made of needs of the several organizations for officers, teachers, leaders, sponsors, helpers. Specialized training classes should then be organized from these lists of prospects and persons invited to enlist for a limited period of special training. The class will not be just a "study course," though naturally study course books will be used. The definite objective will be to get ready a group of people for work in each of the church's organizations and special activities by giving them a three months' course in that particular field, which will involve not only the use of books, but guided experiences in getting acquainted with the organization or field of special activity, becoming familiar with literature and methods, and having opportunities for acquiring practical skills in doing the job.

Who will lead the specialized training class? Obviously the best persons available must be secured. For the Sunday school, it may be the general superintendent, or a department superintendent, or one of the ablest teachers, occasionally the pastor. For Training Union, it may be the director, or the best equipped person who knows Training Union work thoroughly and is able to give practical training to prospective officers and leaders. For the Woman's Missionary Union, it may be the president, or some member of the organization who is competent and zealous in the work of the organized women. For the Brotherhood and deacons, it may be the president or a member who is skilled in developing the possibilities of the men's work. Thus for each of the specialized groups there should be found the one best person qualified to give practical direction to an intensive course in the organization for whom prospective officers and teachers and leaders are needed.

When will the course be given? The time will depend on local conditions. A week night may be set apart and the group meet for an hour once a week. Or the class may be held continuously each evening for two or more weeks. One of the most successful plans is that of conducting the course at the regular Training Union hour for a period of three months. This has the advantage of relating the specialized training directly to the Training Union, enlisting the Training Union's help in securing attendance, and making the course an integral part of the Training Union's program. Since many of those in the special course will not be in Training Union when enrolled, they may well be counted on to remain as members of one of the regular groups at the conclusion of the special course. The only difference between this specialized training course and the regular units will be that instead of the quarterly program materials being used, the group in charge will present a phase of the work of the organization for which workers are being prepared. Records will be taken covering the usual eight points, daily Bible reading will be urged and the quiz conducted, the activities calendar will be emphasized, and the closing assembly attended. Care should be taken in enrolment of members for the specialized course not to take needed officers or leaders from the regular unions, thus crippling them. The specialized course is primarily for prospective workers who are not already in places of responsibility, or who as new workers feel the need of an intensive course to fit them for their duties.

For example, in the orientation course for Sunday school workers, on one evening the group in charge will be pastor, general superintendent, and other general officers. They will present an over-all view of the Sunday school and its needs and lead the discussion. Successively the resource groups in charge will be Cradle Roll and Nursery workers, teachers and officers of Beginner, Primary, Junior, Intermediate, Young People's, Adult, and Extension departments. As each department is presented, appropriate literature and study course books will be displayed. The final periods may be devoted to emphasis on fundamental principles of teaching, its methods and aims. The entire class will thus be exposed to the total needs and opportunities of the whole school. Each member will be in position to make intelligent discovery of the place in the school where he or she can best serve. During the course of the class, members may receive experience as supply teachers and may observe the work of a department or class in which they are especially interested. Thus a reservoir of prospective teachers and officers may be continuously provided for the Sunday school—or for any other organization of the church which may desire to utilize the plan. Care must be taken not to let this plan of specialized training interfere with the regular functions of the Training Union. Although there are obvious advantages, it is not essential that the plan be operated on Sunday evening.

SUGGESTED GENERAL TRAINING ENROLMENT CARD

Recognizing my need of continuous study to the end that as a growing Christian, I may become an ever-increasingly efficient and fruit-bearing church member, I hereby enrol for training in the following general fields, and may be counted on to read suggested books and take study course classes as offered and when possible:

_____Home Missions	_____The Church
_____Foreign Missions	_____The Home
_____Bible Study	_____Stewardship
_____Christian Doctrines	_____Soul-winning
_____History	_____The Denomination

SUGGESTED SPECIALIZED STUDY COURSE ENROLMENT CARD

Realizing that my church needs trained workers in its several organizations and their departments and for the work of the church as a whole, and being aware of my own need of competency as a Christian and church member, I hereby enrol for training in the field or fields checked below:

_____Training Union Efficiency	_____Deacons and Church Officers
_____Sunday school Efficiency	
_____W. M. U. Methods	_____Church Music and Worship
_____Brotherhood Methods	

(Other side of card)

Name _____ Address _____

Age _____ How long church member _____

Now enrolled in _____ Date _____

RECORD OF LEADERSHIP TRAINING PROGRESS

Name _____

Address _____

How long church member _____

Enrolled _____ (date) for courses as follows:

_____   _____   _____   _____

Suggested program of study:

_____   _____   _____   _____

_____   _____   _____   _____

(Other side of card)

Completed satisfactorily courses as follows:

Date	Course	Book	Award

Remarks:

A Church Reaching the Unreached

Jesus's plan of recruitment was amazingly simple and effective. A preacher (John the Baptist) bore witness to the claim of Jesus to be the Messiah. Two of John's followers put these claims to the test in a personal experience, and were convinced. Each then brought another to Jesus, and they in turn were convinced. Through the influence of two of these disciples, a fifth was won. This man was instrumental in winning the sixth. Thus the process went on until there were twelve, later "seventy also," and at length "above five hundred," one hundred and twenty of whom met the conditions of the outpouring of the Holy Spirit at Pentecost, when more than three thousand were added in a day.

Accompanied by the "inner circle" of the disciples, "Jesus went about all the cities and the villages, teaching in their synagogues, and preaching the gospel of the kingdom, and healing all manner of disease and all manner of sickness" (Matthew 9:35 ASV). Relative to possibilities, the results were clearly disappointing. When Jesus observed the unreached multitudes, "he was moved with compassion for them, because they were distressed and scattered, as sheep not having a shepherd." Humanly the task was too great for their meager numbers. Through divine power only could they meet this need, hence the instruction of Jesus, "Pray ye therefore the Lord of the harvest, that he send forth laborers into the harvest" (Matthew 9:38). Proceeding with his plan, Jesus called unto him in still closer fellowship the twelve, to whom he gave "authority over unclean spirits, to cast them out, and to heal all manner of disease and all manner of sickness." He then charged the twelve as he sent them forth, saying, "Go not into any way of the Gentiles, and enter not into any city of the Samaritans: but go rather to the lost sheep of the house of Israel. And as ye go, preach, saying, The kingdom of heaven is at hand. Heal the sick, raise the dead, cleanse the lepers, cast out demons: freely ye received, freely give" (Matthew 10:5–8). Beyond the "lost sheep of the house of Israel" lay the vast multitudes of Gentiles, but to reach them would require recruits from those closer at hand who were in a peculiar sense "his own," whose heritage as Jews should have made them especially susceptible to the call of the gospel. From their number would come the witnesses at Pentecost and beyond.

There can be no improvement on this plan of Jesus for reaching the unreached. His broad principles and his instructions given to meet the conditions of his day must nevertheless be implemented and adapted to the changing conditions of succeeding ages. In the practical working out of Jesus' plan of disciple winning, we need to develop and utilize certain tested procedures.

SYSTEMATIC DISCOVERY OF THOSE TO BE REACHED

In a certain city a group of pastors, representing several denominations, were discussing the history and growth of the community's churches. Baptists had outstripped all others, both in number of churches and in total membership. A pastor of one of the oldest churches in the city, seeking the explanation, said: "When the pioneer missionaries of some of the denominations came to a developing community, they asked, 'Where are the Lutherans, or Episcopalians, or Presbyterians?' But when the Baptist missionary came, he simply asked, 'Where are the people?'"

People without Christ or church affiliation are indeed "distressed and scattered, as sheep not having a shepherd." They did not respond to the invitation of Jesus himself. "Come unto me," he pleaded, "and I will give you rest." "How often would I have gathered thy children together, . . . and ye would not!" Worldly Christians and unregenerate sinners can scarcely be expected to seek out the church uninvited. Active church members, moving into a new community, often feel a hesitancy in aligning themselves with a church. In almost every sizeable community there are enough church members with their membership elsewhere to form several new churches. All these need to be located by name and address, to be cultivated until confidence is established and interest is aroused. This program of discovery has been reduced to near-science, the procedures being thus described, the chief agency used being the Sunday school:

1. *Check the membership roll*, to discover those who are enlisted or unenlisted: in attendance on the preaching services; in the Sunday school; in the Training Union; in Woman's Missionary Union or Brotherhood. Multiple lists of inactive members in each of these organizations should be made, one copy being retained for the permanent files and other copies turned over to the organizations involved.

2. *Take a religious census*, in which all the homes in the community will be visited by visitors who have been carefully trained, who have been assigned definite territory, who will secure firsthand information on census cards concerning every person in every home visited.

3. *Organize the census returns*, eliminating first those who are not the church's responsibility, dividing the remainder into those already enrolled

and those unenrolled, assorting the cards of the unenrolled into age groups, making multiple lists of these groupings to show name, age, address, church member or nonchurch member, prospect for enrolment, in what organization and department, church preference (if any), and how best approached.

4. *Provide enlargement of organization and quarters* on the basis of possibilities discovered, in confident expectation that many of these prospects will be enrolled and with a view to meeting their needs so satisfyingly that they will be held.

5. *Visit systematically and continuously,* using so persuasively the inducements of friendship and good salesmanship to attract those who have been found that they will come once and again, eventually being won into the full life of the church and then going out to win others. (See Arthur Flake, *Building a Standard Sunday School,* Chapter 3.)

WHO GOES TO CHURCH—AND WHY?

The assumption of the enlargement plan described above is that those who are visited persistently and invited attractively will first join the Sunday school, then be led to Christ and into the church, and will then quite naturally take their places in the full life of the church. For a gratifying number this assumption will prove true, but for many others it is unsound. The names may be secured, the visits may be made, not once but often, the invitation to attend may be given ever so attractively, yet many never respond. Another type of inquiry needs to be instituted, another form of census taken. The questions raised might be somewhat as follows:

1. Did you once attend church regularly? _____

2. Do you now attend occasionally? _____

3. Do you not attend because: duties prevent _____ health hinders _____ distance inconveniences _____ need sleep Sunday morning _____ need Sunday for rest and recreation _____ dislike Sunday school _____ dislike church music _____ dislike preaching _____ church-going too expensive _____ cannot dress suitably _____ lost faith in religion _____ feel that church is against my viewpoint and interests _____ can spend my time better otherwise _____ have little confidence in preachers and religious leaders _____ have become absorbed in other things _____ have just broken the habit and lost interest _____ somehow have not

found the right church _____ expect to begin church going some-
time _____

4. Could we do anything to help you overcome your difficulty? _____

5. Would you be willing to discuss your problem with some earnest,
intelligent Christian? _____

6. When could this visitor conveniently call? _____

Certain questions for pastor and people should follow:
Why do many of this community never attend church?
If it is their fault, how can they be made to realize it?
If it is the church's fault, how can we remedy it?
How may we train a group of "counseling visitors" to make contacts
with these nonattendants with a view to getting at their real problems
and help them to see that Christ and the church have the answer to their
deepest needs?

TAKING THE CHURCH TO PEOPLE WHERE THEY ARE

Every church has two constituencies—those who attend its services.
and those who do not. Usually they are about evenly divided. About half
the members of the church are enrolled in Sunday school, with about 50
percent of these, on the average, regularly present. About half the resident members will attend the preaching services on a given Sunday. About
half the members will contribute something to the support of the church,
with some 50 percent of these giving regularly. Out in the community are
many people, members and nonmembers, who for various reasons are shut
out from regular attendance on the church services. A church therefore is
simply following the line of least resistance if it ministers only to those who
come to the house of worship.

The most immediate solution to the problem of nonattendance on the
part of those who are prevented is the *Extension Department.* In view of
the challenging needs and possibilities, this department should be greatly
magnified. Its work cannot be safely entrusted to a Sunday school class or
classes, nor to the missionary society or Brotherhood. The Extension Department of great universities is often on a parity in many respects with
the work done in its classrooms. A church may conceivably reach as many
people through its Extension Department as are reached through its regular services.

Too long has this department been thought of narrowly, its ministry
confined to occasional visits to the aged and the invalid, with hasty

checkup on their Bible reading and the delivery of a magazine and other literature. Fortunately, it is beginning to be recognized that through this department a church may bring to a multitude of people practically all the ministries which it offers to those who cannot attend its regular services. To make this vision of the Extension Department come true, it must be presented attractively to the congregation, given strong leadership and serious support, and made an important and recognized division of the church's work. Efficient organization and fruitful operation of the Extension Department will involve the following essentials:

A superintendent, with vision, ability, devotion, influence, time.

Associate superintendents, to assist the superintendent in planning, to share responsibility of supervision of visitors, to have oversight of the work in each of the several geographical divisions.

A secretary, to keep enrolment up-to-date, to keep and publicize accurate records, to note strong and weak points, to co-operate with superintendent and associates, to keep in touch with visitors, to handle mailing of birthday cards and the like, to order needed literature, to secure and use the necessary record forms and supplies, to foster special activities.

Visitors, who commit themselves wholeheartedly to this spiritual ministry, who form a vital link between the church and the Extension Department, who visit with skill and purpose, who enlist in Bible study and prayer, who encourage family worship, who supply Christian fellowship, who make contacts between members and the pastor, who practice the art of Christian counseling, who utilize every opportunity for soul-winning, who seek to bring the ministries of the church to those who cannot attend and bring to active attendance all who find it possible.

Sunday school support, the department being established as a regular department of the Sunday school, under its leadership and guidance, its officers and visitors a part of the Sunday school forces, its enrolment and records regularly reported and counted as an integral part of the Sunday school's responsibility.

Church recognition and approval, the work of the department being brought before the whole church, its officers elected by the church, provisions for expenses provided in the budget of the church.

EXTENSION THROUGH PLANNED VISITATION

The Extension Department is not a substitute for *systematic, planned visitation.* Some of the most effective plans of visitation are:

Home visitation by officers and teachers of the Sunday school, to cultivate acquaintance with Sunday school members and their families, to care for sick and distressed members, to bring back absentees, to interest and enrol new members.

Home lesson study, the teaching in the home of the Sunday school lesson to those who are unavoidably absent.

Regular, concerted monthly visitation of absentees and prospective members by officers, teachers, and selected workers who will go together from the church to visit on Sunday afternoon every person in whom an interest should be shown.

Special visitation, by pastor and selected members into homes where difficult problems are confronted, or unusual cases are to be dealt with, calling for skill and experience beyond that of the average visitor.

REACHING CHILDREN THROUGH THE HOMES

To the many adult "shut-ins" must be added an increasing number of children "shut-outs." These children are shut out from the privileges of church and Sunday school, not from their own choice, but because of the indifference or difficult circumstances of their parents. Efforts to bring them to the church are often unavailing. Again, ways must be found of taking the church to them.

A plan to reach them through Christian homes in the neighborhood has been found effective and useful. In almost every neighborhood where there are unreached children, a Christian family may be located to whose home the near-by children may be invited. After school hours, or on Saturday or Sunday, children not in Sunday school may be induced to come to the home of a neighbor for a happy Bible story hour. Few parents would object if the time could be arranged conveniently. The "story hour" feature will appeal to the children, and their enjoyment will bring them back again and again. Materials for use of the leader or leaders have been prepared by the American Baptist Publication Society, 1703 Chestnut Street, Philadelphia 3, Pennsylvania, and may be had at nominal cost. These home story hour meetings will of course not take the place of Sunday school attendance, but the series of carefully planned home services should achieve the following results: (1) "Every child should have been introduced to the Christian message in such a way as to make him want to know more about Christ. (2) "Every child should have been enrolled in some church school. (3) "Every child, who is ready to do so, should have been encouraged to accept Christ as his Saviour and declare his purpose to follow him."

It is emphasized that "these few meetings are insufficient for getting the whole program of evangelism accomplished. The neighborhood meetings are only the beginning. We must follow up with a thorough-going program of teaching in the church and in the home."

The young people unattached to any church constitute a great host. Many who have been in Sunday school throughout childhood begin to drop out in the intermediate years and form a swelling volume of losses as they grow to be young people. Some have never had church relationships, hence have no ties that bind them to the church. Over against these are the devoted young people who have found their highest self-realization in Christ and in the service of their church. Better than any others, Christian young people can reach other young people who are adrift or unsaved.

The *youth revival* is one of the best means of utilizing young people to reach young people. Some of the distinctive features of this plan are:

Deep concern, on the part of pastor, deacons, adults, and young people for the unreached youth of the community.

Selected leadership, consisting of a devoted inner circle of Christian young people who have the courage to witness for Christ to their fellow young people, who have found joy in Christian discipleship, who are willing to spend and be spent for Christ.

Originality of plan, not just another "revival meeting," but selection of names of young people to be reached, invitation of these to homes for an attractive social hour, demonstration that Christ brings life to richest fulfilment and is not just an affair of church going and moral rules and regulations.

"Eight great days," with preacher or preachers chosen by the young people, music of high quality, but "different," special features by talented Christian young people, testimonies by young people as to what Christ means to them, personal visitation and invitation to secure attendance of unreached young people, effective advertising of the meetings, special nights featuring special youth groups, full co-operation of pastor and adult membership in making the meeting successful.

Appeals for decision, not just to be baptized and join the church, but to make out-and-out commitment to Christ, to abandon whatever stands in the way, to accept the promised guidance of the Holy Spirit, to enter upon a life dedicated to Christian service, to become an unashamed witness for Christ.

Follow-up, the youth revival serving as a beginning point rather than a terminus, saved young people grouping themselves together as prayermates and personal workers, other unchurched and unsaved young people being found and won, dedications sought for full-time Christian service, places of usefulness found in the church, in the association, in the community, wherever young people are needed.

MEN REACHING UNREACHED MEN

The near-despair of many pastors and churches is the large number of men in the community, who, though claiming to be Christians, are lost to usefulness; and the many men who are outside the Christian fold altogether. These unreached men can usually best be reached by other men. The usual methods of invitation and visitation will be found effective in reaching some of these men, but something unusual is needed to reach many others. One of the most effective plans for reaching men through men is the *Laymen's Revival*.

The Laymen's Revival is a revival in the original sense of the word. It is not primarily a soul-winning campaign, but an effort to reach, enlist, refresh and renew the men of the church. The success of such a revival calls for thorough and careful preparation. Details of the plan have been developed out of wide experience of the Baptist Brotherhood.

Organization for the revival should be simple but effective. A layman should be chosen as chairman, selected because of his influence and spiritual vitality. Certain committees will be needed, to give direction and promotion to publicity, transportation, entertainment, finances, music, visitation. Of course the pastor's leadership is indispensable. Some of the most successful laymen's revivals have begun on Sunday, at the regular morning preaching hour, and have continued through Wednesday. Others have continued through the following Sunday.

The program of the revival should be varied and maximally attractive to men. Laymen will be in charge of the services, laymen will furnish the music, a layman will bring the message at each service, laymen will pray and testify. The entire male membership of the church will be listed and divided into small groups of some seven to ten men. To the inner circle of men of the church will be given these names for personal visitation, invitation, conversation.

The definite aim of the revival will be, not only to secure attendance of the men, but also to deepen their spiritual lives, to lead them to expression of rededication, and to commit them to active participation in the full program of the church. To this end cards will be provided on which may be indicated the determination to read the Bible and pray regularly, to attend the services or worship, to enlist in Sunday school and Training Union, to practice stewardship-tithing, to bear personal witness to other men, to put the principles of Christianity into everyday practice, to give more time to spiritual things, to build a Christian home. Of course the revival will not be for men only, but all others will be welcomed and urged to attend.

REACHING THE UNREACHED THROUGH VISITATION EVANGELISM [1]

The gravest departure by many churches from New Testament evangelism is their dependence on an annual evangelistic meeting, led by a preacher and a singer, with a handful of devoted Christians—usually Sunday school officers and teachers—concentrating their efforts for a brief period on that which should be the church's perennial business, the making of disciples. No greater recovery could come to these churches than that of lay witnessing, the enlistment of an ever-increasing number of laymen and laywomen to go to the unchurched and the unsaved, not just to invite them to hear the preacher's message or to join one of the church's organizations, but to present the claims of Christ and press for decision. The occasional evangelistic meeting will not bring the unsaved multitudes to Christ for the simple reason that they are not present. Evangelism will inevitably fall short of its fruitage even though, during one or two weeks of intensive effort, the people go afield to visit the unsaved. A church that takes its commission seriously must inaugurate and maintain a plan of continuous visitation evangelism.

A plan of this sort must have a beginning. A dependable and consecrated group of men and women may be called together by the pastor, who will discuss with them the possibilities and requirements of a successful visitation evangelism program. Having decided that the time is ripe to begin, they will make a list of members whom they will call together in a larger conference. The pastor will of course present the matter from the pulpit, it will be made the subject of discussion and prayer at the prayer meeting, in other organizations throughout the church it will be presented attractively. From the census returns or otherwise names of unchurched and unsaved people will be gathered. The name of each person to be visited will be placed on a visitation card, with all available information. Simple decision cards will be provided. (See p. 131.)

Preceding the visitation, special meetings should be held for the inspiration and instruction of those who will do the visiting. Climaxing the special season of visitation, an evangelistic meeting of power may be held, with "membership Sunday" as its high peak, when all those who have been won and have presented themselves for membership will be specially recognized. Immediately as many of these new members as possible should be enrolled as helpers in a continuous visitation evangelism program, that they may share in reaching their unreached friends. The heart of the matter lies in selecting and preparing those who will do the visiting.

---

[1] Adapted from tract by Spencer P. Austin, "Organization for Week of Visitation."

RECORD OF COMMITMENT

_____Turning from sin and in faith to Jesus Christ, I purpose with his
help to live a Christian life.

_____I desire to unite with the _____Church, and plan
to present myself for membership on Sunday, _____

_____I wish to transfer my membership to this church. For letter write to

_____ at _____

My name is recorded there as _____

Name _____

Address _____

The following clear and detailed instructions for visitors will be found
stimulating and practical.

The methods described here are neither new nor original. Jesus sent out
visitors in teams of two. The application of this method with many variations has been tried and found fruitful by many churches. The suggestions are intended for the busy pastor who would make use of the experience of others in setting up a week of intensive home visitation
evangelism in the local church.

Advance Preparation

Five things should be done before the date set for the week of visitation.

1. Prepare a prospect list. It should be reasonably complete one month
before the calling begins.

2. At least four weeks in advance, the pastor, church council, and all
committees related to the project should meet and review all plans, clear
the time schedule and arrange for the four supper meetings to be held
during the visitation.

3. Visitors should be enlisted three weeks in advance of the dates they
are to do their calling. There should be approximately 16 callers for each
100 prospects to be visited.

4. Copy information concerning each prospect on _Evangelistic Visitation Cards_.

5. Arrange assignment cards in envelopes for visitors.

Compiling the Prospect List

Begin with a survey of your own church roll and list the names of the
relatives of members who should be won. The rolls of the Sunday school

and other organizations of the church will contain the names of non-members and may also call to mind many others. These should be carefully listed, giving name, address and relationship to the church. After each name it should be noted fully whether or not this person attends church and whether relatives belong or attend. Other pertinent information helpful for the visitor should be indicated. The pastor must supervise the task to insure the completeness of this survey of the church-related homes. Additional names may be added to the prospect list from the names of nonmembers who attend the preaching services of the church. Names of visitors in the Sunday school classes should also be listed and added to the prospect roll. The surest way to secure a complete list of prospects is by means of a religious census of the community.

The size of the prospect list and the care with which the information is recorded will determine the abundance of the harvest possible during the visitation campaign. All persons whose names are included on the prospect list should be cultivated as much as possible in advance of the visitation.

Selecting the Visitors

The minister, perhaps with the help of a small committee, should check the membership roll carefully and compile a list of those who would make competent visitors. Sunday school officers and teachers and leaders of the other church organizations should naturally lead the list. A few names beyond the actual needs of the campaign will be needed in order to allow for those who are unable to accept assignment. As a rule, men will be more successful in visiting than women. The proportion of men visitors should therefore be much larger than that of women. *Do not call for volunteers;* hand-pick the most capable members of the church.

Three weeks in advance of the visitation, the visitors should be called together and completely informed concerning the proposed project. At this time they should be signed up for the Sunday instruction conference and for the successive nights of visiting. Most laymen who are inexperienced in visitation will show a hesitancy and express a sense of inadequacy concerning personal visitation. These are natural reactions from conscientious men, and are probably a mark of qualification for the task. To offset these tendencies, the minister will emphasize the point that no one will be asked to make calls until he has first been instructed in what to say and how to say it. He will also note the example of Jesus in the use of this method and the success which it had then, as well as its effectiveness now. Finally, he should make it plain that the callers are not asked to go forth to argue theology or preach sermons, but to witness to their faith in Christ and to the value of the church in their own lives. No one should be accepted for visitation who will not agree to attend the Sunday training conference.

Preparing the Assignments

The names and complete information from the prospect roll should be copied on *Evangelistic Visitation Cards.* Each card should have the exact address and all information which will help the caller understand the best approach to the prospect. Designate before the name whether the prospect should be addressed as Mr., Mrs., or Miss. Indicate the relationship of the prospect to the church and the religious status of the other members of the family. Do not run the risk of having a call spoiled because of inadequate information.

It will be the minister's personal responsibility to assign the prospects to specific teams of visitors. For his own convenience he may wish to classify the prospects listed on the Visitation Cards into first, second, and third class, depending upon the seeming nearness to church membership. In the first group will be placed the names of those who already have some natural interest in the congregation; i.e., the wife attends, the children are in Sunday school, perhaps the prospect himself attends some of the services. The second group will include the names of older people who have manifested little interest in the church and others who do not seem as ready for membership as those first listed. The third group will be comprised of those who are especially difficult, those who have expressed antagonisms toward the church, those who have had their feelings hurt, some of whom may have been regarded as almost hopeless.

The minister will place those cards in envelopes, on the outside of which have been written the names of the callers. In each envelope he will put a supply of Decision Cards, Church Membership Transfer Cards, and Evangelistic Visitation Cards listing prospects. A team can complete three or four calls in an evening. As many as six assignments will allow for some prospects not being at home. Never give assignments for more than one evening at a time. In the first evening of visitation, using inexperienced workers, it will be best to assign the first class prospects and give them opportunity to develop confidence and experience the joy of victory. Arrange prospective calls so the team has a minimum of travel between assignments.

The Sunday Training Conference

At the beginning of this session the partners for each of the teams will be indicated. At least an hour or an hour and a half should be allowed for instruction in the art of visitation. In instances where some outside leader has been asked to supervise the campaign, he will be responsible for this period of instruction. Where several churches are engaged in a simultaneous effort, the pastors and visitors of all the churches participating will be present.

The Supper Assignment Conferences

Supper meetings are necessary to insure an early attendance, promptness, and an intimate fellowship. If at all possible, the church should furnish these suppers free for the callers. If it is necessary to charge for the meals, they should be served at cost. Let the entire meal, including the dessert, be on the table by 6:15 each evening, with no serving or interruption until the workers are sent out at 7:15. During the first fifteen minutes of the supper period the minister will give assignments to each team and will answer any questions which may arise concerning the address or other information about the prospect. At 6:45 he will begin a brief period of instruction, ending with a fervent challenge and a prayer of consecration not later than 7:15. The workers will leave immediately on their calling assignments.

The first evening of instruction may well be devoted to instruction of visitors. On Tuesday, Wednesday, and Thursday evenings part of the time should be used for reports of successes of the previous night of visitation. The rest may be spent discussing difficult cases, excuses, and other hindrances to decision. Visitors should be sent out each evening with a sense of divine mission.

Each night, at the close of the visitation, the callers will return to the church to report their successes and turn in their cards.

The Public Commitment

The four nights of calling may well be followed by a week or more of evangelistic preaching. In that case the workers will be instructed to have the prospects signify on the card their intention of presenting themselves before the congregation at the opening service of the preaching series, or as early as possible during the week.

If such preaching services are not contemplated, it will be well to designate the second Sunday following the visitation as Membership Sunday. This will give the pastor opportunity to make a personal call on each individual who has signified his intention of making a public commitment. During this visit the pastor will discuss quite frankly the obligations of church membership which are implicit in accepting Christ as Saviour and Lord.

Follow Up

As a part of the visitation campaign the minister will need to plan a program of conservation for the new members. No minister has fully faced his obligation as a shepherd until the spiritual needs of every member are met with adequate pastoral care. Every new member should be immediately enlisted in Bible study, training, giving, and service.

REVIVING THE REVIVAL

For more than a hundred years the revival has been the most successful means employed by evangelical churches, particularly in America, for winning the lost and building up the church membership. The revival, by its very name, is intended first of all to revive the church. Its immediate purpose is not that of an ingathering of new members but renewal of faith and devotion on the part of Christians, of recommitment to Christ and his cause of those already saved. As a consequence, these revived Christians begin to bear their witness anew, to share their faith and joy in Christ with unbelievers, and thus the revival bears the fruit of evangelism. The best way known to Christian experience to revive the drooping spirits of Christians is exposure to soul-winning sermons that present Christ and his way of salvation and life, coupled with earnest intercessory prayer for the lost. Such preaching and concern become a magnet to draw unbelievers to the gospel, and in such an atmosphere the Holy Spirit can work mightily to bring sinners to faith and confession. Organized evil, operating in chain reaction, calls for organized simultaneous evangelism to match it. C. E. Matthews, superintendent of Evangelism of the Southern Baptist Home Mission Board, thus describes the *simultaneous crusade:*

The only method in evangelism, we believe, that is absolutely adequate for this hour is the simultaneous method. A simultaneous revival is one in which all the churches of like faith and convictions within a given territory enter into a revival beginning on the same day and closing on the same day. No other kind of meeting is simultaneous. Sometimes a few churches want to begin a week ahead or close a week later than the others. Some churches want to have a one-week meeting or a ten-day meeting while others go two weeks. This is not a simultaneous revival. We give the following marks and advantages of the simultaneous revival:

1. It is definitely a concerted effort, all the churches in a given territory doing the same thing the same way at the same time (a Pentecostal condition).

2. It is church-centered. The revival is conducted in the local church work and makes possible conservation of results.

3. If properly directed, it will command the attention of saint and sinner.

4. It fixes the responsibility with individuals and churches. The association-

wide simultaneous crusade enlists every church and employs an army of people.

5. The simultaneous method leaves the prospect without excuse. There is a church in every community involved.

6. It gives every church, large or small, the same assistance and direction in leadership. It places every church on an equality.

7. It enables any state, regardless of size, to have at least one revival in every church and unchurched community every year, something that no other method can do.

8. The association-wide revival crusade, properly conducted, we believe, is the answer to the problem of churches making an annual report of no baptisms.[2]

The individual church revival still has and will always have a place of great importance in reaching the unreached. For such a series of meetings the most careful and prayerful preparation should be made. Plans for a revival of far-reaching influence will include procedures and features somewhat as follows:

Preparation. The time having been fixed, the church should be called to prayer and conference concerning the preacher (whether evangelist or visiting minister), the leadership of the music, attractive and effective publicity, co-operation of all the church organizations, canvass of the Sunday school rolls to discover the unchurched and unsaved. Preparation should include listing of others to be reached, prayer covenants on behalf of the meeting, the membership, the unreached.

Training. There should be brought together deacons, church officers, Sunday school officers and teachers, leaders of Training Union, Woman's Missionary Union, and Brotherhood, with other dependable soul-winners, for conference and study concerning problems of contact and approach, materials and methods, doubts and difficulties, mistakes and blunders, prayer and the Holy Spirit, decision and commitment. Prayer meetings and other group meetings may be used for this purpose.

Deepening. As the time for the special meetings draws near, there should be conscious deepening of prayer and concern. Prayer meetings in homes should be held, conducted informally with chief emphasis on specific prayer for the unsaved; special services in the several departments of the Sunday school may be held, the assembly period being used to present the need and the way of salvation; letters may be written by teachers and friends to those for whom concern is felt; the radio may be used for

---

[2] C. E. Matthews, *The Southern Baptist Program of Evangelism* (Atlanta, Georgia: Home Mission Board of the Southern Baptist Convention), pp. 40–41.

spot announcements, and the newspaper may carry brief notices; the choir may be enlarged and rehearsed and all who lead the singing brought to realize how important is their part; the church council will bring representatives of all the organizations to see to it that the total life of the church is geared to the special effort. Deacons and officers will meet with the pastor to pray together for the meetings; of course the pastor will pour out his heart to the people as he presents needs and opportunities.

The harvest. Time of the meeting having arrived, the several organizations of the church will join hands in securing attendance of all available church members and especially those who are on the several prayer lists. An atmosphere of deep reverence should pervade the sanctuary, Christians should come with prayerful hearts, the music should be Christ-centered and powerful in persuasiveness, invitations should be given with simplicity and sincerity, rejoicing should be very great over "one sinner that repenteth."

Follow up. The baptismal service following the meeting (sometimes in the midst of the meeting) should mark a high hour in the life of the church as well as in the experience of those saved; each new member should at once be enlisted in the life of the church. The new members should be formed into a class and given brief instruction concerning their commitments, their faith and relationships, their duties and privileges; those still unreached should be sought with fresh fervor so that additions to the church will become the expected and usual thing week after week. Thus the harvest will be made continuous rather than occasional.

REACHING THE UNREACHED OVER THE AIR

Radio and television have immensely multiplied the possibilities of reaching the unreached with the gospel. Although relatively new, these amazing instrumentalities are rapidly coming into wide favor with churches that are alert to the opportunities of this marvelous age. There are certain requisites to the successful use of radio (and eventually television) for evangelistic purposes. The church that meets these requirements must take certain steps:

A *strong radio committee* should be appointed, with a chairman who is capable, energetic, acquainted with broadcasting techniques, influential in dealing with the station's management.

Desirable time should be secured, not "dead" time when few listen, nor time which will be in competition with nationally popular programs, but time most favorable to reaching people in their homes. While a thirty-minute broadcast is highly desirable, effective presentation of the gospel may be made in fifteen minutes or even less. Of importance second only to the message itself is the music, which should be understandable, familiar, gospel-centered, of high quality.

The gospel message, is, of course, the heart of the matter. Its opening words should be attention-compelling, it should be carefully organized with utmost economy of words, it should be full of human interest and Scripture, it should be directed to the listener with persuasive appeal. Effective radio preaching is an art which must be learned, and the preacher should humbly submit himself to the instruction of technicians in matters of enunciation, articulation, voice control, listener appeal.

"Spot" announcements are in the nature of advertisements and must usually be paid for. Such announcements, to be effective, must be very brief, unusual and original, attention-getting and good-will producing. Properly timed between attractive programs, such spot announcements may prove to be the most fruitful kind of advertising.

A Church Serving the People

The church is for people, not people for the church. The words of Jesus concerning the sabbath may be paraphrased to read, "The church was made for man, and not man for the church: therefore the Son of man is Lord also of the church" (Mark 2:27–28). The tendency throughout history has been to exalt the church as an end rather than as means. Thus the church came to be looked on as a saving institution rather than an institution of the saved. Wherever this has come about, Christianity has become corrupted. Only a serving church can remain a pure church. According to the New Testament pattern, members of a church do not serve the church; they serve people in Christ's name through the church. The worship of the church rather than the Christ of the church has led and will always lead to spiritual perversion.

Christian service through the church is both an art and a science. As an art it calls for insight, imagination, creativity. As a science it calls for investigation, distinction between essentials and nonessentials, foresight of ends and use of appropriate means, experimentation according to sound theory, a policy of consistent action as the outgrowth of validated general principles. In a world of selfish competition, where contending individuals and groups are seeking selfish advantage, and where almost every act of service calls for a fee or a profit, a serving church stands out with the conspicuousness of a city set on a hill. In such a church men and women find opportunity to put into practice the guiding principle of the Christian life —the losing of life in order to save it.

How may a church fulfil its mission as servant of the people? Certainly not by mere good intentions, nor by lip service to the ideal. A church that serves efficiently and fruitfully must plan its program of service, leaving as little as possible to chance. In this planning the Holy Spirit's guidance will be sought and confidently followed.

FIELDS OF SERVICE IN THE CHURCH

A church must serve the people through its people. Pastor and staff are chief servants of the church, but the pastor and his associates serve best when they lead others to serve. Regarding any service activity, the slogan of the minister or ministers might well be, "Don't do this yourself if you can get someone else to do it." Certainly this would not be the easy way on their part, for ordinarily it would be simpler to do the job than to get it done.

Many church members have never rendered service because they have not been called on to do so. Opportunities for service are exhausted in a typical church when about one-fourth of the members have been employed. The remaining three-fourths are quite naturally content to be served, thus depriving the church of their services and depriving them of the privilege of rendering service. The New Testament ideal is that of every-member service. It is inconceivable that Christ should save a person and call him to discipleship and yet expect of him no service and have for him no place of usefulness in his church. A study of fields of service in the church, actual and potential, will prove revealing.

FIELDS OF SERVICE BEYOND THE CHURCH

A church should not exhaust its services on itself. Beyond the church lie greater needs than those within the church. A list of these needs would include some of the following:

Building Christian homes. The home life of a community is fundamental; a church should lend its utmost effort to the establishment of Christian homes, guidance in Christian family life, rebuilding of broken homes, providing homes for homeless children.

Caring for the needy. A church should follow the example of its Lord, who "went about doing good"—in giving first aid in emergencies, in providing help for the helpless, in rehabilitating broken lives, in encouraging the handicapped to become self-supporting.

Seeking social righteousness. A church that does not produce the fruits of righteousness has violated its charter, "for the fruit of the Spirit is in all goodness and righteousness and truth" (Ephesians 5:9); a church should therefore be aggressively concerned to rid a community of lawlessness, immorality, indecency, injustice, and to replace them with "love, joy, peace, longsuffering, kindness, goodness, faithfulness, meekness, self-control" (Galatians 5:22 ASV).

Guiding public opinion. A church should not seek to control public affairs, but it is under inescapable obligation to influence thought and opinion toward the elimination of vice and corruption and for the promotion of good schools, good government, public welfare, right human relations, protection of the weak, a fair deal for all men.

Here are fields of service which challenge the church. Into these areas of need and opportunity the church should send its members with intelligent conviction and unselfish motives.

SERVING THE LEISURE-TIME NEEDS OF PEOPLE

The waking time of the majority of people is divided between doing what they have to and what they want to. Concerning the use of much of their time, they have little choice. The labors of their calling may be pleasant, their duties as citizens and as parents may not be irksome, meeting the demands of health and life may not be exacting, but for the most part these activities are not optional. A church renders an immeasurable service when it helps people in all these areas to have right motives, right aims, right attitude, right ideals and standards, right conduct and character—*right* in the sight of God and men. It is in their spare time, however, that people are more tested morally than in their vocations, for what they do with their leisure is of their own choosing.

A mechanized world has given to multitudes more leisure than ever before possessed. Their use of it may re-create or dis-create, and a church may have much to do with the outcome. Two great opportunities and equally grave responsibilities are opened up: to give guidance to the community in the character of recreational and amusement activities which it fosters; and to provide and foster wholesome Christian recreation as a part of the church program. Both of these ends may be served by a well-planned, well-balanced, well-conducted program of social fellowship and recreation guided by high Christian ideals. The following essentials of a Christian program of recreation are thus summarized: [1]

Carefully planned. Unplanned or carelessly planned social events and recreational activities are almost certain to end in failure.

Properly related. The social-recreational activities of a church are not something apart from its educational-spiritual services, but a vital aspect of the several church organizations, which should sponsor and support them.

Really re-creative. Wholesome enjoyment should be without regrets or violated conscience.

Spiritually purposive. The same high purposes should characterize the social-recreational activities as mark other phases of the church's work.

Consistent with Christian standards. Questionable activities, leading to criticism or becoming occasions of stumbling, should be excluded.

Producing valuable by-products. Growing out of the social-recreational activities should be many accompanying values—Christian courtesy, respect for personality, elevated moral standards, good sportsmanship, fruitful friendships, acquaintanceships that may lead to happy homemaking, contacts leading to soul-winning.

---

[1] T. B. Maston, *A Handbook for Church Recreation Leaders,* adapted from chapters IV and V. Nashville, Tennessee: The Sunday School Board of the Southern Baptist Convention.

Church supported and church centered. Generous provision should be made in the church budget for this aspect of the church's life, and every activity should be centered about the church and under church supervision.

Distinctive in character. A church social-recreation program should not imitate nor compete with commercialized amusements, but should be Christian in purpose, content, leadership, and results.

In the light of the opportunity and responsibility of a church to render much needed service in this field, such questions as these should be answered:

Are commercial agencies the chief dependence of the community for amusement and recreation? Are these commercialized amusements for the most part unwholesome? Is the church meeting its responsibility to raise the standards of social and recreational life? Has the church a planned program of social and recreational activities? Has the church provided competent leadership for such a program? Has the church made adequate provision in its budget for this program? Does the church appreciate the spiritual values of Christian social life? Has the church faced up to this guilt if this phase of its responsibility is neglected?

MEETING THE NEEDS OF PEOPLE FOR CHRISTIAN FAMILY LIFE

The family is society's primary institution. The family was divinely instituted before the state, the church, the school, or any other human institution. Family disorganization brings eventual disintegration to every other human enterprise. Even beyond its concern for itself should be the church's concern for its families. A church should therefore plan intelligently and continuously to render its best possible service in getting young people ready for homemaking, in establishing homes on a sound Christian basis, in preserving the integrity of the home when it is threatened, and in making the home an impregnable defense against the attacks of its enemies. A church may render this service in some of the following ways:

COUNSELING THOSE WHO PLAN TO BE MARRIED

The minister, representing his church, is called on to perform wedding ceremonies because church and state thus unite in their desire to give the marriage binding Christian sanction. Minister and church have no moral right to sanction this most sacred of human contracts unless there is reasonable assurance of divine approval. Ministers should therefore make careful inquiry as to the legal status involved, the moral right to enter into the contract, clear understanding of the significance of the relationship, reasonable assurance of the permanency of the marriage, and ground of hope that the union will result in a happy home. These ideals should be clarified through conference of the couple with the minister or qualified church representative, who in the conversation may lead to a deepened understanding and appreciation of the marriage relationship.

LENDING CHRISTIAN SANCTION TO MARRIAGE

Memorable in the lives of all who participate should be the wedding ceremony. A wedding is not just a private, personal affair, no matter how quietly it may be celebrated. It is a contract involving many lives—the two persons who are being united in a lifelong relationship, their families and kindred, the children who may be born of the union, the state and society. The marriage contract must be legalized by the state, which sets up certain minimum requirements of legality. If solemnized by a minister, representing the church, it should meet the conditions of Christian approval of the matrimonial bonds, otherwise there would be no point in a Christian minister performing the ceremony.

The officiating minister should never forget that he acts for both state and church in legal and spiritual capacity and never just as a private individual. A wedding may be held in a home, or chapel, or church, but if the minister officiates, it should never be a "stunt" affair or under any circumstances that would bring notoriety or discredit to the church which he represents or to the cause of Christ. Care should be taken to make every wedding an event of reverent dignity, never on the one hand a trivial affair, nor on the other a fashion show. If the wedding is held in the church, with special friends or the public invited, there should be careful rehearsal and scrupulous observance of the social amenities.

Marriage laws and customs vary, hence the minister should be well acquainted with legal requirements and social expectations of the state and the community. Forms of wedding ceremonies are also varied, from the simple and informal home wedding to the elaborate and formal church affair. Universally recognized as authoritative is Emily Post's *Etiquette* as regards approved social usage. Concerning all matters that pertain to the minister and the church in weddings, Dr. Gordon Palmer's *A Manual of Church Services* is complete and invaluable. In this book will be found a digest of the laws of all the states of the United States regarding marriage; instructions concerning the rehearsal, preparation for the wedding, correct procedures for both the informal and the formal wedding, diagrams showing exact position of all those taking part, appropriate forms of ceremonies from which choice or adaptation may be made.

The pastor may provide an attractively printed marriage certificate and copy of the wedding ceremony to each couple at whose wedding he officiates:

THIS CERTIFIES
THAT

_____

of _____

AND

_____

of _____

were by me united in
MARRIAGE
according to the teaching of the gospel and the laws of the

State of _____,

at _____ on the

_____ day of _____,

in the year of our Lord 19_____,

_____
Minister

Witness:

_____

_____

THE WEDDING CEREMONY [2]

Appropriate Scriptures: Ruth 1:16–17; Matthew 19:4–6; Ephesians 5:22–27; 1 Corinthians 13:4–7; Hebrews 13:4a.

MINISTER: "Marriage is honorable. God hath declared that 'it is not good that man should live alone.' Marriage is a joyous occasion. Jesus, our Master and Lord, was so greatly interested in mankind that He attended the marriage at Cana of Galilee. It was there that He did His first wonderful work, to the joy and amazement of the guests. Marriage is a sacred and solemn occasion. 'Therefore shall a man leave his father and mother and cleave unto his wife and they twain shall become one flesh.'

"Because marriage is honorable and joyous and yet a sacred occasion, it

---

[2] Adapted from Gordon Palmer, *A Manual of Church Services*, pp. 59–63; full directions given for formal wedding service. See also James D. Morrison, *Minister's Service Book*.

should therefore be entered into thoughtfully, advisedly, and discreetly. Let us invoke God's blessing upon you as you pledge your troth before this company. Let us pray."

MINISTER: "Who giveth this woman in holy wedlock?"

THE FATHER: "I do." (The father then places the hand of the bride in the hand of the groom and returns to pew.)

MINISTER (taking the hand of the groom): "John, do you take Jane to be your wedded wife?"

GROOM: "I do."

MINISTER: "Do you covenant to love her, honor her, cherish her, and comfort her, taking her for richer, for poorer, for better, for worse, in sickness and in health, to have and to hold, from this time forth, cleaving to her alone, till death do you part?"

GROOM: "I do."

Bride gives bouquet to maid of honor to hold until after benediction.

MINISTER (taking the hand of the bride): "Jane, do you take John to be your lawful wedded husband?"

BRIDE: "I do."

MINISTER: "Do you covenant to love him, honor him, cherish him and comfort him, taking him for richer, for poorer, for better, for worse, in sickness and in health, to have and to hold, from this time forth, cleaving to him alone till death do you part?"

BRIDE: "I do."

MINISTER: "What token of sincerity have you?" (The best man presents the ring to the groom and he to the minister.) (For double-ring ceremony see below.) The minister holds the ring in the palm of his hand as he says: "This ring is a symbol of completeness and an emblem of eternity. It is metal that has been tested and proved true. It is a fitting emblem of your love for each other and of your faith in each other. May your love and faith prove as true in the test of time as gold does in fire, and may they endure until death do you part. Jane, do you in evidence of your love and sincerity accept this ring?"

BRIDE: "I do."

MINISTER (giving the ring to the groom): "You will repeat after me—"

GROOM (placing the ring on the third finger of the bride's left hand repeats after the minister): "With this ring I thee wed and with my heart's faithful affections I thee endow."

MINISTER: "As you have mutually assumed the marriage covenant I do as a minister of the gospel, in the name of the Father and of the Son and of the Holy Spirit, pronounce you husband and wife—Mr. and Mrs. Jones."

For Double-Ring Ceremony

MINISTER: "What tokens of sincerity have you?" (The best man gives his ring to the groom, who places it in the minister's hand. The maid of honor or matron of honor gives her ring to the bride, who gives it to the minister.)

MINISTER (holding both rings in the palm of his left hand): "These rings are symbols of completeness and emblems of eternity. They are metal that has been tested and proved true. They are fitting symbols of your love for each other and of your faith in each other. May your love and faith prove as true in the test of time as gold does in fire and may they endure till death do you part."

MINISTER: "Jane, do you in evidence of your sincerity accept this ring?"

BRIDE: "I do."

MINISTER (giving the ring to the groom): "You will repeat after me—"

GROOM (placing the ring on the third finger of the bride's left hand, repeats after the minister): "With this ring I thee wed and with my heart's faithful affections I thee endow."

MINISTER: "John, in evidence of your sincerity do you accept this ring?"

GROOM: "I do."

MINISTER (giving the ring to the bride): "You will repeat after me—"

BRIDE (placing the ring on the third finger of the groom's left hand, repeats after the minister): "With this ring I thee wed and with my heart's faithful affections I thee endow."

MINISTER (uniting the hands of the bride and groom): "As you have mutually assumed the wedding covenant, I do as a minister of the gospel, in the name of the Father and of the Son and of the Holy Spirit, pronounce you husband and wife—Mr. and Mrs. Jones." (Proceed then as with the single-ring ceremony.)

MINISTER: "Let us pray." (The bride and groom should kneel for the prayer of blessing.)

Minister helps the bride and groom to rise and says: " 'Those whom God has joined together let not man put asunder.'

" 'May the Lord bless thee and keep thee. May the Lord make his face to shine upon thee and be gracious unto thee. May the Lord lift up his countenance upon thee and give thee peace.' Amen."

A CHURCH SERVING IN THE CRISIS OF DEATH

Death is never commonplace. Its inevitability and frequency of occurrence do not take from death its mystery and solemnity for all who are sensitive of soul. Most people turn intuitively to the minister and the church in the crisis of death. Few services rendered by minister and church are more significant or fraught with greater possibilities than those attendant on the approach of death, death itself, and the funeral. Never should minister or members be too busy to give time and thoughtful attention in the crisis of death, no matter how humble or unworthy the person or persons involved may be.

The approach of death, when foreseen, lays heavy responsibility on the minister. Sometimes it is his duty and privilege (if not contrary to physician's advice) to make the patient aware of his impending dissolution.

If the patient's mental condition permits, there may be quiet and reassuring information of the probability of death, tactful inquiry concerning the patient's readiness for the experience, the reading of appropriate verses of Scripture, and brief prayer in which the patient may be invited silently or audibly to engage. Of course utmost caution should be taken not to excite the patient nor depress him, but to strengthen faith and courage for the great adventure that lies ahead. Services with the family should likewise be quietly reassuring that they too may be prepared to meet the approaching crisis with Christian fortitude.

The funeral services often call for the minister's counsel concerning preparations and the burial rites. Minister and funeral director should have clear understanding of their mutual responsibilities. The minister, if given opportunity, should counsel simplicity, avoidance of undue expense, brevity, and dignity in the service, the lightening in every way of strain upon the bereaved.

The minister will do well to avoid lengthy obituary, eulogy, Scripture exposition, appeal to emotion. The funeral service is for the living, that they may render this last service of love and respect to one who has passed beyond mortal praise or blame. The principal part of the service should ordinarily be given to appropriate music, the reading of familiar and relevant passages of scripture, and prayer. If the funeral is held in the home, especial care should be taken that the service relieve as far as possible the strain and tension of those present. If the service is held in a funeral parlor (which has become increasingly popular), the church should show no less interest and the minister should not be made to feel that he is performing a mere routine service. If the funeral is held in the church (where it properly belongs for faithful members), it should be made an impressive witness of the Christian's faith in Christ as the "resurrection and the life." If the one to be buried lived apart from the church, or had never made a profession of faith in Christ, or had taken his own life, or met death violently, the minister is under the obligation of love to omit details that would embarrass and hurt, and leave judgment where it alone must rest, in the hands of God.

SUGGESTED ORDER OF FUNERAL SERVICE [3]

Soft music, the playing of some of the great and familiar hymns.

Prayer of thanksgiving for the gift of life, of praise of God for his grace in Christ and the comfort of the Holy Spirit; intercession for the bereaved; petition on behalf of any who may not have "made their calling and election sure."

---

[3] Adapted from Gordon Palmer, *A Manual of Church Services* (New York: Fleming H. Revell Company), p. 80.

Obituary, consisting of brief statement concerning the deceased, his or her church membership (if any), facts of special significance concerning his or her life, mention of survivors.

Solo or hymn or reading of hymn.

Scripture message, appropriate, selected passages read preferably from the Bible.

Solo or hymn or reading of hymn.

Appropriate poem, inspiring and comforting.

Benediction.

Recessional, pallbearers in charge, congregation standing, service to be concluded at cemetery.

Services at the grave should be brief and simple. Immediate relatives having been seated, and the casket having been placed over the grave, the minister will again read passages of scripture and offer brief prayer, followed by dismissal. In most instances, the casket will not be lowered until after family and friends shall have gone.

Bereavement is often hardest to bear during the lonely days following the funeral. The thoughtful minister will arrange to call on the bereaved person or family within a week or two to bring counsel and comfort, and thereafter on anniversaries of the event if possible and desirable.

A CHURCH EXPRESSING ITS CONCERN FOR THE CHILDREN

Another major event in human experience is the birth of a baby. Before the child's birth, at its birth, and in the days and months that follow, a church has unusual opportunity and obligation to render appreciated and fruitful service. Preceding the baby's birth, the expectant mother often longs for a bit of attention, for spiritual counsel and encouragement, and for reassurance concerning the experience through which she is to pass. The husband would likewise welcome friendly interest on the part of thoughtful Christian friends, and conversation with the minister will be timely. Frequently a "baby shower" may be arranged by a group of church women, whose gifts for the baby's wardrobe will be treasured.

Following the baby's arrival, the minister and his wife should call as soon as practicable, for congratulations and prayer. The Cradle Roll superintendent or visitor should also call within the month, possibly presenting an attractive "Baby Book" in which are pages for the recording of notable events in the youngster's life. The birth of the baby should be recognized at the prayer service and special prayer offered for parents and child.

The Nursery department or class has come to be an established feature in many churches. In an attractive and properly equipped nursery room or rooms the babies under four years of age are cared for while their mothers attend Sunday school and worship services. Realizing that the foundations of personality are being laid in the first three years, the church nursery is designed to be far more than merely a place to keep the children safe and comfortable; it is an opportunity of far-reaching importance for the child's ultimate spiritual destiny. The best-trained workers available should be assigned to the Nursery department, and contacts thus made through the babies followed up for the winning of parents to Christ and the deepening of their loyalty to Christ and to his church.

An annual "Children's Day" or "Dedication Service" may be held with great profit. Conducted early during the morning worship, this service finds the children less tired and restless.

FOLLOWING UP THE CHILDREN'S DAY SERVICE [4]

"Provide a well-worded and attractive certificate of dedication containing the names of the child and parents, date of birth, date of dedication, place of dedication, name of officiating clergyman, and two of the witnesses.

"Have the certificate completely filled out and present it to the family before they leave the church auditorium. If you have an assistant he can make the presentation. Moreover, he should direct the family to their proper position for the service.

"Keep a complete record of these services, including time, place, and participants and date of child's birth, etc.

"Visit the parents after the service. It is good to show your parents that their minister desires to be their friend as well as their preacher. Encourage them to become active in the Sunday School class or special organizations for young adults. Young parents need the influence of the church more than ever. Let them know that your church offers much to meet their spiritual and intellectual needs."

A CHURCH GIVING GUIDANCE TO LIFE ACTIVITIES

A relatively small proportion of the time and interests of average people is spent at church or in church work. A church, therefore, that is primarily concerned with what goes on within its walls or for its support and welfare is largely missing the mark. A church should be something like a telephone exchange, receiving many calls, making connections and transmitting the calls to points near and far. That the exchange should be maintained efficiently is a matter of great importance, to be sure, but of far greater

---

[4] For an attractive children's dedication service, see Gordon Palmer, *A Manual of Church Services*, pp. 85–87.

importance is its faithful transmission of the messages entrusted to its wires. Likewise, it is of high importance that a church be maintained in strength and health, its services well attended and its program generously supported; but the supremely important matter is that the church send its saving and healing influences out where the people are, in their homes, in their places of business, in their fields of labor, in the major areas of their interests and responsibilities.

The ultimate test of a church's usefulness is not to be found in its popularity and prosperity but rather in the changes that it produces or prevents in the lives of people, individually and collectively. A church should keep always before it, therefore, the broad range of human experience, and its responsibility for ministries to the whole of life.

A Church Enriching Its Worship

A church may have many attractions, but the quality of its worship remains perennially the magnet with which to draw the people to its services. Sensationalism may get quick and cheap results, but worthy and satisfying worship is an absolute essential for a church's permanent growth and usefulness. The Bible is a book of worship. More of its contents are devoted to purposes of worship, private and corporate, than to any other subject. Prayer and worship were central in the life and teachings of our Lord and must be given primacy in his church if it is true to him.

Worship in the churches tends to two extremes. One extreme is that of ornateness, ceremonial elaborateness, complicated formalism. Such worship may have the form of godliness without the power thereof. At the other extreme is formless worship, extemporaneous and unplanned, often confused and poverty stricken. Lacking the elements of unity and dignity, such worship proves empty and unsatisfying to those who come to church seeking an experience with God.

Obviously there is needed a middle ground between ornateness and poverty of worship. Minister and people should give frequent, prayerful attention to the total worship program of the church, from the training of children in worship to the practice of worship by the adult congregation.

THE STATUS OF WORSHIP IN THE CHURCH

The two contrasting dangers of formalism and formlessness must be guarded against in the worship services of a church. Hindrances to worship may develop almost unnoticed, and familiarity may breed indifference. The building may not be conducive to worship, pews and lights may bring discomfort, heating and ventilation may be improperly adjusted, the atmosphere of the building may detract from worship. Again, bad habits of worship may have been formed—beginning the service late and running it overtime, carelessness in the timing of the several features, unpreparedness and blundering on the part of the leaders, inexcusable inattention and distractions, faulty participation by the congregation. A church should take stock frequently to evaluate the several elements that enter into its worship.

Following this evaluation, certain questions may be discussed: Could

CHECKING UP ON THE CHURCH'S WORSHIP

Items for evaluation	Yes	No	To some extent	Don't know
1. Has the church a committee responsible for study and improvement of worship?				
2. Is the place of worship kept clean, comfortable, well arranged?				
3. Are ushers present, punctual, helpful?				
4. As the people enter, are they quiet and reverent?				
5. Before the service begins, is everything in readiness?				
6. Does the choir contribute positively to the experience of worship?				
7. Do music and singing definitely aid in worship?				
8. Are the songs and hymns, in both text and tune, worthy of use in public worship?				
9. Does the congregation join heartily and reverently in the singing?				
10. Has the worship program been so planned as to produce unity and harmony?				
11. Does the leader show good taste in his selection and arrangement of materials of worship?				
12. Does he avoid introducing distracting irrelevancies into the service?				
13. Does he secure the hearty co-operation of all who share responsibility for worship?				
14. Is there sufficient variety in the order of service?				
15. Is there an attractive bulletin giving guidance to the worshipers?				
16. Is there careful economy of time in the worship period?				
17. Are sermon and other features of the service carefully co-ordinated?				
18. Is the service brought effectively to a conclusion, with persuasive invitation to response?				
19. Is there friendliness, yet reverence, following dismissal?				
20. Do the people feel that in the worship service they have had an experience with God?				

the building be made more worshipful? Could the decorum of the people be improved? Is the music fully satisfactory? Are the materials of worship varied and worthy? Is the leadership of worship skilful and pleasing? Do the people take part intelligently and happily? Is the total worship unified, harmonious, impressive? What can be done to send the people away with a sense of spiritual glow and uplift?

HINDRANCES TO WORSHIP

Spiritual worship has little appeal to the natural man. The strange thing is not that so many people stay away from worship but that so many attend. Worship is not true worship that seeks to attract attendance by inducements that appeal to pleasure, pride, profit, prominence. The worshiper should not ask, "What will I get?" but "What will I give?" It is debatable as to whether churches should undertake legally to close places of business and amusement on Sunday in order that church attendance may thereby be increased. Sunday laws may be desirable from the standpoint of public welfare but not as a means of filling the churches with those who attend because they have nowhere else to go. Hindrances to attendance on services of worship and hindrances to worship on the part of those who attend should be analyzed with thorough objectivity and results of the analysis employed to meet conditions as they are. Such an analysis would take into account the following circumstances:

Hindrances within the community. Hindrances in the way of worship have greatly multiplied in most communities during the past decade. Sunday has become increasingly secularized. Standards have been generally lowered regarding the sacredness of the Lord's Day. Competition for the time of people on Sunday has been intensified. These facts call not for surrender but for a bolder challenge to the community to "keep Sunday for the soul."

Hindrances within the homes. The home has largely ceased to be a place of worship for many people. The life of many families is organized so as to leave out worship, at the family altar or in church. Many men take Sunday to catch up with chores about the house. Both men and women "remember the Sabbath to sleep it wholly." For many families Sunday is a holiday. Again, complaint that this is true is of little use. The churches need to put on a vigorous campaign for the recovery of worship in the home and for attendance at worship by the family.

Hindrances within the church. The church itself may not be blameless in the decline of worship. Its building may be uninviting and uncomfortable, its people may be unfriendly, its music may be second-rate, its order of services may be stereotyped, its leadership may be inept, the message from the pulpit may be without gospel dynamic, the content of its worship may be unrelated to life. A church can come to close grips with these internal hindrances and effect their removal. To do so will make possible a service of worship, divinely powerful and humanly attractive, at both the morning and the evening hour, year after year.

Worship is more satisfying when the surroundings are appropriate or the forms are planned but flexible, the content is thoughtful and inspiring, the leadership is reverent and confident, participation is spirited and general. Broken down into details, what are some of the most valuable aids to worship?

Appropriate surroundings. The externals of worship are not all-important, but they are important. The building should be constructed as a house of worship, and both exterior and interior should be conducive to worship. There is no one Christian style of architecture, but a church building should be so distinctive that it will at once be recognized as a church and be easily and naturally associated with worship. Symbols become a hindrance to worship when they attract attention to themselves and tend to become objects of worship. Symbols are useful aids to worship when they help to concentrate attention, when they reveal hidden meanings, when they represent truth and beauty, when they become charged with tender memories and holy association. Such appropriate aids to worship may be in the form of stained glass windows, simple pulpit with Bible upon it, choir made uniform in dress by means of modest robes, a spotless communion table with candelabra, a baptistry that lends beauty and dignity to baptism, a communion service worthy of the Lord's Supper, hymnbooks that are well kept, air that is fresh, light that is subdued, pews that are clean and comfortable. These externals will not produce worship, but they may serve to encourage worship.

Forms of worship. Public worship must have some form. No matter how informal and extemporaneous the worship may be, it must follow some order or become disorderly and cease to be worship. In general, there are two forms of worship—prescribed and free. The order of Catholic worship, for example, is prescribed—those who lead it have little or no liberty to make changes. Protestant worship, for the most part, is free —ministers have considerable liberty both in following and in devising orders of service. Baptist churches have been historically completely free in the order of their services of worship, though actually forms of worship have developed that, with variations, are rather generally followed. Whatever the form of worship, it should be orderly, moving from reverent beginning with musical prelude, call to worship and invocation, through congregational singing, Scripture reading and prayer, offering and offertory, congregational singing or special music, to the climactic sermon, coming to its close with appeal to decision and action and invitation to church membership, with reception of members (if any), a moment or two of quiet meditation, benediction, and postlude. Two cautions should be observed: the order should not be so varied as to confuse and embarrass the congregation by unexpected demands; yet it should not become so stereotyped as to lose freshness and interest.

The content of worship. The content of the worship service is as important as the content of the sermon. In fact, people generally get their religious ideas and convictions more from their participation in the worship service than in just listening to the sermon. Two questions may well be raised concerning every element of the worship program: Does it represent reality? Is it inspiring? Songs may be tuneful, yet the words may be superficial, poorly related to scriptural truths, of inferior quality as poetry, bringing little or no spiritual uplift. The several parts of the worship service may be so unrelated to one another and to the sermon as to distract from rather than aid in worship. A worship service of value cannot be just "thrown together" carelessly and hurriedly. Let it be insisted that the service of worship is not a "preliminary exercise" to the sermon, but should be given the same sort of careful and thoughtful planning as is given to the sermon.

The leadership of worship. Not only is sincerity demanded of the leader of worship, but also a high degree of artistry. As a rule, the minister is the leader of public worship. He should not be so consumed with concern for his function as prophet as to forget that he is also, in the true Old Testament sense of the word, God's priest. The minister, as leader of worship, seeks to bring together God and the people in a sacred experience of worship. To do this, God must be real to him that he may make God real to the congregation. He must remember that response depends on interest, hence the service of worship must never be dull or wooden. He must be intensely conscious of the people's need of Christ and that his business is to represent Christ, not himself. Of course, the leader should be careful about his personal appearance, dressing so as never to be conspicuous, avoiding mannerisms that attract attention away from worship to himself, prepared in mind and heart so that he deeply feels what he would have the people feel; intelligent in purpose, to the end that every service shall have an aim toward which each part progressively moves. Perhaps nothing that the minister does so tests his leadership in every phase of his personality and calling as does his conduct of public worship. He should therefore have the most sympathetic possible co-operation from those who assist in the leadership of worship—chorister, musician, choir, ushers, congregation.

Participation in worship. In Catholic theory, worship is primarily objective, directed to God himself, with the congregation as worshipful spectators. If no one but the officiating priests were present, the worship would go on just the same, since God is its object and the presence of people is incidental. In our free church theory, worship is more likely to be subjective. It is, of course, the worship of God, but the service of worship is usually intended primarily to stimulate and produce responses of reverence, thanksgiving, petition and intercession, understanding and appreciation, decision and expression. Sometimes the worship may be so congregation-conscious as to be scarcely at all God-conscious. Ideally, a balance should be sought—the presence of God in Christ through the Holy Spirit consciously and objectively realized, yet the elements of the service so planned and projected as to stimulate subjective response on the part of the congregation.

If the highest values of worship are to be secured, therefore, participation must be provided for all. Perhaps everybody cannot or will not take part in everything, but care should be taken to make possible participation of every member at some point. Songs should be selected that at times appeal to children as well as adults, to those who know music and to those who do not, to those who prefer the great hymns and to those who like to sing the more popular gospel songs. The minister should be reminded that he is not praying privately but is leading the congregation in prayer, hence should make thorough preparation of the pastoral prayer so as to include the interests and needs of the varied congregation.

The Scripture reading should be with more in view than the reading of a passage from which the sermon text is to be chosen. Many may not read the Bible for themselves at all unless they be given the opportunity in the worship service. Selected Scripture passages related to the theme of the service may nearly always be found in the hymnbook, or, if not, may be printed in the bulletin, from which the people may read responsively or in concert. The offering should be made a high moment of worship in which all may participate with a sense of devotion, as they offer themselves through their money to God in partnership with Christ for his kingdom purposes. Participation through testimony may at times deepen the experience of worship and should not be excluded to the point where the only oral witness is borne by the preacher. A worshiping church at its best is a church in which participation is spirited and general.

TRAINING IN WORSHIP

Skill in public worship is attained through instruction and practice. Many people do not participate in worship because they do not know how. A church may have low standards of worship because it has had little opportunity to establish a higher standard. Considering the tremendous importance of worship, is it not strange that many churches have given so little attention to the training of their people in the practice of worship? As a rule, it is too late to instruct a congregation as to how to worship when they are in the midst of worship. The spirit of worship tends to disappear when too much attention is called to its method. A program of fruitful training in worship would take advantage of these resources:

Worship in the home. Children who have learned to worship at home will not find it difficult to worship in the church. Children from worshipless homes cannot be led easily to appreciate the meaning and the value of church worship. A mark of the decadence of our civilization is the decline of family worship. Its revival would be one of the most significant signs of spiritual recovery. The use of one of the popular aids to family devotions, with suggestions for daily Bible readings and prayer, would prove of inestimable value in the promotion of worship in the home, where the best of all training in worship may be received.

Worship in the Sunday school. The assembly period for the school as a whole or in the several departments affords excellent opportunity for training in worship. Here groups may learn to sing and to love the great hymns of the church, to read together with spirit and intelligence, to enter into prayer individually and collectively, to discover reasons for giving and become informed as to the causes to which they give, to become acquainted with worship symbols and their uses and values, to acquire skills in participation in worship and eventually in its leadership.

Worship in other organizations. The Training Union offers unusual opportunity for training in worship. Its assembly periods, like those of the Sunday school, are occasions for practice in the art of worship. Its devotional programs give opportunity for better acquaintance with the worship materials of the Bible and for discussion of the meanings and the problems of worship. A feature of every meeting of Woman's Missionary Union and its organizations, of the Brotherhood, of committees, of the choir, of the deacons and the church council, should be at least a few moments of well-planned worship. Worship may frequently be the theme of the midweek prayer meeting, as fresh discoveries are made of the relation of prayer and worship, of preaching and worship, of evangelism and worship, of giving and worship, of service and worship, of Christian character and worship.

Special studies in worship. Worship is worthy of study in an occasional school. Churches have found it exceedingly worth-while to set apart a week when on two successive Sundays special programs of worship are presented, and during the evenings of the week classes and discussion groups are held for the children, the Intermediates, the Young People, the Adults. Textbooks for this graded study are available, and the school may be conducted in the same fashion of the School of Missions or a training course.

Worship through reading. The literature of worship is abundant and rich. If there is a church library, of course it should contain some of the choicest of these books. Occasional efforts should be made to get the literature of worship before members of the church. Especially should books and manuals dealing with worship for the several age groups and in the church organizations be placed in the hands of the respective leaders. The building of worship programs should be a subject of continuous interest to all who are charged with this responsibility, and there should be made available for them the best and latest materials.

THE ORDINANCES AS OCCASIONS OF WORSHIP

The emphasis of Jesus was not on form and ceremony but on the inwardness of experience in worship. "Neither in this mountain, nor in Jerusalem, shall ye worship the Father," he said. "But the hour cometh, and now is, when the true worshippers shall worship the Father in spirit and truth; for such doth the Father seek to be his worshipers. God is a spirit: and they that worship him must worship him in spirit and truth" (John 4:21, 23-24). Jesus swept away the accumulated mass of ceremonials that had gathered about worship in Judaism, and replaced it with two simple, beautiful, meaningful ceremonies, which he obviously intended to be symbolic of the heart of Christian experience. The first of these, baptism, is the initial ordinance which "stands between the two great experiences of regeneration (make disciples) and sanctification (teaching them to observe all things). Standing on this lofty position, baptism symbolizes the essential facts of Christianity in the past, present, and future. That is, it embodies three fundamental ideas: (1) The fact of Christ's death and resurrection—historical Christianity; (2) the regeneration of the soul, buried with him by baptism and raised to walk in newness of life—living Christianity; (3) the final resurrection of the body —prophetic Christianity. Baptism is an epitome of Christ's message to the world: 'More beautiful than figures of speech, more accurate than any statement of the lips, more complete than the articles of any creed.' We show our love by obeying Christ implicitly, who said, 'Go ye therefore, and make disciples of all the nations, baptizing them into the name of the Father, and the Son and the Holy Spirit: teaching them to observe all things whatsoever I commanded you: and lo, I am with you always, even unto the end of the world.' " [1]

The recurrent Christian ordinance, the Lord's Supper, is inseparably connected with the initial ordinance. Its observance is a memorial, "a proclamation of a past act, the pronouncement of a present experience, the prophecy of a future event. Those who sit at the Lord's table are to turn their opened eyes of faith back to the cross, are to lift up their opened eyes of hope to Christ's coming again, and are to open their hearts of love to fellowship with his Spirit. The Lord's Supper deals with believers in three tenses—past, present, and future. As to the past, it is a commemoration; as to the present, it is a meditation; as to the future, it is an anticipation. . . . Each communicant at the Lord's table who partakes of the broken bread and who drinks from the cup becomes a new messenger to the truth of the everlasting gospel 'that Christ died for our sins according to the Scripture.' The Lord's Supper speaks a universal language, and those who observe it proclaim a universal message." [2]

One of the highest moments of worship in the experience of the Christian and of the church gathered together collectively should be when a new member of the family of God and of the local fellowship of faith is received following his or her testimony through baptism. Next to this experience of worship stands that which is undergone in the Lord's Supper, when the individual and the church collectively are reminded of the one ground of their hope, the death and resurrection of Christ. For each of these beautiful and meaningful ceremonies the most careful and prayerful preparation should be made.

OBSERVING THE ORDINANCE OF BAPTISM

Preparation of the church. A church should not be permitted to accept the administration of baptism as a mere routine matter. There should be keen realization on the part of the church of its responsibility to those who are coming into its fellowship. Those to be baptized, having been received on vote of the church, should become the deep concern of the membership. At the prayer service, they should be mentioned by name,

---

[1] George W. McDaniel, *The People Called Baptists* (Nashville, Tennessee: The Sunday School Board of the Southern Baptist Convention), pp. 79–80.

[2] M. E. Dodd, *Christ's Memorial*, (Nashville, Tennessee: The Sunday School Board of the Southern Baptist Convention), p. 11.

and special prayer had for each of the candidates. So far as is humanly possible, pastor and church should be satisfied that those to be baptized are truly saved and understand the significance of their decision and action.

Preparation of those to be baptized. Those who have requested baptism, and whose request has been granted by the church, should be carefully instructed as to their part in this meaningful event in their Christian experience. This instruction (usually by the pastor) will include clear explanation of the symbolic nature of baptism, the seriousness and sacredness of the ceremony, just how the baptismal act is performed, how the one being baptized may co-operate to make the ceremony maximally impressive and honoring to Christ.

Preparation for the occasion. The place of baptism should be made ready with care, to the end that nothing unseemly will occur. An experienced committee should assist those to be baptized in dressing appropriately for the service, in assisting the minister in every needful way, to aid those who have been baptized in dressing again. The choir should be rehearsed to provide appropriate music, a stanza of a beautiful hymn being softly sung in the interim between the baptism of one candidate and the next. It is usually better to have the baptismal service just preceding the sermon, so that it may be made the center of the worship service and not come as an undue prolongation of the service. The service of baptism should be joyful but profoundly reverential. It should be permitted to speak its message simply, clearly, eloquently, persuasively. All who take part in it or who witness it should be deeply moved as having undergone a memorable experience of worship.

The baptismal ceremony. Practice in Baptist churches varies as to the administration of the ordinance. As soft music is played or as the choir sings softly, the minister may enter the water, face the congregation, and repeat such passages as Matthew 3:5–6; Mark 1:4–5; Luke 3:12–21; John 1:25–26; John 3:23; Matthew 28:19; Acts 2:38–41; Acts 8:36–38; Romans 6:3–4; Colossians 2:12. As the one to be baptized enters the pool, he is met by the minister, who leads him to that position and depth of water most suitable. The candidate having been previously instructed to clasp his hand, with fingers intertwined, the minister slips his left hand underneath the clasped hands of the candidate. With right hand uplifted, the minister may say, having first given the name: "Upon confession of your faith in Jesus Christ as Saviour and Lord, and in obedience to his command, I baptize you, my brother (or sister) in the name of the Father, and of the Son, and of the Holy Spirit. Amen." Slowly and impressively the candidate is then lowered beneath the water, and again quietly and gently lifted from the symbolic watery grave to his feet, to go up out of the water rejoicing as did the eunuch of old.

Reception into the church. At the conclusion of the baptismal service, or at the next convenient service, the new members should be welcomed into the church. This reception of members will include those coming through transfer by letter. As their names are called, they will come forward and stand facing the congregation. The minister will read an appropriate passage or passages of Scripture (from the Sermon on the Mount, or Romans 12, or Ephesians 4, or Philippians 2). The church covenant will be read, and assent made to it by the newly received members. On behalf of the church, the pastor will then welcome each member, giving the right hand of fellowship, after which members of the church will come forward to give the hand of fellowship. The service will be concluded with a season of prayer for these who have become members of the church family and for the church that it may not fail in its duty toward these who have thus been received.

OBSERVING THE MEMORIAL SUPPER

Few directions are given in the New Testament for the observance of the Lord's Supper. The institution of the Supper is described in detail in Matthew 26:17–30, with other slightly variant descriptions in Mark 14:22–24; Luke 22:19–20; John 13:1–4. Reference is made to the observance of the Supper in Acts 2:42, 46, 47; Acts 20:7; 1 Corinthians 10:16–22. Paul, in 1 Corinthians 11:20–34, tells of the institution of the Supper, condemns its unworthy celebration, and sets forth its spiritual significance and value. Jesus gave no details concerning the manner of the observance. Luke reports that he said simply, "This is my body which is given for you: this do in remembrance of me" (Luke 22:19). Paul adds, "This do, as often as ye drink it, in remembrance of me" (1 Corinthians 11:25). Thus no time is fixed, no ceremony is prescribed, no accompanying details are given. A church may therefore observe the Supper weekly, or monthly, or quarterly, or annually. Experience indicates that the observance should not be so often as to become commonplace or so seldom as to be lost sight of. That it was intended for baptized believers only is abundantly evident.

Early in Christian history the Supper was given a place of exalted importance in the services of the churches. Later, the simple ordinance was perverted into a saving sacrament, the bread and the wine believed to be magically transmuted into the actual flesh and blood of Christ, the taking of which was necessary to the sustaining of the communicant's spiritual life. Revolting from this doctrine of transubstantiation, the free churches, particularly Baptist churches, tended to swing to the opposite extreme in making observance of the Supper merely incidental to the preaching service.

Recovery of the high spiritual values of the memorial service should be made without endangering its simplicity and symbolic nature. In many churches it is observed less often than monthly, usually quarterly, the entire morning or evening service being devoted to the celebration. In other churches, the worship program and the sermon are shortened, with every feature of the service gathered about the observance of the Supper, leaving ample time for its unhurried administration. To the end that the Supper may be an occasion of enriching and ennobling worship, certain procedures are appropriate:

Preparation of the church. Preceding the observance of the Supper, on the previous Sunday and at prayer meeting, announcement should be made and the people called to prepare their minds and hearts for the anticipated occasion.

Preparation of the ministrants. Pastor and deacons should meet for prayer and planning so that there will be perfect understanding of each step in the procedure, thus insuring dignity and orderliness. As the pastor takes his place at the table, the deacons will come forward and take their places. It is impressive to have them march together as a body and surround the communion table.

Preparation of the table. The individual communion service has become all but universal. The bread and the "fruit of the vine," symbolizing our Lord's body and blood, will be on the table in suitable vessels. Over the table will be a spotless white covering. Two of the deacons will carefully remove the covering and lay it aside.

Preparation for the observance. The opening order of service may be followed as usual—doxology, invocation, response of choir, offering, prayer. Invitation to church membership may then be given. The pastor may then announce the theme of the service, e.g., Love, Discipleship, Faith, Sacrifice, Loyalty, Forgiveness, Worship, God's Grace, Christ's Salvation, The Church, The Incarnation, The Holy Spirit. The pastor will then lead in brief meditation concerning the chosen theme, after which an appropriate Scripture will be read followed by the singing of an appropriate hymn, followed by brief meditation and prayer. This may be repeated as the people draw closer and closer to him whose "real presence" they seek in their hearts.[3]

The serving of the Supper. At the anticipated time, the minister may thus preside over the administration of the Supper:

The deacons standing, the minister will proceed with:

The Scripture: 1 Corinthians 11:23–24

---

[3] Adapted from Robert E. Keighton, *The Minister's Communion Service Book,* Judson Press, Philadelphia.

The prayer of thanksgiving

The breaking of bread: "As together we eat this bread, let it be to us a solemn reminder that 'when we were yet without strength, in due time Christ died for the ungodly. For scarcely for a righteous man will one die: yet peradventure for a good man some would even dare to die. But God commendeth his own love toward us, in that, while we were yet sinners, Christ died for us' (Romans 5:6–8 ASV). Ministering in his name, I give you this bread, the symbol of his body given for you." (The minister, having broken a piece of the bread, hands the plates filled with fragments of the bread to the deacons, who will distribute it to the people who sit in reverent silence). Upon returning, the deacons will place the plates on the communion table. The minister will serve the deacons and return to the table. One of the deacons will then serve the minister. Standing, the minister may recite John 6:58, or a similar appropriate verse, after which he eats the bread, the members following his example.

The Scripture: 1 Corinthians 11:25–26

The prayer of thanksgiving

The taking of the cup: " 'Much more then, being now justified by his blood, shall we be saved from the wrath of God through him. For if, while we were enemies, we were reconciled to God through the death of his Son, much more, being reconciled, shall we be saved by his life' (Romans 5:9–10 ASV). Ministering in his name, I give you this symbol of Christ's shed blood, which you will drink in remembrance of him." (The deacons will make distribution as before, returning to be served by the pastor, the pastor in turn being served, and all partaking together as the minister, standing, recites: "But if we walk in the light, as he is in the light, we have fellowship one with another, and the blood of Jesus Christ his Son cleanseth us from all sin" (1 John 1:7).

Fellowship offering (if this is the custom of the church)

The dismissal

After the Supper, it is recorded that our Lord sang a hymn and went out. (Without music, "Blest Be the Tie" may be sung. The pastor may shake hands with the deacons as all stand, each deacon successively with his fellow deacon, all then marching two by two to the rear of the building, where they will greet those who go out quietly, without conversation, with a handclasp and a "God bless you!"

REVITALIZING THE CHURCH THROUGH MUSIC [4]

Our church songbooks contain some splendid hymns, and also some which kill a congregation's enthusiasm. From the psychological angle, a good song

---

[4] George W. Crane, *St. Louis Post-Dispatch,* December 31, 1948.

is one which has harmony and a stirring rhythm which lends itself to untrained male voices, as well as to graduates of conservatories of music.

Recently I have been visiting various churches for the purpose of observing their music. Just from my listening to the half-hearted singing in many of them, I have felt sorry for the congregation, since many of the men were really trying to participate in the music but couldn't because it was so difficult or so lacking in a strong, essential rhythm. It would be a great boon if our churches limited themselves to a few dozen of the good old hymns in which people can really participate. For church music should be sung with delight and gusto, so that the very walls almost burst outward with the hearty music. Churches need more men's music.

There are two chief psychological purposes of music in the church. The first is its value in producing wholehearted participation by the congregation, for a crowd that has cooperated in music and ritual is much easier for the speaker to influence. A clergyman thus deserves to have a strong musical build-up before he delivers his address, for when the musical prelude to the sermon has been weak and half-hearted, the clergyman's task is far more difficult.

Second, music is valuable chiefly because of the old emotional memories and moods which are reinstated by it. Thus, idealistic thoughts of one's childhood and the moral precepts of one's mother, should be resurrected by the music.

But this demands the singing of familiar hymns! Effeminate hymns, too often employed today, handicap the clergyman, kill the interest of the congregation, and fail to call up religious memories.

Some clergymen, too, are guilty in this connection, for they select hymns whose titles fit into the sermon topic but whose music is listless. Just hear the French Foreign Legion sing the Marseillaise and you will understand what I mean by whole-hearted singing. Why, the Marseillaise has such inspiring power that its singing has actually been forbidden in times past because it inflamed the French soldier too much.

A living church thus needs well-lighted auditoriums which suggest that people are alive and friendly. And it should have music that both inspires and evokes 100 per cent participation by men, women, and children. Besides, this music should include the familiar hymns of our childhood, to open the storehouse of our emotional memories.

SUGGESTIVE TYPES OF WORSHIP SERVICES

ORDER OF SERVICES

Morning Worship—11:00 A.M.

Prelude—Chorale, "St. Cross" . . . . Parry
Doxology
Invocation and The Lord's Prayer
* Hymn No. 37—"A Mighty Fortress Is Our God" . . . . .Luther
Scripture Lesson
Quartet—"While the Earth Remaineth" . . . . Tours

Prayer
Choral Response
* Hymn No. 244—"The Church's One Foundation" . . . . . . Wesley
Tithes and Offerings
Offertory Soprano Solo—"Consider the Lilies" . . . . Scott
Sermon—"OUR FATHER'S BUSINESS". . . . . The Pastor
* Hymn No. 380—"Saviour, Thy Dying Love" . . . . Lowry
The Lord's Supper
Hymn No. 81—"Break Thou the Bread of Life" . . . . Towner
Broadcast over WRNL-FM

Evening Worship—8:00 P.M.

Prelude—Chorale, "O God, Thou Holy God" . . . . Karg-Elert
The Ordinance of Baptism
* Hymn No. 282—"On Jordan's Stormy Banks I Stand" . . . . . Arr. Dale
Scripture Lesson
Quartet—"The Day is Past and Over" . . . . Marks
Call to Prayer
Evening Prayer
Vesper and High School Choirs—"Songs of Praises" . . . . . Arr. Jones
* Hymn No. 249—"Faith of Our Fathers, Living Still" . . . . . . Henry
Tithes and Offerings
Offertory Quartet—"Fierce Was the Wild Billow" . . . . Noble
Sermon—"OUR FATHERS' FAITH" . . . . The Pastor
* Hymn No. 169—"My Faith Looks Up to Thee" . . . . Mason
Benediction
* The congregation will please stand with the choir.
—First Baptist Church, Richmond, Virginia

TODAY'S WORSHIP SERVICES
MORNING
Sunday School—9:30   Worship Service—11:00

The Lord's House   *Enter to Worship*
Quiet Moments for Personal Prayer: "The earth is the Lord's and the fulness
thereof; the world, and they that dwell therein." Psalm 24:1
Organ Prelude: "Our Father Who Art in Heaven". . . . . Bach
Call to Worship: "The Lord Is in His Holy Temple" . . . . Root
Invocation
Choral Response: "Hear Our Prayer" . . . . Whelpton
Doxology: "Old Hundred". . . . . Choir-Congregation
Morning Hymn No. 46: "Onward, Christian Soldiers". . . . . . Sullivan
Scripture Lesson and Pastoral Prayer
The School of the Church . . . . .Supt. Gale Dunn

SUGGESTIVE TYPES OF WORSHIP SERVICES—(*Continued*)

Greeting Our Guests
Service of Giving:
Offertory Hymn No. 393: "Trust, Try, and Prove Me". . . . . . . Leech
Offertory Prayer
Offertory Organ: "Were You There?". . . . . Wingwold
Anthem: "He Shall Reign Forever" . . . . .Simper
Sermon . . . . The Pastor
Invitation Hymn No. 57: "Jesus Is Calling" . . . . Stebbins
Benediction, Choir: "The Lord Bless You and Keep You" . . . . .Lutkin
Postlude, Organ. . . . . Bach

EVENING

The Lord's Work	*Depart to Serve*
Training Union—6:15	Evening Worship 7·30

Organ Prelude: "Evening Meditation" . . . . Arranged
Call to Worship: "Near to the Heart of God" . . . . Choir
Evening Prayer
Choir Hymn: "Leaning on My Saviour" . . . . Dunn
Training in Church Membership
Songs You Request. . . . . Led by Gale Dunn
Greeting Our Guests
Gathering of Tithes and Offerings
Offertory Hymn: "Devotional Medley" . . . . .arr.
Offertory Prayer
Offertory, Organ: "Softly and Tenderly". . . . . .Thompson
Hymn-Anthem: "The Voice of My Saviour" . . . . .Ackley
Sermon . . . . The Pastor
Invitation Hymn No. 29: "Let Him In". . . . . Excell
Benediction
Postlude, Organ. . . . . .Waring
(Please remain through the invitation. This is the most vital and serious moment
of the entire service. We are asking that you pray earnestly for the salvation of the
lost and to remain perfectly quiet.)
—Gaston Avenue Baptist Church, Dallas, Texas.

CORRELATED CHURCH PROGRAM *

I. *Wednesday Family Night*
9:00 A.M.   Staff conference: Bible reading, prayer, discussion of plans,
problems, calendar of activities, and other matters necessary to promote a smoothly-functioning, graded ministry
serving the needs of all.

---

* Adapted from plan of Immanuel Baptist Church, Tulsa, Oklahoma.

5:00 P.M.   Intermediate R.A.'s and G.A.'s meet.

5:40 P.M.   Minister of education meets with department superintend-
              ents of the Sunday school to outline plans for the coming
              week, to be passed to the departments in their meetings
              following supper.

6:00 P.M.   Meal served cafeteria style, at cost, to all of church family
              desiring to attend.

6:10 P.M.   New church members are welcomed and visitors recog-
              nized.

6:15 P.M.   Intermediates go to chapel choir rehearsal, Juniors to G.A.
              and R.A. meetings, younger children to Sunbeam meet-
              ings, and babies to nursery. Minister of education, pastor,
              and general Sunday school superintendent present matters
              of interest and importance to entire Sunday school.

6:30 P.M.   All Sunday school workers go to their several departments
              for a forty-five-minute departmental meeting. Those not in
              Sunday school departmental meetings, missionary auxilia-
              ries, or chapel choir are invited to visit church library or to
              attend a training course taught by the pastor.

7:15 P.M.   All come to sanctuary for midweek worship service of
              prayer, praise, and Bible study. Service is followed by re-
              hearsal of sanctuary choir, composed of young people and
              adults.

II. *Other Weekday Activities*

1. Weekday activities of W.M.S. and its auxiliaries will include general
and circle meetings on Thursday; business women's circles and Y.W.A. on
Monday night; other W.M.U. groups will meet on Wednesday night as
indicated above.

2. The Brotherhood holds a monthly dinner meeting on Tuesday night,
followed by Brotherhood visitation.

3. Weekday recreational activities include scheduled games and practices of the three softball and hardball teams in season, the basketball
team, and the numerous socials conducted by the various departments
and classes and missionary organizations. A youth fellowship hour also
follows the Sunday evening services.

4. Tuesday is visitation day. Groups gather for the visitation assignment at 9:30 A.M., 1:30 P.M., and 6:45 P.M. On the first Tuesday in each
month the Sunday school gives special emphasis to visiting prospects; the

Brotherhood, on the second Tuesday; the W.M.U., on the third Tuesday; Training Union, on the fourth Tuesday. This is in addition to visitation of absentees promoted weekly. One of the staff secretaries keeps the master file for visitation up to date, records the reports of visits, and assigns new prospects to appropriate groups. A vital part of the total visitation ministry is that rendered by the Extension Department and the Cradle Roll Department.

III. *Sunday Activities*

1. Sunday starts with Sunday school at 9:30 A.M., followed by the worship service at 11:00 A.M.

2. Two choral groups rehearse each Sunday afternoon—the Young People's choir, 4:00–5:00 P.M.; the Junior Carol Choir, 5:30–6:15 P.M.

3. The Training Union meets at 6:30 P.M.; the evening worship hour follows at 7:30 P.M.

PROGRAM OF PRAYER MEETING [5]

Convene with call to order, 8:00 P.M.

Two or three hymns from hymnal, led from platform (7 minutes)

Vocal or instrumental music (4 minutes)

Prayer period—one-minute silent prayer, then prayers by individuals in the congregation (short prayers) ending with the Lord's Prayer led by pastor (10 minutes)

Scripture lesson, either read by the pastor or responsively; or given by the congregation in verses (3 minutes)

Business and announcements (5 minutes)

Children's or Young People's Chorus—sacred music (4 minutes)

Singing of "Favorite Hymns," called for by the congregation, and led from the platform without music and use of hymnals (6 minutes)

Testimonies by the congregation (7 minutes)

Address by the pastor (15 minutes)

Welfare, sick-and-needy reports, etc. (4 minutes)

Closing hymn and benediction (3 minutes)

The meeting closes at nine o'clock or within a few minutes of the hour. No time is lost, no "drag" is experienced. The hour is all too short. The service is alive!

---

[5] Adapted from Arthur Thomas Brooks, *The Practical and Profitable in Church Administration* (Philadelphia: Judson Press), pp. 170–175.

A Church Promoting and Practicing Christian Stewardship

Church members have accepted partnership with Christ. This partnership involves all of life—time, talents, influence, family relationship, social fellowship, professional or business practice, property, and money. Discipleship recognizes Jesus as Teacher, stewardship acknowledges him as Lord. As faith-salvation is the "good news" to the sinner, so stewardship-living is the "good news" to the saved. According to the former, the sinner is saved by grace apart from any merit of his own; according to the latter, the Christian enters into a life of service in which all that he is or has is put at the disposal of God the owner to be used for the purposes of Christ the Saviour under the guidance of the Holy Spirit the teacher.

Both Old and New Testaments make this covenant relation of the believer with God central in the divine purpose and essential to fulness of life of the believer. Implementation of the doctrine of stewardship by a church is a primary responsibility. If this doctrine is not preached and practiced, the church limps along in weakness and its members grow lean of soul.

The practice of stewardship involves far more than financial support of the church and its enterprises. By it is given reality to the profession of the church members, who may say with their lips that they trust the salvation of their souls to Christ, but who by their failure in stewardship-living and -giving declare that they cannot trust God with their lives and possessions. God and the world will know which of these declarations to believe.

Christian stewardship involves tithing as "an equitable minimum." The Christian is not bound by the law of tithing any more than he is bound by the law of the sabbath; yet the Christian who gives less under grace than the Jews of old under the law, or who observes the Lord's Day as being any less sacred than the Jews held their sabbath to be, would be unworthy of the Name. A church that provides ways and means of putting into practice the central doctrine of the Christian life is doing high service to Christ and his people.

CHURCH FINANCING MUST REST ON STEWARDSHIP FOUNDATIONS

Trying to finance a church by spasmodic money-raising appeals and methods would be like trying to raise a crop without regard to seed and soil and season. Churches using traditionally approved methods of financing are often disappointed because the church's income remains meager and inadequate. Perhaps they have overlooked the truth that church financing is not an occasional affair but a perennial major activity.

A church whose members give regularly and worthily is a church with a stewardship conscience. Many earnest Christians who have a sensitive and enlightened conscience concerning other great Christian doctrines have somehow failed to develop an active conscience concerning their duty to "render unto God the things that are God's." People generally are quick to recognize the strategy of pastor and deacons who ring the changes on certain verses of Scripture with the obvious purpose of getting money from unwilling givers. The worthy giving of money through the church for the support of its ministry at home and abroad is like the practice of any other great Christian principle—it is the fruit of knowledge, conviction, inspiration, determination, satisfaction.

The two great correlative Christian responsibilities are *evangelism* and *stewardship*. The first responsibility, evangelism, is to share in the bearing of Christian witness to the end that the lost may be saved; the second, stewardship, is to share in bringing the saved under the Lordship of Christ to the end that his mastery may extend into and over every area of life. Concerning every service of worship, every sermon, every program, every lesson, every activity or enterprise of a church, the searching question should be asked: How is it related to the promotion of evangelism and stewardship? Just as there are special seasons for evangelism, so there should be special occasions for the emphasizing of stewardship. The "stewardship revival" should become as well established in a church as the "soul-winning revival." In the plan of study courses, books on stewardship should be regularly included. Any church can be grown into a great giving church whose leadership is willing to undergird its financial program with a long-range stewardship emphasis program.

SUCCESSIVE STEPS IN SUCCESSFUL CHURCH FINANCING

Church financing is beset with many perils, chief among them being *haphazardness*. An intuitive fear lies at the heart of the minister lest he be accused of being "money-minded." Deacons and other church officers advise cautiously against saying too much about money, since to do so might drive some people away. The general attitude is thus created that the finances of a church are a sort of necessary evil—the less said about

CHECKING UP ON STEWARDSHIP AND FINANCES

Items for evaluation	Yes	No	To some extent	Don't know
1. Are sermons on stewardship preached regularly?				
2. Are special seasons set apart for stewardship emphasis?				
3. Are tracts on stewardship circulated?				
4. Are special programs on stewardship presented in Sunday school, Training Union, W.M.U., Brotherhood, assembly periods?				
5. Are Sunday school teachers made aware of their duty and privilege to emphasize stewardship?				
6. Are stewardship books regularly included in study course plans?				
7. Is the church developing increasingly a stewardship conscience?				
8. Has careful analysis been made to determine exactly how many members are tithers, nontithers but regular givers, occasional contributors, noncontributors?				
9. In the light of the facts thus revealed, has the church a definite plan to enlist all the irregular and noncontributors?				
10. Has a study been made to determine the giving possibilities of the church?				
11. Has the church a unified and inclusive budget based on its giving possibilities?				
12. Are all members fully informed about the budget?				
13. Is the budget such as to make unnecessary special designation?				
14. Are the people kept well informed concerning the causes represented in the budget?				
15. Is the "fifty-fifty" ideal (as much for missions and benevolences as for local expenses) kept steadily in view?				
16. Has the church an effective system for collecting the weekly offerings?				
17. Is the ceremony of collecting the offerings made dignified and worshipful?				

Items for evaluation	Yes	No	To some extent	Don't know
18. Is there an accurate and adequate system of accounting for all money received and disbursed?				
19. Is the church kept informed concerning all financial transactions?				
20. Are statements made available to members showing relation of gifts to pledges?				

them, the better. Since a church is the Lord's business, it is assumed, he will see that ample resources are provided for its success. Perhaps back of some of this reasoning is the unholy fear that a system of church financing will call for more money from some than they are willing to give. A haphazard financial program, it is easy to see, leaves many to enjoy the privileges of the church free of charge while others get them at bargain rates.

Let the minister settle it with himself once for all that he cannot preach a full gospel and omit heavy stress on stewardship-giving. He is as duty bound to preach and to teach this doctrine and to secure its practice as any other basic doctrine of the Scriptures. Money is life transmuted into currency, and it is absurd to speak of "consecration" apart from systematic and proportionate giving. Deacons and other church officers would have little business in a church if they did not lead out in implementing this central doctrine of the Christian life, without obedience to which the individual Christian denies Christ's Lordship, and the church and the denomination risk bankruptcy. A sound, systematic plan of church financing develops the Christians who give, lends vigor and power to the church, makes possible fulfilment of Christ's great commission, and wins favor with God and men.

The successive steps in a successful plan of church financing, confirmed by the experience of countless churches that seek both spiritual and monetary returns, may be thus enumerated:

1. Establish a stewardship-tithing basis.
2. Determine giving possibilities.
3. Build a worthy unified budget.
4. Publicize the Christian causes.
5. Secure the adoption of the budget.
6. Plan to enlist every member.
7. Utilize the church organizations.

8. Make "Loyalty Week" a great occasion.
9. Follow up until every member is accounted for.
10. Let giving be an act of worship.
11. Keep alive the personal relationship.
12. Maintain confidence through competent accounting.

The several items in this comprehensive program may be developed as follows:

PUTTING THE CHURCH ON A WORTHY BUDGET BASIS

The minister may preach stewardship-tithing with great earnestness, the scriptural ideal may be agreed to in principle by the church, yet the doctrine practically denied by the church's plans, goals, and gifts. A church may in effect be saying: Stewardship-giving, with the tithe as an equitable minimum, is *right* according to the Scriptures; but you may do as *wrong* as you please about it, your church is indifferent.

To be *wrong* in this area of stewardship-giving is to be *wrong* at the very heart of the Christian life. It is therefore the sacred duty of a church, through its deacons or other qualified committee, to study the church membership roll each year to discover (1) the tithers, (2) the nontithing regular givers, (3) the irregular givers, (4) the noncontributors. This list should be carefully made and studied, not for publicity purposes nor with the thought of exalting by praise or embarrassing by blame, but as symptomatic of spiritual health or ill health calling for prayerful concern.

With this analysis before them, a small, discreet, trusted stewardship survey committee, pledged to keep the discussion sacredly confidential, will sit together in an honest effort to determine the giving possibilities and probabilities of all those whose names are on the membership roll. First, there will be laid aside the names of those who may ordinarily be expected to give nothing—non-resident and unlocatable, and those without income; second, resident members who gave nothing of record during the past year who should be lovingly visited to discover reasons for their unenlistment; third, those with limited incomes whose giving will probably fall within the range of one cent a week to one dollar a week; fourth, those whose incomes will warrant expectation of $1.00 to $5.00 a week; fifth, those who might well give $5.00 to $10.00 a week; sixth, those who, as faithful stewards, might be led to give $10.00 to $25.00 a week; seventh, those who can and should go beyond $25.00 a week. Of course, the upper brackets will be determined by the range of incomes in a given situation.

The process of devising a tentative budget will then be simple. The number will be set down successively of those who, as matters stand, could, if they would, give one cent a week, five cents a week, ten cents a week, twenty-five cents a week, fifty cents a week, seventy-five cents a week, one dollar a week, above $1.00 to $5.00 a week, above $5.00 to $10.00 a week, above $10.00 to $25.00 a week, and so to the highest expectancy. Multiplying these "possibilities" by fifty-two weeks, the *tentative* budget total will be arrived at. This constitutes the church's financial *goal,* which will be discounted for the immediate year ahead as experience and common sense may dictate.

With this *tentative* budget goal before them, the budget committee will meet to propose its worthy distribution. The ideal will be a fifty-fifty division—as much for missions and benevolences (the "Cooperative Program") as for local expenses. Beginning with the one-half tentatively apportioned for local expenses, every foreseeable item will be listed with an amount allocated according to agreement and need: salaries, upkeep of building, insurance, literature and supplies for each of the organizations, public utilities, office and transportation expenses, music, library, fellowship and recreation, printing and publicity, extra-pastoral services, local missions, radio, incidentals, unforeseen contingencies. Of course, interested groups will be consulted as to their needs and given opportunity to present their requests.

On the other side of the budget will be listed all the causes among which will be divided the other 50 per cent of gifts. It is not enough simply to lump all these together under "Cooperative Program." Here again the ideal is a fifty-fifty division—one-half of the money given to be used for state purposes, the other half to be used for Convention-wide purposes. Under "state missions" will be included all the causes supported by the churches of a given state—officers and employees at state headquarters; state Sunday school, Training Union, W.M.U., and Brotherhood work; Christian institutions within the state—schools, orphanages, hospitals, and the like; direct missions in needy places—neglected city areas, neglected rural sections, work among Negroes, Jews, foreigners, concerted evangelistic efforts, etc.; aid to new and struggling churches; publicity and promotion as represented by the state paper, participation in state radio programs, printing and distribution of tracts and pamphlets, etc. Under "Convention-wide" causes will be listed foreign missions, home missions, ministerial education, hospitals, relief and annuity provisions for ministers and others, expenses of administration and promotion, Convention radio programs, Convention committees, miscellaneous items. The proportion of distributable receipts to each of these agencies or institutions or activities varies from year to year according to needs, hence the budget committee should have at hand a copy of the latest agreement concerning percentages of gifts for each of the several causes.

People do not give with enthusiasm to a percentage table. Of utmost importance is the attractive publicizing of these Christian causes to which they give. A familiar poster device may show the dollar divided into two halves, each half then divided into segments indicating each of the major causes to which that proportion of the dollar will go. A series of letters may be prepared and mailed to the membership, each letter setting forth a phase of the budget, making clear that the members do not give *to* the church but *through* the church, not *to* the Cooperative Program but *through* the Program. Tracts may be had for the asking which set forth clearly and attractively the causes which the churches are called upon to support. These may be mailed or otherwise distributed. Of course the pastor will preach occasionally on the work and needs of the church, and the specific causes at home and abroad which are supported by gifts made through the church. Likewise, teachers in the Sunday school and leaders in the other organizations will make frequent opportunity to present educationally and inspirationally the objects which church members are called upon to support by their gifts. At midweek prayer meeting mention should often be made of the work and the workers, and earnest and intelligent prayer offered in their behalf.

With such a background of knowledge of giving actualities and possibilities, with such a unified budget carefully and thoughtfully proposed, with such appreciative understanding of the items and causes included in the budget, the church is now ready to adopt it. The adoption of the budget should be no mere routine affair. Having been proposed by the budget committee, and having been approved after thorough discussion at the church business meeting, it should then be presented to the congregation as a whole for adoption at a climactic Sunday morning hour in an atmosphere of high inspiration and deep consecration. Few services of a church should be looked upon as more important than this hour when the whole church votes to support its whole program. Into this hour pastor and people should pour their best of intelligent committal to their church as Christ's instrumentality for the achievement of his kingdom's purposes.

SECURING EVERY-MEMBER PARTICIPATION

The budget having been adopted, the next step is to get it subscribed. Nothing short of every-member enlistment will satisfy the Christian ideal. A church, like the good shepherd, should not be content if there are ninety and nine who are safe in the fold of stewardship giving and living, but should seek with deep concern to bring back into the Way the last, least, straying member. Every effort should be made to locate the "unlocatables." Concentration of prayer should be upon the noncontributors. If a number *cannot* give, the church should throw its arm of love and support around them until self-support again becomes possible.

The "every-member canvass" as once conducted had many faults. It savored too much of a shrewd "money grab." Canvassers were recruited from the church membership at large, groups of canvassers were placed under leaders, each group was given a list of members, the canvassers were intensively trained to go forth simultaneously to visit every member and to secure, if possible, a signed pledge card. After the first flush of interest in this type of campaign, the difficulty of securing canvassers usually increased. To visit the faithful members to secure their pledges appeared to be a waste of time and sometimes was resented. Indiscreet canvassers with the best of intentions sometimes blundered frightfully.

Inevitably it dawned upon thoughtful pastors and church leaders that it is not best to undertake to secure systematic giving by a spasmodic campaign. The persistent, perennial aspect of stewardship-tithing calls essentially for consistent educational undergirding. Those closest to the majority of the church members are the teachers, officers, leaders of the several organizations. As a rule they are the church's convinced, practicing tithers. To them the church may turn with greatest confidence to carry out, quietly and effectively, its plans for every-member enlistment in giving. The wise church will therefore, through pastor and finance committee, summon the responsible "inner circle" of its several organizations and place upon them responsibility, together with the deacons, for getting the budget subscribed.

Each year a week should be set aside to seek commitment of every member to the financial support of the church and its causes. Many churches designate this "Loyalty Week," with its climactic Sunday known as "Loyalty Day." Certain procedures are suggested in making this an epochal week in the life of the church:

1. Prepare for the special week over a period of at least three months, back of which will be nine months of continuous concern.

2. Bring together under leadership of pastor, deacons, and finance committee, all elected teachers and officers of all the organizations, with whom will be discussed in detail the plans for "Loyalty Week."

3. To this "inner circle" group add faithful members of classes, departments, unions, circles, committees of the several organizations.

4. Publicize attractively and effectively the importance and purpose of "Loyalty Week," seeking to have present on "Loyalty Day" the largest possible attendance.

5. Let all officers and teachers of the Sunday school be present ahead

of time on "Loyalty Sunday," with a copy of the adopted budget and a pledge card for each member with his or her name already on it.

6. The opening service (for the school as a whole or in the department assemblies) should concentrate attention and prayer on the supreme purpose of the day—to secure a worthy commitment for the support of the church from everyone present.

7. Superintendents, teachers, and other workers with children of beginner, primary, and junior ages should have made previous visits into the homes to explain carefully to the parents the objective of the church in developing in each child the grace of giving, the character traits of generosity and unselfishness, the joy of sharing in the church's kingdom program, the habit of carefulness in the use of money. Make clear that the amount is not most significant but rather the spiritual results in the life of the child. Assure the mother that the child is just as welcome without the regular gift as with it, but that the child's moral development will be quickened by participation in the full program of the school through regular gifts, preferably from an allowance which the child will look upon as its own. The card may be brought back by the visitor or sent by the child on "Loyalty Day."

8. In the Intermediate, Young People's and Adult classes, teachers may take the lesson as a point of departure, but they should devote the major part of the class period to an explanation of the budget, a clear statement of the principles of stewardship-tithing, and attractive presentation of the privilege of sharing in the church's kingdom program, with especial emphasis on the missionary aspects. Questions should be invited as to how the money will be used, how the tithe may be determined, the meaning and value of the pledge, how each one decides for himself the amount of the weekly offering, how and when the offering is to be made, how and what happens if one finds the amount pledged cannot be paid, what is meant by "tithes *and* offerings," what rewards may be expected from worthy and faithful giving, etc. No effort should be made to overpersuade anyone, pledging beyond reasonable ability to pay should be dissuaded, care should be taken that what is done is "not to be seen of men." While class and department quotas may be set, there should be no mere rivalry to outdistance others, but a deep sense of desire to know and to do the will of God.

Some fifteen minutes before the preaching service, all classes, juniors through adults, should assemble in the sanctuary, joyfully reports should be given, with special recognition of those classes and departments that have met their quotas. Inevitably some will be absent, and these should be visited by teachers or class representatives during the week ahead.

Following the worship service, the pastor will present his appeal, based on Scripture, for the faithful fulfilment of their pledges by those who have already signed, and for signing of cards by all present who have not yet done so. With a pledge card and a detailed statement of the budget in their hands, with the plea of the pastor ringing in their ears, and with the call of Christ stirring their hearts, all who are present should "make it unanimous" by signing the cards. It is a glorious sight, then, to witness all who have signed, at the Sunday school or the worship hour, marching single file past the communion table and placing on it their cards of commitment.

What of those who are absent, or who for any reason have not signed? A selected group of deacons, church officers, Sunday school officers and teachers, Woman's Missionary Union, Training Union, and Brotherhood members, will have been invited to remain after the preaching service to participate in the follow-up. For them a light luncheon will be prepared. While they are eating, a competent committee will quickly check the signed cards against a master list. Within an hour or less they should check the names of all resident members for whom there are no signed cards. These names are at once distributed to those who can best make the contacts, and they are prayerfully sent forth to visit each person and bring back a report of results. These visits should be made with great tact, not just to secure pledges but even more importantly to show the church's concern for their spiritual welfare, to discover opportunities for service on the part of the church, and to re-establish church relationships where broken. At the Wednesday prayer service and on the following Sunday reports of these visits should be made and additional pledges reported. Names of those still not signing cards should be turned over to the deacons, who with the pastor will seek continuously to remove difficulties of enlistment on the part of these spiritually derelict members.

MAINTAINING GIVING THROUGH SPIRITUAL SATISFACTIONS

It is a law of life that activities tend to be discontinued if not accompanied by satisfactions. A glow of enthusiasm will pervade the church when its stewardship-giving program has been carried through to success as described above. Then follow the fifty-one weeks when temptations to laxity arise. For some money may become scarce, others may experience unexpected misfortune, the spiritual ardor of a number may cool, a few may have their feelings hurt, worldly interests may crowd out spiritual interests for others, some may be overtaken by sin. When a member falls behind in his or her giving, "there's a reason." To discover the reason and remove the difficulty is far more important than for the church to receive the gift. A delinquent member is a challenge to the church to discover the cause and remove the stumblingblock.

In what ways may the church provide satisfactions that will sustain stewardship-giving?

1. The pledge of the member should be gratefully acknowledged in a letter from the church, signed by pastor and chairman of the finance committee, with explanation of the use of the carton of weekly offering envelopes as a means of personal accounting.

2. Giving should always be made an act of worship. Gifts through the Sunday school, especially in the younger departments, should be received in a happy ceremony consisting of Scripture verses, prayer, music. The high moment of dedication in the worship service should be when the people offer themselves to God through their gifts in simple but dignified worship. Never should giving be incidental, commonplace, irreverent. When the small group or the great congregation give, they should do so as unto God, in the realization that he who sat over against the treasury still watches and evaluates those who give. Much should be made of the motive of giving, of the objects of giving, of the joy of giving, of the spiritual rewards of giving.

3. Members should be kept informed as to their record of giving. Care should be taken that this information is not construed as a "dun" or "bill," but is simply to the end that each one may know how his account stands on the books of the treasurer. Gratitude should be expressed for whatever has been given and the needs of the church and its causes restated attractively and winsomely.

4. "Honor rolls" of tithers or other givers are of doubtful value. They may tend to spiritual pride rather than to spiritual satisfaction. Such publicity may wound the feelings of those whose names do not appear. Some churches publish at regular intervals the names of all who have given anything with no reference to amount. Would not a more satisfactory plan be to write a note of thanks personally to all who have given and a personal note of regret, with loving statement of the church's desire to be of service, to all who have made no gifts of record?

5. The financial affairs of a church should be entrusted to duly elected officials in whom all have complete confidence. The treasurer, for his own protection, should usually be bonded. Monthly reports of the church's finances should be made regularly, and semiannually a complete detailed report should be printed or mimeographed and mailed to every member. This report should usually be certified by a qualified auditor, or, if not by an auditor, by a competent committee of the church. That the church's finances are in safe hands is a matter of deep satisfaction to the givers.

6. Those who give should be reminded in a multitude of ways that they are making investments that will yield eternal dividends. The money that one is surest of having saved and invested beyond the possibility of loss is money that has been given through the church to the cause of Christ. Convinced that this is true, those who give will do so systematically, proportionately, intelligently, not spasmodically nor grudgingly as of necessity.

7. Returns on their investment should often be brought to the attention of those who give. They should be kept informed as to the achievements of the church locally, and made to rejoice that they are having a real share in winning the lost and advancing God's kingdom around the world. Kingdom men and women do not have to be coaxed to give— they realize that they are privileged to invest in an enterprise which will bring the highest of satisfactions both here and hereafter.

THE LORD'S ACRE PLAN [1]

1. Let each church elect or appoint a strong Lord's Acre committee to put the Lord's Acre plan into effective operation. In order to gain a full measure of success, this work must be made an important, vigorously executed activity of the church, with thorough preparation in planning and in prayer.

2. The Church should decide which are the most important of its financial needs, for which the Lord's Acre plan can most suitably be used. It is almost always desirable to use a portion of the Lord's Acre money for improvement in the church building, or better equipment, or landscaping the grounds. Such an objective appeals especially to the young people. It is also recommended that some of the Lord's Acre money be used for local expenses, and some for benevolences. This gives to each one training in supporting the whole life of the church.

3. Every one in the church and Sunday school who can find it practicable to have a project should be expected to have a part. The Lord's Acre committee should enlist workers in worthy projects by enthusiastic, determined week-by-week effort. Many churches have found it most practical to enlist workers through the Sunday school classes. Others who are not members should be reached by special visitation. Such visitation often gives an effective Christian approach to those who have not been interested in the church.

4. The Lord's Acre plan provides a practical means of support, summoning young and old in the country church, as well as others who re-

---

[1] Farmers Federation, Asheville, North Carolina, Religious Department.

ceive its blessings, to carry through dedicated farm projects, so enabling each one to have a worthy part in advancing the Divine Mission.

"This plan can open and fill weak, closed rural churches in America today and help to give the United States again the spirit, purpose and power of our forefathers, who came here seeking a place where they would be free to worship. The Lord's Acre can do it."

STEWARDSHIP EDUCATION FOR CHILDREN [2]

Boys and girls learn to live by living. Education is a continuous ongoing process. It is a teaching-learning process. Christian educators, like other educators, have come to believe that the boy or girl does not gain at one time or in one situation sufficient knowledge to last him the rest of his life. Christian educators guide children in living today on their level of understanding and ability in order that they may be the Christian adults of tomorrow, for it is day by day out of their experiences that boys and girls are building concepts, habits, purposes, and attitudes which will make or mar life for them.

Each day a child comes into perplexing situations. He is confused by conflicts and tensions in the world in which he lives. He is forced to make choices, and is subject to the consequences of his decisions. This ability to arrive at a Christian solution of his problem depends upon how real God is to him. If the child knows God as his friend and leader, he will seek, with God's help, the solution of his personal problems. His ability to solve in Christian ways the next problem to arise will depend upon his satisfactory handling of today's choices. This is the law of growth and habit formation. Christian stewardship is subject to the same laws.

The child has his first lessons in the stewardship of time when he is first taught to pray and is first taken to church school. He has his first lessons in the stewardship of talent when he sings his first songs of praise to God or participates in the sharing experiences of the home and church school nursery class. He has his first lessons in the stewardship of possession as he shares a favorite toy with another child or when he places in the offering receptacle at church school the money which has been given to him. From these beginnings on through each day and year, the child grows and develops as a partner and worker with God and, as such, is a Christian steward.

Objectives

Undergirding any work with boys and girls should be definite objectives. Study of and experiences in stewardship should lead boys and girls:

1. To appreciate God's gifts to them and to use these gifts as a sacred trust from God
2. To understand the responsibility that having time, money, and talents brings to each person and to develop a partnership with God in the right use of life and possessions

---

[2] Adapted from *Children and Stewardship*, a pamphlet published by the American Baptist Convention Council on Finance and Promotion.

CHECKING UP ON THE CHURCH'S PROGRAM OF TITHING-ENLISTMENT [3]

Items for evaluation	Yes	No	To some extent	Don't know
1. Are we familiar with and committed to the Forward Program of Church Finance as adapted to our church needs?				
2. Have we decided what would be a reasonable budget goal for our church?				
3. Have we talked and prayed with church leaders about the stewardship effort?				
4. Has our church set a definite tithing goal for this year?				
5. Has a stewardship chairman been appointed, and has he consented to serve?				
6. Have we appointed a stewardship committee representing the several organizations or departments in our church?				
7. Have we instructed this committee concerning its privileges and duties?				
8. Has the pastor planned a series of appropriate stewardship sermons?				
9. Have we planned to place a stewardship item in every piece of literature we get out?				
10. Has the stewardship poster been prominently posted, and has attention been called to it?				
11. Has careful selection been made of the stewardship and tithing literature sent to the pastor?				
12. Has stewardship and tithing literature been ordered from our state secretary?				
13. Have we planned to have a study course or a stewardship revival in our church?				
14. Are our Sunday school, Training Union, Woman's Missionary Union, and Brotherhood all committed to this effort and working at it?				
15. Have we planned to have three-minute stewardship talks in all organizations at least once a month?				
16. Have we planned for a special Stewardship Enlistment Day?				

[3] Adapted from J. E. Dillard, *Building a Stewardship Church.*

3. To establish right attitudes toward and appreciations of material possessions, values, and other persons
4. To determine choices and actions upon principles of Christian stewardship
5. To learn ways to increase, practice, and share skills and abilities
6. To accept Christ as personal Saviour, and then to become a part of the church fellowship through the use of possessions in the work of the church and in bringing others to the church
7. To feel a kinship with all peoples of the world who receive Christ as Lord and worship God as Father.

EXAMPLES OF CHURCH BUDGETS

A Small Quarter-time Church Budget

Pastor's salary	$ 600.00
Janitor and upkeep	100.00
Literature and supplies	100.00
Light, heat, insurance	50.00
Pastor's car expense, stationery, stamps	100.00
Annuity Board	25.00
Incidentals	50.00
Total	$ 1,025.00
Cooperative Program	400.00
Local missions and benevolences	100.00
Grand Total	$ 1,525.00

A Larger Half-time Church Budget

Pastor's salary	$ 1,800.00
Janitor and upkeep	200.00
Literature and supplies	200.00
Light, heat, insurance	150.00
Pastor's car expense, stationery, stamps	250.00
Annuity Board	50.00
Incidentals	100.00
Total	$ 2,750.00
Cooperative Program	1,200.00
Local missions and benevolences	250.00
Grand Total	$ 4,200.00

A Small Full-time Church Budget

Pastor's salary	$ 4,000.00
Janitor and upkeep	600.00
Literature and supplies	300.00

EXAMPLES OF CHURCH BUDGETS—(*Continued*)

Light, heat, insurance	300.00
Office expense	300.00
Pastor's car expense	300.00
Bulletin and printing	200.00
Fellowship and social expenses	150.00
Pastor's Convention expense	100.00
Supply in pastor's absence	100.00
Incidentals	200.00
Total	$ 6,550.00
Cooperative Program	2,000.00
Local missions and benevolences	500.00
Grand Total	$ 9,050.00

A Larger Full-time Church Budget

Pastor's salary	$ 6,000.00
Church secretary	3,400.00
Musician	750.00
Janitor and upkeep	1,000.00
Literature and supplies	600.00
Light, heat, water, insurance	600.00
Office expense	600.00
Advertising and printing	600.00
Fellowship and social expenses	500.00
Pastor's car expense	600.00
Supply in pastor's absence	100.00
Pastor's Convention expense	100.00
Library and visual aids	100.00
Annuity Board	75.00
Upkeep of pastor's home	400.00
Incidentals	500.00
Total	$ 15,925.00
Cooperative Program	6,000.00
Local missions and benevolences	1,000.00
Grand Total	$ 22,925.00

A Still Larger Full-time Church Budget

Pastor's salary	$ 7,500.00
Church secretary	3,600.00
Minister of Education	6,000.00
Musician and music	1,200.00
Janitor and upkeep	1,500.00
Literature and supplies	1,000.00
Light, heat, water, insurance	1,000.00

EXAMPLES OF CHURCH BUDGETS—(*Continued*)

Office expense	1,200.00
Advertising and printing	1,200.00
Fellowship and social expenses	600.00
Pastor's car expense	600.00
Pastor's Convention expense and other travel	150.00
Supply in pastor's absence	150.00
Library and visual aids	200.00
Annuity Board	150.00
Upkeep of pastor's home	600.00
Incidentals	600.00
Total	$ 27,250.00
Cooperative Program	7,000.00
Local missions and benevolences	1,500.00
Grand Total	$ 35,750.00

A Large Church Budget

Missions Here

Salaries	$ 42,000.00

Minister, minister of education, minister of music, age-group directors, secretaries, hostess, and janitors

Printing and office supplies	3,600.00
Repairs (building, roof, and painting)	3,000.00
Electricity	1,000.00
Fuel	1,500.00
Insurance	2,000.00
Convention expense	600.00
Pulpit supply	250.00
Music	2,000.00
Miscellaneous	10,000.00

Debt retirement, water, fuel, light, telephone, janitors' supplies, car expenses

Literature and supplies	2,000.00
State paper	1,200.00
Meals	1,500.00

Sunday school, Training Union, W.M.U., Brotherhood, committees, etc.

Organizational work and activities	2,000.00
Parsonage upkeep	1,500.00
Revival	500.00
Equipment replacement	1,000.00
Unallotted	500.00
Total Local Budget	$ 76,150.00

Missions There

Cooperative Program	$ 30,000.00
Orphanage Special	2,500.00
Baptist Council	500.00
District Association	600.00
Baptist Hospital	750.00
Unallotted missions	750.00
College Special	5,000.00
Total Missions and Benevolences	$ 40,100.00
Grand Total	$116,250.00

A Still Larger Church Budget

For Church Expenses—

For preaching the Christian gospel, for leadership in the work of the church, necessary expenses, and pastorium care...................$ 18,000

For the Christian education and training of our people, minister of education's salary and expense, Training Union, nursery, Vacation Bible school, Scouts, educational secretary, and library.................. 12,000

For the ministry of church music, including salaries of directors and morning choir, the cost of music and equipment................... 12,000

For the administration of the activities of the church, including necessary office expenses, such as printing, supplies, telephones, postage, auditor, financial secretary, church secretary, collection envelopes, and a great number of smaller items...................................... 15,000

For keeping the membership informed of its activities, including *Church News*, and advertising... 5,000

For keeping the houses of worship and work neat and orderly and supplying them with necessary conveniences, including hostess' salary, janitors' salaries and supplies, dining room, heat, light, water, cooling, and care of lawn.. 16,000

For keeping our buildings attractive, in good repair, additional equipment, and properly insured...................................... 8,000

Total Current Expense Budget.................................$ 86,000

Cooperative Program, including missions and benevolences, foreign missions, association, local Chinese work, American Bible Society, Baptist Children's Home, Baptist Hospital, home and state missions, seminaries and colleges... 80,000

For expansion and building program, including payment on property, architect fees, parking areas and driveways..................... 40,000

For new building, annual payment............................. 125,000

Total proposed budget...$331,000

A SEVEN STEP PLAN FOR GROWING A STEWARDSHIP CHURCH *

Out of their experience, Southern Baptists have matured a program of stewardship development which is scriptural, comprehensive, balanced, simple, and practical. It incorporates principles which are as old as the Scriptures and methods which have been proved through long and widespread experience in Baptist life. These principles and plans have been gathered into a comprehensive statement, with the aid of state secretaries, experienced pastors, and other leaders in stewardship promotion throughout the Convention. They constitute a balanced program of stewardship development for any church whether large or small, urban or rural. It is the approved comprehensive Southern Baptist program of stewardship development.

1. *Teach Bible Stewardship.*—(1) Teach Bible stewardship, which includes tithing and full Christian living. It is taught in Old and New Testaments. It includes all of life. Its expression begins with the tithe and goes beyond. (2) Teach Bible stewardship, missions, and the Cooperative Program. The fundamental principles of all three are found in the Bible. (3) Teach Bible stewardship through the pulpit and church agencies. Preach it. Teach it in each church agency. Use study courses. Many churches use stewardship revivals. Magnify Christian Stewardship Week each fall.

2. *Enlist Tithers.*—(1) In worship services. Have a dedication day. Ask members to commit themselves to God's plan of Christian stewardship and tithing. (2) In church organizations. Give opportunities for committal in all church organizations at any time during the year and especially when the church budget is being subscribed.

(3) Through Tithers Enlistment Visitation. Utilize personal visitation and witnessing in stewardship as in evangelism. This plan uses the scriptural methods of visiting personally, showing what the Bible teaches, giving one's personal testimony, and asking for decision. Visual aids make clear the Bible teachings and their meaning in one's life. The plan results in greatly increased giving and spiritually enriched living. As one pastor testified, "The use of the Tithers Enlistment Visitation plan doubled our budget receipts, salvaged inactive members who had been lost to the church, and helped to develop the best band of personal soul-winners I have had in my pastoral experience." Another testified: "This plan reached one member whose tithe amounted to $5,000 the first year. Far more important, it reached hundreds of others whose income was not large, but whose importance to the Kingdom was just as great."

3. *Plan Church Finances.*—(1) Prepare a budget. Jesus encouraged

---

* Adapted from a tract by Merrill D. Moore.

planning. Have church to name a budget committee. Instruct it to study the needs and possibilities of the church and recommend a budget. (2) Adopt a budget. Study the proposed budget in a business session of the church. Be sure it is comprehensive, adequate, and worthy. Make any necessary changes. Then adopt it. (3) Follow the budget. Use it throughout the year as the authorized financial guide. Spend only as approved in the budget or in subsequent action of the church.

4. *Increase Cooperative Program.*—(1) Incorporate the Cooperative Program in the church's plan. The Cooperative Program *is* missions. The members of a missionary Baptist church give to missions *through* the Cooperative Program. Through it, offer every member an opportunity to give regularly to all the work of the Kingdom. (2) Include the Cooperative Program on the basis of a definite percentage of the budget. The percentage basis rather than a specified number of dollars for the Cooperative Program is fairer to all causes, local and worldwide, under all conditions. Make the percentage a worthy one. (3) Increase the percentage each year. Set up a definite plan—and follow it!—for increasing each year the percentage of the total budget going to missions through the Cooperative Program.

5. *Ask Every Member to Give.*—(1) Emphasize individual responsibility. Christianity is an every-member religion. None can be left unreached without damage to himself and the cause of Christ. (2) Tell every member about the church and its budget program. By all available publicity, promotion, and teaching methods show each member the value of the work the church is doing, and why it needs and deserves the support of every member. An informed member is an interested member. (3) Conduct an every-member canvass. Reach the last member. He is important.

6. *Make Offerings Weekly.*—(1) For local expenses. Weekly offerings mean more faithful stewards and better church support. (2) For the Cooperative Program. Weekly offerings will produce more mission dollars. (3) Through the Sunday school and worship services. Such a plan puts the financial program of even the smallest church on an every-Sunday basis and helps to enlist the entire membership of the largest or the smallest church. It will mean a better response, more funds, more participating members, greater spiritual blessings, and a stronger church.

7. *Handle Funds Well.*—(1) Keep accounts carefully. Have a committee help in counting funds. Keep all mission funds separate. Make detailed monthly and annual reports to the church. Make quarterly reports to each individual of his own gifts. (2) Send mission funds promptly. At least once each month send all Cooperative Program and designated mission funds to your state mission office.

CHURCH FINANCE RECORD SYSTEM

A few year ago Dr. Merrill D. Moore, now secretary of the Stewardship Commission, and Dr. J. M. Crowe, administrative assistant at the Sunday School Board, worked together in developing some record forms for church accounting and a manual to explain their use. The preface of the *Church Finance Record System Manual* states its purpose as follows: "It describes a financial record system which will be useful to churches with congregational government. Sound accounting principles are recommended, but certain circumstances peculiar to churches which use volunteer workers who are not accountants are recognized. An effort has been made to use terms and to suggest procedures that can be understood and used by a person who has had little formal or professional training in accounting. In addition to the necessary textual material, a complete set of record forms is included, and their use is described."

Available at religious book stores, this whole system has already proved its usefulness in many churches.

A Church Managing Its Affairs

A church, at its best, is a spiritual democracy. Its government is of the people, by the people, for the people. In a democratic church, the rulers are the ruled. Leadership is necessary, but the leaders are selected by the people and are amenable to them. Authority is necessary, but it resides humanly in members themselves who may delegate certain aspects of it as they see fit. While the will of the majority is ordinarily determinative, the rights of the minority must always be respected. Differences of opinions, in a free church, are to be resolved in open discussion, completely free from violence or coercion. To the members of such a democracy, persecution is utterly abhorrent.

The church may look to the state for protection of its rights and in turn may inculcate and defend the principles of good citizenship, but neither must infringe upon the prerogatives of the other nor seek material or political advantage one from the other. In the management of its affairs, the local congregation is autonomous and sovereign, if it accepts the New Testament pattern. A church should exhibit to the world the best possible example of intelligent self-government, such as would form an acceptable model for organized society.

The pages of history are darkened by stories of violations of this ideal of the church as a spiritual democracy. In the light of the past, churches should highly resolve that history must not repeat itself. Yet churches committed to the ideal have often been torn by strife and controversy, frequently as attributable to bad management as to bad motives. The well-managed church should be a peaceful, harmonious, progressive, fruit-bearing church. The principles of good business administration should find their best demonstration in a church managed by Christian people under the leadership of a competent and consecrated pastor.

BASIC REQUIREMENTS OF A CHRISTIAN DEMOCRACY

Too often democracy has been conceived in terms of a political philosophy only. This conception of democracy emphasizes certain inalienable rights of men, the function of government to protect and promote these rights, the limitation of authority in government by the will of the people, the assumption that the majority expressing itself intelligently is bound to be right. Political democracy, lacking Christian idealism and motivation, may ruthlessly override the rights of minorities, may create social barriers and foment class struggles, may exalt the wealthy and degrade the poor, may sway public opinion by propaganda rather than by truth, may cultivate selfishness instead of sacrifice, may make property rather than persons the test of the good life, may put Caesar rather than Christ in authority.

If democracy is to survive the fierce onslaughts of its modern enemies, it must rethink its philosophy and reconstitute its bases. Christless democracy has little more to commend it than atheistic communism. Christian democracy is the nearest approach that men have yet found to conjoint right living. A Christian church should therefore set the example of a Christian democracy in action. If Christian democracy will not work in church life, how can it be expected to work in society and the state? Yet history demonstrates that few church bodies have undertaken consistently to operate according to Christian democratic principles. Indeed, some of the most powerful religious bodies ("churches") have been and are deliberately organized and operated as autocracies ("hierarchies"), while the polity of others has been democratic only to a limited degree. Some Christian bodies have given lip service to the democratic ideal, but actually the rulership has not been that of the ruled but of one man or a family or a clique or a faction. It is not enough to say, "Ours is a democratic church." Democracy is more than the rule of the many by majority vote. Christian democracy is essentially a Christian way of life. Its basic requirements may thus be stated:
1. Respect for personality
2. Protection of minorities
3. Many and varied common interests
4. Healthy cells making up a healthy body
5. Freedom of discussion
6. Devotion to truth
7. Decisions reached through the democratic process
8. Voluntary sacrifice for the common good
9. The Spirit of Christ in all things
10. Christian persons in a Christian society the ultimate objective

DEVELOPING SKILLS IN THE DEMOCRATIC PROCESS

Many church members would be surprised to learn that they are expected to take part in shaping their church's policy, in discussing alternatives, in suggesting more effective ways and means, in originating new enterprises, in changing traditional but outworn procedures, in arriving at conclusions and making and enforcing decisions. It is somehow assumed

Items for evaluation	Yes	No	To some extent	Don't know
1. Is each new member made aware of his or her democratic privileges and responsibilities?				
2. Is there conscious or unconscious distinction among persons in the conduct of the church's affairs?				
3. Are some members looked upon as too insignificant to be taken into account?				
4. When the majority votes, is the minority then ignored?				
5. Does a wilful minority sometimes try to defeat the will of the many?				
6. Is "the church" looked upon as apart from its smaller unit organizations?				
7. Do the church organizations or "auxiliaries" seek to operate independently of "the church"?				
8. When issues involving differences of opinion arise, is there entire freedom of discussion?				
9. Have members been taught that it is both their privilege and their duty to participate in discussion?				
10. Is there thoroughgoing devotion to truth in all proposals and presentations?				
11. Do discussions take the form of sharing rather than debate?				
12. Are the principles of group discussion known and followed in church meetings?				
13. Are committees wisely chosen and carefully instructed?				
14. Do committees function faithfully for the welfare of the whole church?				
15. Is there evidence of voluntary sacrifice for the common good?				
16. Is the spirit of Christ apparent in all church discussions and decisions?				
17. Is the conscious objective in all church affairs the enrichment and development of Christian personality?				
18. Would "the good society" be established if worthy social and civic organizations (including the state) were to follow the example of your church in the conduct of their affairs?				

that a vague group known as "they" will do all these things. Obviously the first step in the growing of a democratic church is to enlighten each member concerning his or her inalienable rights and duties as members of a democratic body. A democratic church owes to each member, from the beginning and continuously thereafter, the duty of clear definition of privileges and responsibilities in the conduct of the church's affairs.

What is the democratic process? In brief, it is decision and action by all members of the body who can be induced to participate in the conduct of a church's affairs. Preceding decision there must be trustworthy information, unbiased statement of the issues involved, discussion to clarify difficulties, objective desire to do the right and best thing, willingness to subordinate prejudice and selfishness, the spirit of sacrifice for the common good. Action following decision should be immediate, hearty, intelligent, unanimous, ungrudging, loyal, devoted, in accordance with the spirit rather than the letter of the decision. Both decision and action should seek the total welfare of the church as a whole, to the end that its local affairs and worldwide interests may maximally prosper.

If skills are to be developed in this democratic process, pastor and church leaders should understand that they must be learned by the rank and file of church members. Group thinking is not essentially different from individual thinking. Persons who think together in a group, as a committee or council or congregation, must be given facts which they are led to interpret; they must be confronted with the problem or problems involved; they must be led to share with one another in the suggestion of alternative possibilities; they must be led skilfully to reason together toward a tentative solution; they must then devise practical ways and means of trying out the tentative plan until it has been confirmed and improved; they must learn how to do teamwork and to discover the joys and satisfactions of achievement together.

The easier and apparently more efficient way is for pastor and deacons and a small "inner circle" to discuss, decide, and then bring the results to the congregation. Some pastors and churches are afraid of the democratic process. Granted that it is slower and riskier, it yet has the tremendous advantage of being the Christian way, with its objective the development of every member into an intelligent, autonomous disciple. When this conviction lays strong hold on ministers, deacons, Sunday school officers and teachers, leaders of the several church organizations, and ultimately the church as a whole, it will eventuate in the building of democratic Christian bodies through which God in Christ through the Holy Spirit may accomplish whatever needs to be done in the consummation of the kingdom of God on earth.

LEARNING DEMOCRACY IN THE CONGREGATIONAL BUSINESS MEETING

Most congregationally-controlled churches set apart a time, usually once a month, for reports and the transaction of business. To officers and committeemen who must make reports, the business meeting is often looked upon as a chore. To many others it is frankly looked upon as a bore. Perhaps the majority of members, in typical churches, simply accept the business meeting as a sort of necessary evil. The moderator takes charge, the meeting is called to order, minutes are read and approved, various statistical reports are read and approved, unfinished business or matters of reference are brought up, opportunity is given for introduction of new business, letters of dismission are granted and receipt of letters acknowledged, the meeting is then adjourned with a sigh of relief. Sometimes the meeting is enlivened by election of officers, or the calling of a pastor, or discussion and decision on some controverted issue. When controversy arises, the faithful become alarmed and the careless become interested. The prayer meeting may suddenly develop into a full-grown congregational assembly, with opposing factions bent on out-arguing and out-voting one another. In some churches pastor and deacons are kept constantly anxious lest the business meeting open the door to a church quarrel.

What can be done to make the congregational business meeting both democratic and spiritually enriching?

First, its tedium may be relieved by careful preparation. Little expense would be involved in having all routine reports mimeographed or otherwise duplicated so that each one present might have a copy. Instead of the tiresome reading of these reports, attention could be called to certain interesting highlights—increases or decreases, strong or weak points, unusual achievements or features, special needs or opportunities. Commendation for faithfulness and good work is always in order.

Second, the causes of the church should be briefly and attractively noted—the church's local activities, the associational program, statewide interests, convention boards and institutions, some phase or phases of missions. The treasurer's report, for instance, takes on new interest and significance when it is related to the causes for which the money has been given.

Third, notable events since the last meeting should be reviewed. There may be a brief word about the minister's sermons, notice may be taken of members received or baptized, weddings and funerals may be noted, unfinished business or matters of reference may be brought to attention, letters may be granted or receipt of letters reported, all of this in the consciousness that the church is writing its history for future generations to read.

Fourth, matters of new business may be introduced. There may be recommendations from the deacons, the finance committee, the Sunday school, the Training Union, Woman's Missionary Union, Brotherhood, committees, members at large. The best rule is that when such matters provoke difference of opinion, they be immediately referred to a fairly-chosen committee to resolve the differences if possible before bringing the matter back to the church. Intelligent discussion is, of course, always in order, but acrimonious debate is out of order in assembly. As soon as debate begins to develop, the invariable rule should be, let the matter be referred.

The key to the success of the church business meeting is *prayer*. A report having been made, it becomes immediately a call to prayer. Needs, problems, difficulties having arisen, become a challenge to prayer. Events in the life of the church having been reported, become immediately the occasion of prayer. The causes of the church at home and abroad having been mentioned, become instantly objects of prayer. New proposals having been introduced, they become a summons to prayer for wisdom and guidance. Tensions can best be relieved by laying the matter aside for the moment and calling the assembly to prayer. When members are dismissed to unite with another church, or when members are received, the event should be marked by earnest prayer on their behalf. A business meeting thus characterized by prayer at every turn of the procedure will be dynamic, distinctive, democratic, deepening the spiritual life of the church.

PARLIAMENTARY LAW

A Christian assembly can do what it wants to do, regardless of parliamentary law. However, long experience has established certain principles and rules in conducting the affairs of a democratic deliberative assembly that should not be disregarded. The general rule is that the business of the assembly is expedited through orderly procedures.

The assembly should be properly organized, with presiding officer (moderator), clerk, committees. Time and place of meeting and requirements of voting should be determined. The presiding officer should be well acquainted with the several kinds of motions and their precedence.

KINDS OF MOTIONS

The *main question* is that under immediate consideration, no matter how trivial or important.

Subsidiary motions are those which grow out of and relate to the main question and are intended to dispose of the main question by amendment, by a substitute motion, by delaying its consideration, by limiting its consideration, by committing or referring it, by reconsidering or rescinding some former action concerning it, by bringing the question with or without its amendments to a vote of the assembly. Subsidiary motions, in the nature of the case, are debatable.

Privileged motions are highest in rank and take precedence over all other motions. They are intended to preserve the dignity and conserve the comfort and welfare of the assembly. Privileged motions are those which call for the orders of the day, for adjournment or recess, for objection to the consideration of a question, for division of the motion, for appeal from the chairman's decision, for personal privilege in the protection of an individual member's rights or the dignity of the assembly.

Incidental motions are so-called because they grow out of the effort to deal with the main question through subsidiary motions, and are usually differentiated from the latter by the fact that they admit of only limited debate. Incidental motions are classified as points of order, reading of papers, withdrawal of motions, suspension of rules, division of the question, method of consideration, limiting speeches, closing debate, taking vote, etc. These incidental motions take priority over all other except privileged motions.

The best chairman of a Christian deliberative assembly is not a stickler for strict adherence to the letter of parliamentary law, but is a Christian gentleman skilled in the practice of courtesy, fairness, considerateness, able to guide consideration and discussion happily to the end that the will of the body may be reached and declared in Christian spirit. He should firmly insist that members rise and address the chair before speaking, that only one member speak at a time, that proposals be introduced by proper motion, that discussion be dignified and orderly, that discussion not be monopolized by a few, that participation be brief and general, that the rights and dignity, of each member be held inviolate, that by consent the deliberation be turned from discussion to prayer whenever needful.

The members on their part should be taught to practice the golden rule always, to be courteous and considerate, to seek truth rather than triumph, to put the church's welfare and the cause of Christ ahead of personal gratification, to take part not to be seen and heard of men, but in order to share in reaching the best possible conclusion.

Pastor and church leaders should look upon the congregational meetings as the church's school in Christian democracy. In this school each member is learning to put into practice the principles of Christian self-government and the teachings of Christ concerning social relationships. Even occasional tensions and estrangements of fellowship may be viewed as lessons in the curriculum leading eventually to the degree of Master of Christian Living.

PRACTICING DEMOCRACY IN THE WORK OF CHURCH COMMITTEES

A church may follow either of two extremes in its policy concerning committees—the appointment of too few or too many. If there are no church committees, or very few, the tendency may be toward centralization of responsibility in the officers; if too many, responsibilities may be so scattered as to be virtually lost. Middle ground calls for just so many committees as may be needed to provide effective media through which a church may accomplish what is needful in such matters as would not ordinarily be cared for by general officers and heads of organizations. It is usually better not to have "standing" committees that continue year after year until they either lose interest or assume undue authority. All major committees should operate under church appointment, for a limited time, usually for a specific purpose, and should report to the church on occasion.

What are the functions of a church committee? As the term implies, a committee consists of one or more persons to whom the church has referred or committed responsibility. This responsibility may be for investigation, discussion and report or recommendation to the church as to conclusions reached. The committee, by order of the church, may have its powers extended to action at its discretion concerning the matter placed in its hands. As a rule, committees are not appointed with power to act, but are expected to bring their decision, with or without recommendation, back to the church for its action. Committees sometimes overlook this limitation of authority and thus overstep their bounds.

In general there are two kinds of committees—permanent and occasional. The personnel of the permanent committee may and should be changed from time to time, but the committee serves a continuous or recurrent need in the life of the church. The occasional committee is raised up to meet an immediate need and is automatically dismissed when its work is done.

The deacons of a church form an example of the permanent committee. To the deacons are committed all matters pertaining to the general welfare of the church—its peace and harmony, its fellowship and good order, its pastoral and lay leadership, its property and finances, its worship and ordinances, its benevolences and ministries. This is indeed a large order.

Next to the minister, the deacons are charged by the church with gravest responsibility for its spiritual and material welfare. Yet by their very name they are *servants* of the church, never managers or dictators. The church has the right to refer to them any problem that arises, and they are duty bound to consider every need and opportunity of the church which comes before them. They should constantly be on the alert to forestall difficulties or divisions. Next to the pastor, deacons are charged most heavily with responsibilities for the church's prosperity, both spiritually and materially. Deacons do well to remind themselves frequently that they are a permanent committee of the church, with changing personnel but with constant responsibilities, seeking not their own will but to know and to do the will of the church which under Christ they serve.

The trustees of a church constitute another type of permanent committee. Usually but not necessarily the trustees are a sub-committee of the deacons. Their function grows out of the legal status of a church as a corporate body. Title to the church's property is usually held in the name of its duly constituted trustees. Should occasion arise for the church to sue or be sued, the trustees are its legal representatives. Responsibility may be assigned to the trustees as custodians of the church's property, the church thus looking to them for upkeep and repair of buildings and equipment, insurance, and other forms of protection, rules and regulations regarding the use of church properties, and the like. Trustees should not come to be a group rivaling the deacons, but should work in close cooperation with the deacons. They, too, should never forget that they are a committee of the church, subject to the church's direction and with no authority except as it is granted them.

A permanent committee on administration of the ordinances is desirable. This committee may be subdivided into a committee on observance of the Lord's Supper and administration of baptism. Under careful instructions of the pastor, these committees should make detailed preparation for the observance of the ordinances. Well in advance they should see that all is in readiness, that those who are to participate are notified and properly instructed, and that the pastor's part is facilitated in every possible way. The chairman of this committee will ordinarily be a trusted deacon, and serving with him on the committee will be men and women chosen because of their thoughtfulness and dependability.

A permanent committee on worship is of high importance. This committee again may well be divided into two groups—the music committee and the committee of ushers. The committee on music will work in closest co-operation with the minister of music or choir director and with the musicians and choirs. Music is a significant aspect of the church's total life and should be given support and direction in all the age groups in every church organization. The music committee should study the needs and possibilities of the church in all its departments, should provide adapted songbooks and other materials, and should seek constantly to lift the level of both music appreciation and performance. The highest point of service will be reached when graded and trained choirs, with deeply spiritual purpose, lead the congregation in worthy worship, the climax of which is the minister's preaching of the Word. The committee of ushers will co-operate with minister and director of music in creating the most favorable possible atmosphere for both song service and sermon. Under the leadership of skilled and devoted chairmen, these two committees may be of inestimable service to minister and choir and congregation.

The finance committee supplies a permanent need. The head of this committee may well be the church treasurer, with whom may be associated certain deacons, representatives from each of the church organizations, and two or three members of the church at large. This committee will plan a continuous program of stewardship-tithing education and promotion, and will give leadership to the annual processes of determining the budget goal, devising the proposed budget, getting the budget adopted and subscribed, and following through until ideally every member is enlisted.

A membership or fellowship committee is permanently needed. This committee will work with the church clerk in continuous study of the membership records, in analysis of the membership in accordance with their degree of enlistment or unenlistment, and in never-ceasing efforts to reduce inactivity and backsliding through both prevention and cure. This committee, under authority of the church and guidance of the pastor, may render a quiet service beyond all estimation in preserving and deepening the fellowship of the church, in the exercise of preventive discipline, and in dealing with "problem" members. To this committee may be entrusted the use of the church's fellowship fund with which to relieve need and render Christian service in special cases.

A committee on community missions is often needed. Nearly every church has one or more fields of need beyond its immediate reach. The need may be for a branch Sunday school, or a mission, or for services in an institution, or for aid to struggling near-by churches, or for evangelistic meetings in streets or shops, or for some other discoverable form of missionary service. A committee charged with this responsibility, backed by the church, may render service comparable to that of the church within its own walls and distinctive field.

Wisdom would indicate that these committees function best when they are vitally related to and work normally through existing organizations— deacons, choir, Sunday school, Woman's Missionary Union, Training Union, Brotherhood. Unrelated committees may become competitive, divisive, overlapping, or merely nominal. Special committees may be appointed as needed, but care should be taken not to name a special committee when the need could be met by a committee already existing.

How should the work of a committee be conducted? Here again is opportunity for schooling in Christian democracy. The chairman should preside, not dominate. Discussion should be factual rather than emotional. Each member of the committee should be impressed with his or her responsibility for sharing and deciding. The burden of responsibility should be borne by all alike. Prejudgments and partisanship have no place in the work of a Christian committee. The chairman of a committee is at his best as a skilled group discussion leader. He will therefore seek to get the issue fairly presented, to indicate alternatives, to elicit discussion which will represent honest effort to reach the best conclusions. From time to time the chairman will summarize the discussion, pointing out fairly reasons adduced for and against the undecided issues. The chairman will be constantly alert to recognize creative suggestions out of which may come a better solution than any yet offered. Members of the committee may well be reminded often of their responsibility, not to themselves or to a faction, but to the church as a whole.

The slogan, "The greatest good for the greatest number," states the ever-present committee ideal. When the committee reaches its decision, the report should ordinarily be reduced to writing. It will then be presented to the church for discussion, possible revision, adoption, or rejection. Should there be strong minority dissent, this lack of concurrence should be brought to the church's attention. After all, have not minorities been more often right than majorities in the course of history?

DEMOCRACY EXPRESSING ITSELF IN TEAMWORK

A baseball or football team is a good example of democracy in action. In a winning team, each is for all and all are for each. "Star performers" are a hindrance. Any player must be willing to sacrifice his chance to score if to do so would help the team to win. Nowhere is this spirit of team play more essential than in the work of a Christian church.

Who shall be called as pastor? Let the decision be made in the light of the best interests of the whole church. Who shall be elected as officers, teachers, leaders? Let the answer be made in the light of needs to be met and the qualifications of available persons to meet these needs. Shall a

church house be built, or its site changed, or shall it be remodeled or re-
paired? Let the decision be reached, not on the basis of sentiment or tradition, nor of personal convenience or desire, but on the basis of what is
best for the church's future. How much money shall be raised, and how
shall it be expended? Let the budget be built through conference with
representative members, in the light of giving possibilities and the needs
of the several objects represented. How shall a contention among members
be resolved? Let the instructions of Christ be followed, that the offended
one first seek out the offender, after which, if this fails, the intervention of
close friends will be sought, and then at length the matter brought to the
church for concerted prayer and concern, and if all these measures
fail, the one who thus stubbornly harbors unforgiveness is to be accounted
as outside the Christian fold, to be prayed for and won to Christ as any
other unsaved sinner. In every situation the test questions become: What
is called for by the spirit of Christ? What will enrich the personality of
each member involved? What will best conserve our fellowship? What will
create and maintain the fullest measure of teamwork in carrying out the
purposes of Christ through his church?

A church thus managing its affairs through clear understanding of the
basic requirements of a Christian democracy, by developing skills in the
democratic process, by learning democracy in the congregational business
meeting, by practicing democracy in the work of church committees, and
by demonstrating its democracy in action through Christian teamwork,
will do more than build a successful church—it will set an example of
democracy in practice that will prove the best of all answers to the false
philosophies of socialism and communism. The welfare of humanity awaits
this demonstration.

TEN ITEMS IN A FULL-ROUNDED CHURCH POLICY [1]

1. The church shall make a thorough survey of its own life and organization.
2. The community and its life around the church shall be studied.
3. A definite plan of work and program of activities shall be made each year.
4. Much greater care shall be exercised before new members are admitted.
5. A minimum standard of worship, service, and giving shall be set up and
lovingly maintained for all members, based upon a definite educational basis
preceding and following regeneration.
6. The work of the minister shall be studied by each church and a program
established for him which will include in his work the training of all lay officers
to enable them to produce a worshiping, working, and giving membership. The
minister's chief task shall be to maintain a spiritual message and ministry.

---

[1] Frederick A. Agar, *The Local Church* (New York: Fleming H. Revell Company)
pp. 82–83.

7. The church shall finance its work upon a maximum basis by making a budget based upon the work to be done, the needs of the local and world situation, and the prosperity of its members.

8. An every-member plan shall be used to enlist the members, with the understanding that there shall be only two classes: those contributing to the support of the church and its missionary program, and those receiving charitable aid from the church because they are too poor to give.

9. The church, in the exercise of its brotherly love, shall, after prayer, by means of personal lay ministries, aim to keep in close touch with every member on the church roll. Where members exhibit an utter lack of fellowship, a loving disciplinary practice shall be used to help them in accordance with the New Testament plan.

10. The church shall minister to the poor, the afflicted, the neglected, and the foreign-speaking people in its neighborhood.

Experience has proved that when such processes and plans as these are utilized, the local churches justify their continuance and are worth maintaining. Their members are spiritual, the world is their parish, they love one another, and they give joyfully and generously without expectation of return in kind, because Christ is the great dynamic of their hopes and lives.

A Church Providing Adequate Building and Facilities

The English word "church" did not derive from the Greek *ecclesia* ("the called out"), but from a related word, *kurios* ("lord"), *kuriakos* ("belonging to a lord or master"). Through a series of changes, the old English *cirice* became middle English *chirche* and modern English "church." Thus the original concept of the church as "assembly" came early to be identified with "the Lord's house." To most of us, a church is inseparably associated with its place of meeting.

The house of worship and work is, of course, not the church, but it gravely affects the life of the church. A church house that is too small bears witness to the people's lack of vision. A church house that has grown old and out of date testifies to their lack of progress. A building that is unsightly, unattractively located, or in poor repair speaks pointedly of the people's lack of appreciation of spiritual values. A building that is out of proportion, failing to provide for a full-rounded program of worship, teaching, training, fellowship, service, and enrichment for all age groups, defies pastor and people to achieve satisfying results.

A church building, like the spiritual body it houses, cannot be "finished" and thereafter let alone. Every generation of church members should add some new value to their church building. In the course of time the old building should be replaced by a new structure. Whether building anew or remodeling, the operation calls for utmost care in careful planning of a multitude of details.

An adequate building calls for attractive furnishings and efficient equipment. No longer may a church house be looked upon as just a meeting place—it is a workshop where life is being remade according to the Christian pattern. The workmen in this destiny-determining laboratory of life need and deserve the best of working conditions and tools. The building should therefore be supplied with comfortable seating, lighting, summer and winter air conditioning, simple but attractive decorations. It should be furnished with books, maps, blackboards, audio-visual aids, recording and filing systems, communicating and duplicating devices, teaching materials and helps, handwork supplies, and other needed facilities.

Especial attention should be given to the weekday uses of the building

—library, reading room, prayer room for quiet and meditation, provision for social fellowship and Christian recreation, kitchen and dining room for preparation and serving of meals. The church building is incomplete without study and office for pastor, members of the staff, and church officers. The pastor's study should make possible privacy during the time required for concentration on prayer, meditation, preparation of sermons and addresses. The study may also serve as the pastor's consultation room, where he meets individuals and groups for purposes of soul-winning and counseling. The church office should be accessible, attractive, as well equipped as any other good business office.

The location and setting of the building are important. At the least, there should be twice as much yard as the building occupies, and five to ten times as much, or even more, wherever possible. The location should be within easy reach of the majority of the constituency, near the highway or highways but not too close, easily seen by passers-by but not too conspicuous. Wherever possible the lot should be beautified by trees, shrubbery, flowers. The problem of parking has become increasingly difficult, hence parking space should be provided on the church property if at all practicable. Most churches have too little real estate. Unfortunately, for many this lack cannot now be supplied; others should proceed at once to acquire more land; occasionally a church should move to another site more spacious and convenient; new churches planning to build should seek a maximum rather than a minimum amount of land.

BUILDING TO MEET PRESENT AND FUTURE NEEDS

Few church buildings, erected twenty-five years ago or more, are now adequate; if still large enough, the space will almost certainly need to be rearranged to meet changed methods of church work. The one-room meeting place, or the church house with scattered rooms, is outmoded and should give place to a departmentized structure. Whether the old building is to be replaced by a new one, or the present building remodeled, or a building erected *de novo*, it is unwise to say, "This will meet all our needs for the foreseeable future."

The first question that arises concerning a building is, To what extent is it adequate to take care of our present responsibilities and possibilities? The answer can be arrived at in two ways: (1) an analysis of the church and Sunday school membership rolls; (2) a thorough house-to-house community census. On the basis of these returns it can be confidently said that the church needs certain space and equipment for its nursery babies (birth to three); its Beginners (4–5); its Primaries (6–8); its Juniors (9–12); its Intermediates (13–16); its Young People (17–24); its Adults (25 and above). Totaling those of Junior age and above, both actual and potential attendants on the worship service, the size of the sanctuary can be determined. Considering the needs of the various groups to be served by the church in a variety of ways, desired departments, classrooms, furnishings, and equipment can be listed. A church taking its commission seriously should then undertake to provide ways and means to meet these present needs, if not all at once, then progressively as circumstances permit.

Future needs may not be accurately forecast, but they may be measurably anticipated. In the light of the past growth of church and community, it may be foreseen that within twenty-five years the building will need, say, a 50 percent enlargement. Whatever the estimate, when present plans of building and remodeling are made, they should include the possibility of future enlargement.

The architect will thus provide for removal of walls or erection of additional units according to a long-range over-all plan that will minimize difficulty and cost when the need for enlargement arises.

ORGANIZING TO BUILD OR REMODEL

Time is an indispensable element in a satisfactory building project. Perhaps in no other undertaking is it truer that haste makes waste. Sometimes a church simply decides to build or rebuild, and then turns the matter over to the pastor and a building committee. Such a procedure is an invitation to dissatisfaction.

A church having recognized the need of building or rebuilding, and having committed itself to the undertaking, would do well first of all to appoint a large and representative *survey committee*. This committee should represent all the major organizations and phases of the church life. There should be those who know thoroughly the needs of the several age groups in Sunday school, Training Union, Woman's Missionary Union, music department; others should feel special responsibility to see that adequate provisions are made for worship, fellowship and recreation, comfort and convenience, furnishings and equipment, design and decorations. The large committee will be divided into appropriate sub-committees according to these needs and interests. Their business will be to answer first of all the question: What sort of building and equipment do we want in order to meet our needs?

Next in order will be a *planning committee*. This smaller committee will bring together the findings of the survey committee, analyze and synthesize them, harmonize conflicts, eliminate nonessentials, and after much conference and consideration emerge with a proposed answer to the question: What kind of building and equipment do we need?

The need now for a *finance committee* is obvious. The building or re-modeling project will cost money. The first question to be answered is, How much? Before detailed plans are made, estimates may be secured based roughly on type of structure, total number of cubic feet, and quality and amount of furnishings and equipment. The building committee must then confront the church, and in turn be confronted, with such questions as these: Is this estimate in line with the church's expectations and ability to pay? If not, how can it be revised? When estimated cost is found acceptable, when and how will the money be raised? What schedule of building operations should be adopted? The finance committee, perhaps reconstituted to include several members who are especially gifted in money matters and in the soliciting of funds, will then lay careful plans for the successful financing of the building project.

We thus come at length to the actual *building committee*. Upon this committee will rest the heavy responsibility of securing the services of a competent architect or architects, of securing bids from contractors and at length awarding the contract and continuously supervising operations until they are able to turn over the finished job to the church. The other committees will continue to function as needed, but great care should be taken to avoid conflicts of authority in dealing with architect, contractor, dealers.

SECURING COMPETENT GUIDANCE

The first form of guidance should come from the denominational architectural department. From these offices may be had, usually at little or no cost, help that is literally indispensable. In the light of the church's needs and resources, widely experienced and highly qualified supervisors and architects are in position to answer many questions, advise on difficult problems, make valuable suggestions, and check and recheck floor plans to correct errors and guarantee maximum usefulness. It is a mistake to send completed plans to this department, requesting revision or confirmation. To do so is to invite possible conflict and confusion. The wiser plan is to send to the architectural department a description of the church site (with photographs if possible), detailed description of needs to be met, queries as to difficulties and problems, rough outline as conceived by the planning committee, and statement of limits of cost. Based on these and other facts and needs which may be developed through correspondence and conference, the department of architecture will be in position to give intelligent and impartial guidance.

The most important single person upon whom final satisfactoriness depends is doubtless the *architect*. No money that the church spends will be a wiser investment than that paid for this man (or firm) who from beginning to end is the building committee's chief guide. The architect should of course be a licensed member of his profession; he should have had experience in the building of church edifices; he should possess sensitivity to spiritual values; he should be well acquainted with the genius and distinctives of the denomination and its organizations of which this local church is a member; he should not have fixed ecclesiastical notions, but should be able to combine traditional concepts of church architecture with modern demands for utility. The architect's business is not to tell the church *what* it wants, but, after having discovered what the church wants, to show *how* best to secure the finished product. The good architect will welcome preliminary sketches from the department of architecture and will be happy to have his plans checked and rechecked. Of course, the architect should not be subjected to arbitrary demands, nor should his ideas of correct architecture be ignored or underrated.

A final word may be said about the building *contractor*. This person or firm should possess unquestioned reliability and experience, and should be in position to build expeditiously and faithfully according to the architect's plans and specifications. It is customary for the contractor to give bond for the performance of his duties in exact accordance with the terms agreed upon. The architect, who will not ordinarily have any connection with the contractor, will supervise construction step by step to see that everything is in strict accordance with the blueprints. So carefully should the plans and specifications have been made in advance that few if any changes will be required as the work progresses. Unplanned changes are expensive both of time and money and should be kept to an absolute minimum. Lighting, heating, cooling, plumbing, and the like are usually included in the general contract. Furnishings and equipment as a rule are bought by the church through separate dealers. Utmost care should be exercised in these purchases, for an otherwise excellent building may be all but spoiled by ill-chosen and unsatisfactory furniture, pews, and other facilities.

Guidance in all these matters should be sought through continuous prayer. "Except the Lord build the house, they labor in vain that build it." Never for a moment should it be forgotten that a church house is not an ordinary building, but is being planned and directed for the glory of God, for the service of Christ, for the spiritual welfare of the people. Christ has promised guidance to those who ask and seek and knock in his name. Of all the mistakes in building, the most grievous would be to build without prayer.

FINANCING THE BUILDING PROJECT

Not many worthy church buildings would have been constructed had it been required that full payment be made on or before completion. A worthy house of worship and work is not built for one generation. Each succeeding generation should put a proportionate amount of sacrificial giving into the building. Those who come later may have their share in two ways: they may help to pay the debt originally incurred; or they may pay for improvements and additions. What are the essentials of success in financing a building project?

There should not be too much *debt*. The maximum debt for safety would ordinarily be not more than 50 per cent of the total cost. There should be reasonable assurance that the remainder will be paid off in not more than ten years. A burdensome, long-continued debt is a handicap to a church. It would be still better if the contract were let when 50 per cent of the total is in hand, with united effort to add another 25 per cent upon completion of the building, than to fasten upon the church a crippling debt.

The building operation should not seriously interfere with other giving. Some may argue that since the church must strain itself to build, after the building is completed and paid for more can be given to missionary and benevolent causes; therefore the church is justified in curtailing or omitting all other giving until this job is finished. Such fallacious reasoning overlooks the command of Christ, the needs of a lost world, the encouragement to selfishness, the limiting of the church's vision, the sense of guilt and dissatisfaction that will inevitably arise. Let the church tighten its belt and give steadily and sacrificially for the advancement of Christ's kingdom causes, and in the end it will emerge happier, stronger, more prosperous.

The financing of the church building should stress the *spiritual* note. Commercialized money-raising schemes should be resolutely avoided. High pressure methods of money-raising should be rejected. Giving for the church building should be placed on a stewardship basis—the investment of life through money in an enterprise that represents partnership with Christ which will yield eternal dividends. The tithe, it should be stressed, represents an equitable *minimum*. *Offerings* should be made for such a permanent investment as the church building. Where else may one put money and be so assured of its safety? From what other form of investment may one be guaranteed such returns of satisfaction now and forever? What other monument will so worthily preserve one's memory in the long years past this life? How better may one pay the debt due to posterity? These are valid spiritual arguments for worthy and sacrificial giving, voluntarily and joyously, to the building of the Lord's house.

Of course, thoughtful attention will be given to *ways and means*. The cause will be presented persuasively from the pulpit. The proposal will be carried to departments and classes of the Sunday school. All other organizations of the church will be enlisted. The appeal may be very simple: Pray earnestly about it and give as the Holy Spirit directs you, not as little as possible, but as much as possible. "Schemes" to induce gifts from unwilling givers are usually a disappointment. Long-term pledges should ordinarily be avoided. The point of safety having been reached, the debt may be financed easily with a bank, an insurance company, or other reputable lending agency. The amount required annually for amortization of the debt may be placed in the budget, with special occasions when extra offerings are made to speed up the debt's liquidation. Let it always be borne in mind that a debt is a sacred obligation and should be paid promptly, regularly, in full. The honor of Christ is involved in the payment of a debt incurred for the building of his church, hence no slightest shadow should ever be allowed to fall across this obligation.

ASSURING SATISFACTORY RESULTS

Cases are on record when the building of a church house has been marred by misunderstandings, jealousies, dissensions. It is not unusual for the minister to find it necessary to resign and move after having led the church building enterprise. Even though these tragic consequences are avoided, the church may move into its new or remodeled edifice with expectations of improvement and enlargement that are not fulfilled. How may disappointment be avoided and maximum satisfactions assured following the building's completion?

Let the congregation be fully informed at every important point. The people who are called on to pay like to feel that the enterprise is theirs, not that of a chosen few. Resentments arise when a committee or a self-appointed group arrogate to themselves the right to make all the decisions. To be sure, there are technical matters which must be decided by the qualified few, but the congregation should be taken into full confidence concerning major matters of policy. The committee would better wait a while and carry the congregation with them than to speed up construction at the cost of good will. The church is on safe ground when the people at large speak of the building project as "ours" rather than "theirs."

Let limitations of authority be clearly defined. The survey committee should not invade the domain of the planning committee. The finance committee should not interfere with the duties of the survey and planning committee, the building committee should not be expected to take orders from any other of the committees. There should be frequent conferences among the committees, and each should seek to aid the other, but conflicts will be prevented at their source if clear understanding is had from the beginning concerning both interdependence and independence, with the church as final authority in every case.

Let the pastor delegate responsibility wherever possible. His most valuable role is that of spiritual leader, impartial counselor, respected inspirer. There may be situations in which the pastor finds it necessary to take over major responsibility for planning, financing, buying, supervision of building. Necessity, of course, is subject to no rule. Yet the pastor who takes over this direct leadership in the church building enterprise may be rudely awakened by the realization that his zeal outran his knowledge, that he is personally charged with mistakes which are almost certain to occur anyhow. Instead of admiring his sacrificial labors, members with leadership qualities may inwardly resent the pastor's forwardness as having deprived them of their right to lead and to serve. The wise pastor will usually stay in the background, deeply concerned and always available for counseling, but careful not to be conspicuous. The pastor who follows this policy will be much more likely to avoid personal criticism, to maintain more influential spiritual leadership, to discover and develop devoted and competent lay leadership, and to enjoy the fruits of his labor and wisdom in the years that follow the building's occupancy.

Let much care be given to maximum use of the building when completed. With the same measure of intelligent preparation as that made for the physical building, preparation should be made for using it to best advantage. New departments and classes will no doubt be needed, new units of other organizations will be made possible, changed methods will be required by new and improved equipment. All of this will demand increase in the number of officers, teachers, leaders, special workers. These needs, both personal and organizational, should be accurately forecast, and while the building is in process of being planned and constructed, "blueprints" should be devised showing internal requirements to be met by the time the building is occupied. This calls for the discovery, enlistment, and training of new personnel, and the development of skills in the utilization of new resources and equipment. A church thus moving into its new quarters with full preparation for maximum use will make adjustment from the old to the new without losses that would almost certainly otherwise occur. Moving in with this spirit, the chances are that the church's chief disappointment will be that it did not build large enough.

CHECKING UP ON THE CHURCH'S BUILDING EQUIPMENT

Items for evaluation	Yes	No	To some extent	Don't know
1. Is the church well located?				
2. Would it be wise to consider relocation?				
3. Is the church lot large enough?				
4. Could more land be secured if needed?				
5. Could the site of the church be made more attractive?				
6. Is the building large enough?				
7. Is it kept in good repair?				
8. Does the building need to be replaced by a new structure?				
9. Should the present building be remodeled?				
10. Is the sanctuary worshipful, comfortable, adequate?				
11. Does the building provide for all departments of a fully graded Sunday school?				
12. Does the building provide for all needed departments and units of a fully graded Training Union?				
13. Is there an assembly room for each Sunday school department?				
14. Is there an assembly room for each Training Union department?				
15. Are assembly rooms soundproof?				
16. Has each assembly room a good musical instrument?				
17. Are assembly rooms equipped for audio-visual aids?				
18. Are classrooms soundproof?				
19. Are classrooms equipped with teaching aids— table, blackboard, maps, etc.?				
20. Are classrooms planned to give at least seven square feet per pupil?				
21. Is adequate provision made for meetings of the men?				
22. Is adequate provision made for meetings of the women?				

NOTE.—See W. A. Harrell, *Planning Better Church Buildings* (Broadman Press, Nashville) for complete and detailed check list for guidance of building committees.

Items for evaluation	Yes	No	To some extent	Don't know
23. Is there a room where Royal Ambassadors and Boy Scouts may meet?				
24. Is there a library, adequate and conveniently located?				
25. Is the pulpit designed to give maximum effectiveness to preaching?				
26. Is there need of a public address system?				
27. Are hearing aids provided for those who need them?				
28. Is the choir space well located?				
29. Does the musical instrument in the sanctuary need attention?				
30. Is there a music room for use of choir?				
31. Is the baptistry well located?				
32. Is the lighting of the building satisfactory?				
33. Is the heating of the building satisfactory?				
34. Is the building kept comfortable in summer?				
35. Is janitor service satisfactory?				
36. Are there adequate recreation facilities?				
37. Is there a well-equipped kitchen?				
38. Is there adequate space for the serving of meals?				
39. Are there sufficient toilets, conveniently located?				
40. Are stairways difficult for handicapped persons to climb?				
41. Is there comfortable pastor's study conveniently located?				
42. Is the church office attractive and accessible?				
43. Is the church office supplied with modern office equipment?				
44. Is an intercommunications system needed?				
45. Are filing and recording systems up-to-date?				
46. Is there ample supply of graded literature, teachers' helps, leaders' guides, etc., for the church's educational program?				
47. Are there ample and convenient cabinets and closets for literature and supplies?				
48. Is there an attractive weekly church bulletin?				
49. Is there an attractive sign giving name of church?				
50. Is the church protected against disturbing noises?				

THE CHURCH LIBRARY [1]

The church library is the book ministry of the church.

As a ministry of the church the promotional program of the library should be determined largely by the church program. The life and usefulness of the library will be measured by the reinforcement it is able to give to the church in its program of worship, missions, teaching, training, evangelism, and recreation. The book ministry of the church has a distinct contribution to make to this program.

As a library it should be made up of a selection of books and materials which have been chosen to help meet the spiritual, cultural, intellectual, and recreational needs of the membership of the church of which it is a part.

The purpose of the church library—the book ministry of the church—is to help lead the unsaved to a saving knowledge of Jesus Christ, and to help develop the saved so that more abundant living will be their experience. Through guided reading this purpose may be accomplished.

The library, through its staff, can help each church member to become rich— for true riches consist of expanding horizons in each of life's areas—spiritual, physical, mental, and social. Through these expanding horizons there will be an ever-enlarging circle of ideas, purposes, and concerns.

Church Controlled and Financed

1. Library in budget of church
2. Room and furnishings provided by church
3. Staff selected and elected by church
4. Librarian on church council
5. Hours and rules voted on by church
6. Library report made in regular church business meetings
7. Library Emphasis Week each year fostered by church

Correlated with Church Program

1. Committee should know needs of each organization in church
2. Book recommendations made to help meet these needs
3. Revivals and other general church meetings assisted through reading suggestions
4. Book lists for Sunday school lessons, Training Union, Woman's Missionary Union programs, and Brotherhood meetings provided
5. An awareness and alertness at all times to meet situations arising in individual and organizational life of church

Furnished Attractively

A person usually enters the church library only because of interest. Care should therefore be taken to arrange and furnish the library so that it will offer

---

[1] Prepared by Florida Waite, Secretary, Church Library Service, Baptist Sunday School Board.

as much persuasion as possible to even the "chance" visitor. Make the room friendly, welcoming, and as attractive as possible.

The library should have the *best* location in your church. By that is meant that the library should be located in an accessible room near entrances that are used frequently. If at all possible, locate the library where all age groups can conveniently pass.

Books Selected Discriminatingly

1. The book selection committee should select new books regularly.
2. First consider the spiritual, cultural, and recreational needs of your constituency.
3. Keep your book selection well balanced. These percentages may help you:
   25% books for ages 3–9 (all classifications)
   25% books for ages 10–15 (all classifications)
   15% fiction and biographies for group 16 and up
   30% books of religion, philosophy, fine arts, useful arts, history, literature, science, social science, and philology
   In fiction and biography, especially biography, you will have books that cover subjects in the 30 per cent group. This repetition raises that percentage. You will also be governed by the needs of your membership as to the division of this 30 per cent group among the listed classifications. For example, usually a student dictionary and possibly one other book on synonyms or better speech will be the only books needed for a small library in the 400-Philology group.
4. Test the book for value. Buy only books that will contribute to the main purpose of your library.
5. Select books that are positively constructive in influence, definitely helpful and useful.
6. Books that have the slightest doubtful quality should not be chosen.
7. Do not accept a gift book that does not measure up to the standards set by the committee for new books.
8. Do not encourage book showers of books that have not passed the selection committee's approval.
9. Do not accept, or at least try to avoid, the gift or memorial books that are presented with specifications on how and where they are placed and used.
10. Do not select books without giving prayerful consideration to the needs of your readers.
11. Encourage church workers to suggest books they would like to have in the library. However, be sure the committee approves these before they are purchased.
12. In a library of limited space and funds, carefully weigh the advantages of having a great many books by the same author. Just because these are popular does not mean that they have the greatest value for your aim of raising the reading level of the reader.

DEDICATING A NEW CHURCH BUILDING [2]

A new church building has been erected and is to be dedicated to God as a place of worship. This dedication is an act of the members of that church, including, of course, the pastor.

It is usually desirable to invite a denominational leader or a well-known minister to preach the dedication sermon. Neighboring pastors may take part. But the actual service of dedication is an act of the membership. It is they who have dreamed of a new house of worship, who have prayed for it, who have planned for it, who have sacrificed for it. It is they who offer it to God to be a place of worship, a place where his honor dwelleth.

The pastor should lead the prayer of dedication. The members should have the privilege of dedicating to the Lord the building which they have erected.

In order that the members may have a vocal share in this dedication, I have prepared a brief service through which the pastor and members may express the purpose of their hearts. Part of it I have taken from other similar services.

The Service of Dedication

(The pastor and members stand and read responsively.)

To the Eternal God our Father, Maker of heaven and earth, Author and Giver of life, who in the person of Jesus Christ his Son has made known to us the patience and power of his redeeming love, and who by his gracious Spirit is ever seeking to bring light into our darkness,
We dedicate this church.

To the preaching of the gospel of Christ, and to our belief that the principles of his gospel will bring light, healing, and peace to mankind,
We dedicate this church.

For the training of youth and the building of character, for the giving of hope and courage to all human hearts, and for the teaching of morality, justice, and righteousness,
We dedicate this church.

For comfort to those who mourn, for strength to those who are tempted, for help in right living, for the welfare of the home, for the guidance of youth, for the salvation of all the people,
We dedicate this church.

For the furtherance of the worldwide program of Jesus, for the encouragement of missionary endeavor at home and abroad, for Christian evangelism and education, for the promotion of social righteousness and the building of human brotherhood,
We dedicate this church.

For the promotion of that Christian unity which sees beneath all formal differences a bond of fellowship and endeavors to keep the unity of the spirit in the bond of peace,
We dedicate this church.

---

[2] Ryland Knight, Pulaski, Virginia, in *Baptist Program.*

In grateful remembrance of all those who have gone before us in the faith of our fathers, without whose sacrifice and piety we could not have built, and with glad thoughts of those who shall come after us to enjoy the benefit of this which we have done,
We dedicate this church.

That this may be for all people a House of Prayer, that men may be conscious that God is in this place, that it may be to them none other than the House of God and the Gate of Heaven,
We dedicate this church.

The God of peace, who brought again from the dead our Lord Jesus, that great Shepherd of the sheep, through the blood of the everlasting covenant, make us perfect in every good work to do his will, working in us that which is well-pleasing in his sight, through Jesus Christ; to whom be glory for ever and ever. Amen.

An Appropriate Order of Service

Doxology
Invocation followed by the Lord's Prayer
The Scripture Lesson (any of these three passages is suggested: 2 Chronicles 6:14–21; Matthew 16:13–26; Ephesians 4:1–16)
Special Music or Hymn "All Hail the Power"
The Service of Dedication
The Prayer of Dedication
The Lord's Offering
Hymn "The Church's One Foundation"
Sermon
Prayer
Hymn "I Love Thy Kingdom, Lord"
Benediction.

I should like to add this further suggestion: It is the custom of some churches not to dedicate their building until it is completely paid for. Thus they sometimes worship for years in a building which has not been dedicated. It seems to me that this is not desirable. The loan on the building is a business matter between the church and some bank or other lending agency. But the building which they have erected and for which they have assumed financial responsibility is a church erected for the worship of God, and as soon as it is completed it should be dedicated to him.

A Church Extending Its Reach

A church's reach, like a man's, should exceed its grasp. Its Founder declared that "the field is the world." He commissioned his disciples to "go . . . into all the world, and preach the gospel to the whole creation" (Mark 16:15 ASV). If his salvation is not sufficient for all men everywhere who meet its terms, it is not sufficient for any man anywhere. A church whose concern does not extend beyond its local field has abrogated its right to be called a church of Jesus Christ. Church members, if Christians, hold the gospel in trust. That they should share it with others from "Jerusalem . . . unto the uttermost part of the earth" is not optional. The most tragic betrayal of Jesus by his churches has been their neglect of and disobedience to his missionary commission. The all but desperate state of the world bears eloquent testimony to the churches' relative failure to be missionary.

EXTENSION THROUGH PUBLICITY

Perhaps it may be objected, on first thought, that publicizing the nature and work of a church smacks too much of the commercial. Shall a church lower its dignity by entering the field with articles and advertisements like those that clamor for attention in the public prints? Shall it indulge in "commercials" over radio and television? Are not these things of the world? The methods of much modern publicity may be questioned and rejected, but the end in view is essentially that of all church promotion— to make known and desired an offered value. All worth-while publicity has three objectives: to attract attention, to develop interest, and to effect decision and action. Are not these precisely the objectives of a Christian church?

Perhaps the chief difference between "publishing the glad tidings" in Bible times and now is in the vast increase of modern methods and media. Publicity in its multiform branches has become one of the world's biggest businesses. Two thousand years ago a message could be made known to the public in just two ways—by word of mouth and by the slow process of handwriting. Today these means have been immeasurably multiplied— witness the amazing developments of the printing arts, the sound-motion picture industry, the near-miracles of radio and television. Combined with all these are the marvels of rapid transit, all but annihilating barriers of space and making the world a community. With what guilt would we be chargeable if we ignored these vast potentialities for making Christ and the gospel known to all men!

A church should organize for publicizing just as it does for preaching, teaching, training. A large church should have a director of publicity, a consecrated and qualified person devoting all or part of his time to this major matter. A smaller church should have a publicity committee, headed by the best available person, devoting time and thought to this interest with the same degree of intelligence and devotion expected of those in charge of the church's principal departments. For their use should be provided a few essential books on journalism, radio, television, techniques of publicity and advertising. In their workshop should be necessary tools— typewriter, duplicating machinery, photographic equipment, art materials, filing devices. The church should approve a long-range publicity policy, according to which the work of the committee would be made constructive and continuous rather than unplanned and sporadic.

The church budget should provide generously for publicity expense, which in turn will be budgeted according to need, opportunity, expected returns. The pastor will ordinarily be ex-officio counselor of the committee, giving his close personal guidance to all their plans and productions. If all this sounds too ambitious, let a beginning be made on a smaller scale, with a view to expansion as results justify. Experience has proved that a broadly conceived, wisely planned and spiritually conducted program of effective publicity ultimately costs the church nothing because of returns in increased giving, and extends the church's reach immeasurably.

EXTENSION THROUGH MINISTERIAL RECRUITMENT

God uses human instrumentality in making known his call to full-time Christian service. It may be argued that the exercise of human influence in "the call" would be presumptuous, if not dangerous. If God selects a certain man or woman as his servant, will he not make it known inevitably and irresistibly? The answer is that God makes known his will through natural channels in the call to service as in the call to salvation. Men might be saved apart from human agency, but the Bible and human experience make it clear that this is not God's way. God might appear to an individual in miraculous fashion, as he has in a few extraordinary cases, but the Scriptures and history indicate that the divine will is usually revealed through observable circumstances given interpretation and guidance by Christians sensitive to the Holy Spirit's leadership.

A church should therefore recognize its responsibility under God for "calling out the called." The prayer commanded by Jesus should often be prayed that the Lord of the harvest send forth laborers into the harvest (Matthew 9:38). A church unconcerned for ministerial recruitment will not be as likely to have its youth recognize and yield to the call as a church with this matter on its heart. One of the holiest privileges of Christian parents is to dedicate their children to the service of Christ, and then help the children to find their place in the will of God in whatever vocation they may follow. Many of Christ's choicest servants give human credit to parents whose conscious and unconscious influence opened their minds and hearts to the call to the Christian ministry.

Occasional opportunity should be provided by every church to present the challenge of Christian service to its young people. "Youth Week" in a church presents such an opportunity. For an entire week the youth of the church will take over responsibility for its operation. They will be in charge of the Sunday worship services, one or more of their number bringing the message. They will conduct the midweek prayer meeting, they will meet with the deacons to learn the duties of their office, they will confer with heads of departments and general officers of the several church organizations—Sunday school, Training Union, Woman's Missionary Union, Brotherhood. They will consider the finances of the church, examine and evaluate the budget, study the denominational causes and their support, look into the needs of the field for community missions, and discuss with the pastor the call to full-time Christian service and how it is to be recognized and obeyed.

Another opportunity is presented in the "Youth Revival." Under pastoral guidance a selected group of devoted young people plan and conduct "Eight Great Days" designed to bring about a far-reaching spiritual awakening among their own members. The "Youth Revival" does not follow traditional lines. The young people who lead invite other young people, for instance, to house parties, where they have a good time, and then, without apology, tell what Christ means to them, discuss problems in the light of Christ's example and teaching, and present the claim of Christ to be Lord of all of one's life. During the morning hours prayer groups meet, and much intensive visitation is done. At the evening hour the young people put on a varied program of song, prayer, testimony, exposition of the Christian way of life, concluding with straightforward appeal to accept Christ as Saviour and Lord or to rededicate life to his service. The week of meetings is then followed up by earnest effort to enlist those who responded in forms of definite Christian service. Out of such an experience young people will begin to reply to the question, "Whom shall we send, and who will go for us?" "Here are we; send us!"

After seasons of spiritual refreshment, in the regular course of the church's work, or following special seasons of religious emphasis and revival, opportunity should be given for the young people of the church to offer themselves publicly for Christian service. Many will desire to make commitment to put Christ first in whatever vocation they may follow, seeking guidance through prayer in the choice of a lifework in which they can glorify God. Others will feel the call to full-time Christian service and are trying to discover whether it shall be as pastor, teacher, or missionary; whether in the ministry of education, ministry of music, ministry of writing, ministry of healing, administrative work, youth leadership, chaplaincy, evangelism, or other type of specialized service. Utmost care should be taken in the counseling of these young people. Should their commitment be made at a service away from their church, responsibility rests just as heavily on pastor and associates for their guidance.

"The call to preach is the call to prepare," a great preacher and teacher of preachers once said. This truth applies to the call to any phase of Christian work. High school graduation should be followed by four years of college, preferably in a high grade church-related institution. College disciplines should lay broad cultural and spiritual foundations, after which the young man or woman will attend a school that specializes in the training of ministers and other Christian workers. The church should follow each of its students with prayer, love, encouragement, and financial assistance when needed.

A program of recruitment of Christian workers, thus broadly conceived and continuously carried on, will constitute kingdom statesmanship of the highest order. Scarcely anything that a church may do will so guarantee Christian advance at home and abroad as this far-seeing plan of recruitment.

EXTENSION THROUGH SOCIAL INFLUENCE

A community may exist without a church, but obviously a church could not exist without a community. Today a given community is so interrelated with other communities that isolation is all but impossible. The community of a church therefore extends in ever-enlarging concentric circles until it takes in the world. By this community and for this community a church lives. Communities are made up of persons with common interests, common needs, common purposes, common problems, common destinies. It is because we have so much in common with one another, whatever our differences, that a church must be concerned with the social life of people.

In general, there are two kinds of social forces in a community—constructive and destructive. Some may be classed as borderline, having both constructive and destructive aspects, but in the long run they will be discovered as on one side or the other. "He that is not with me is against me," said Jesus; "and he that gathereth not with me scattereth" (Luke 11:23). A church of Jesus Christ has no option—it must be with him, it must gather and not scatter the forces that make for the abundant life and the good society. This a church does chiefly through its influence. A church has no business using any sort of coercion or violence, even against its avowed enemies. Its true power is like that of the seed or of the leaven— vital and pervasive. Yet it dare not leave to chance the exercise and consequence of its influence.

A church may project its influence into areas of social need in the following main ways:

By focusing attention on the facts. Facts made effectively known are dynamic. What are the facts about delinquency and crime, about conditions that stultify life, about exploitation of the weak, about prejudice and injustice toward the underprivileged, about bigotry and intolerance? Not only from the pulpit and in the classroom may social facts be presented and interpreted, but they may be given wide hearing through the public press and over radio. Sometimes even more effectively the facts can be laid before individuals and key groups, who will thus be moved to bring about needed changes.

By mobilization of public opinion. Public opinion has always been one of the most powerful instruments of social welfare. Public opinion does not usually exert its greatest power for good as the result of a spectacular campaign. Public opinion is strongest when it is aroused by quiet, persistent appeals to inherent goodness and justice, in which the common man is not made to feel that he is merely the follower of a champion of a cause, but that he is the champion of that cause himself. A church may confront the community, quietly but firmly, with such inescapable questions as these: Is this situation right? Is its existence detrimental to the welfare of children and young people? Is it being used to harm the many for the benefit of the few? Is it in violation of common decency? Can *you* the individual afford to let it go unchanged? What further damage will it lead to? Is it contrary to the example and teaching of Christ? The church may not so much state the answer as insist that the community face the questions honestly and give its own answer. In the process of leading the community to make up its mind, the church (or churches) will powerfully mobilize public opinion.

By the quickening of conscience. Conscience in itself is not of necessity a safe guide. Men may conscientiously practice and defend social evils.

They may in all earnestness argue for licensed liquor, forms of unre-strained gambling, the segregation and protection of some kinds of vice, unjust racial discriminations, the perpetuation of economic wrongs. Con-science is enlightened and quickened when God is brought into the pic-ture. What is his will? How does the situation or practice square with the standards of Christ? What does the Bible say? What happens to the argu-ment when submitted to the test of prayer? How will support of this po-sition look in the bright light of the divine judgment? What satisfactions will be derived when a seemingly justifiable practice has produced an unmanageable brood of corrupt offspring? A church may confidently ex-pect conscience to sting and burn when pricked by such questions as these, especially the conscience of Christians who may have been misled by false arguments. Conscience thus quickened will begin to produce needed social change.

By guidance of action. It is not the business of the church to turn de-tective or take over the functions of the police department. Separation of church and state is not just a negative doctrine. The state has responsibil-ity for the church in the exercise of its rights; the church has responsibility for guidance of the state in the exercise of its prerogatives. The church discharges its civic obligation not directly but through its influence on its members as Christian citizens. Principles of good citizenship are but high sounding phrases until they begin to be translated into action.

A church's duty is to confront the Christian citizenry with such ques-tions as these: What candidate for office does Christian conscience call on you to support? Can you honestly vote for the wrong man even though he belong to the right party? Have you had a citizen's share in naming the candidate or candidates? Do you exercise as a sacred duty your right to vote? Do you insist that platform promises be fulfilled? Do you stand by officers in the discharge of their duties? Are you law-abiding, and do you take a personal interest in law enforcement? Do you take time to protest civic wrong and to commend civic right? Would you be willing to stand for public office if the community wanted you? Are you willing to sacri-fice some of your rights for the good of others? A church, through public pronouncement and private conversation, may tremendously contribute to social welfare through guidance of Christian social action.

By judgment of outcomes. The New Testament speaks emphatically of Christians as judges. Jesus warns against censorious judgment, the attitude of fault-finding accompanied by self-righteousness. But Christians are to "judge the world," in the sense that by them all men and institutions are to be tested and measured. Complacency is the worst foe of Christian so-cial progress. Institutions of society and government are established, men are placed in charge of them, laws regulating social relations are enacted, the machinery of justice is devised and set in motion. The typical citizen then goes serenely on his way, consumed with his personal interests, assuming that all is well with society and the state. Occasional public revolts bring some measure of relief from evil conditions, but soon the situation lapses back to its former estate.

A church must continuously disturb this complacency of its people with such questions as these: Is the will of the people being obeyed? Have those in authority become morally careless? Is corruption creeping into public affairs? Is it time to make a change? Are we honestly informed about social and civic conditions? What should be done with those guilty of malfeasance in office? Are general moral standards being raised or lowered? Are Christians of the community noticeably better citizens than non-Christians? Are we intelligently exercising our right and duty to "judge the world"? What could be done to make life today compare more nearly to New Testament standards in all areas of human conduct and relationships? A church thus turning the light of Christian judgment on social conditions and practices will go far toward sustaining change and consolidating improvements as these are progressively brought about.

EXTENSION THROUGH VITAL CO-OPERATION

A church, by its very nature, must be related to and work with some other churches. To isolate itself completely would be to void its charter as a church. Such isolation would bring inevitable death. The question therefore is not co-operation or no co-operation, but the kind and extent of co-operation. Several views are held concerning church unity.

A church may practice co-operation on a very limited scale, associating itself for fellowship and service with a few neighboring churches of its own kind. The boundaries may be enlarged to include churches of like faith and order in a given region. Regional limits may then be removed and co-operation extended to all churches of the same denomination throughout the world. Co-operation may be based on a doctrinal rather than a denominational basis.

Another group seek what has been termed "federal union"—the uniting of the churches after the fashion of the United States of America. Each co-operating denomination would maintain its identity within a determined sphere, but would surrender its independence to the larger federated body. This larger body would operate as a world council, made up of representatives of the co-operating denominations, possessing no ecclesiastical authority but seeking to present a united Christian front in the advancement of the cause of Christ around the world. A union of all the

"Protestant" church bodies is advocated by some churchmen. They conceive of the world divided according to continents into "the Church of Christ of North America," "the Church of Christ of South America," "the Church of Christ of Asia," "the Church of Christ of Western Europe," "the Church of Christ of Australia," "the Church of Christ of Africa." According to this scheme, present denominations would eventually disappear, resulting in one evangelical Christian body to match the vast Roman Catholic empire.

Over against all these schemes is the New Testament concept of free, independent local bodies (churches), made up of baptized believers, working together on a purely voluntary basis, bound together by vital ties of faith and purpose, doing together those things that no one church could do alone. The unity which these early churches achieved and demonstrated was not legislated but experienced. "The church" was primarily local, not synodical or diocesan, or national, or continental. Of course, they did not have the same problems of division which we confront, but they were plagued with divisions. Principles which emerge from these pattern churches are clearly seen to be: (1) the autonomy of the local congregation; (2) a church as local and not regional; (3) vital unity based on common experience, common faith, common purpose, common activity; (4) voluntary co-operation without surrender of conviction or independence. Would not the application of these simple principles go far toward solving our present troublesome problems of denominational and interdenominational co-operation?

That Christians having as much in common as the evangelical denominations of Christendom should learn to work together in defense of Christianity against its enemies, in the application of Christian principles to matters of human welfare, and in the propagation of essentials of the Christian faith throughout the world, would seem to need little argument. That such co-operation would be brought about by resolutions passed in supradenominational meetings would seem to be a vain hope. That Christian bodies holding to the lordship of Christ, to salvation by grace through faith, to the unique authority of the Bible, to the infinite worth and savableness of man, to the eventual Christianizing of the world, to the consummation of the divine purpose in Christ's return, and to other like doctrines concerning which there is maximum agreement and minimum difference, should be drawn closer together with the passing years would seem to be a promise capable of fulfilment. That they should all adopt one name, accept one confession of faith, come under one great ecclesiastical organization, would appear as unlikely as undesirable. The New Testament key to the problem, confirmed by history, is simple: voluntary co-operation without compromise of conviction or surrender of economy in enterprises involving human welfare for Christ's sake. Co-operating thus, a church may extend its reach into all the world and into all areas of life more effectively than it could possibly hope to do if standing alone.

EXTENSION THROUGH WORLDWIDE MISSIONS

There are two consequences of a church's wholehearted committal to the missionary enterprise: the lost are saved who would otherwise not have known Christ; the church itself is saved from pettiness, narrowness, weakness. Predestinarian arguments lose their force in the presence of Christ's commission and the Macedonian call: "Come over and help us!" When Christ says "Go!" and the lost cry "Come!" a church that calls itself Christian has no alternative—it must be missionary. Intelligent Christians no longer oppose missions, but they may ignore and disobey the missionary imperative. A church worthy to be called *missionary* should have a definite, continuous, aggressive program of missionary promotion and participation.

The growing of a strong missionary church calls for certain essential procedures. The pastor must be unequivocally missionary-minded. If the minister is fully committed to missions as central in the intention of Jesus and the purpose of the church, he can eventually gather about him a group of people possessed of similar convictions and devotion. The true minister of Christ will feel that he is no less a missionary at the home base than his brother or sister in the mission field, and that in the support of these fellow missionaries he is fulfilling his call to be a missionary. No church can measure up to its possibilities whose pastor is omissionary or antimissionary.

Missions must be made real to the church. All too often the word *missions* connotes to many people a collection or an item in the budget, or the picture of some faraway place where certain peculiar people are undertaking the impossible. As a rule we begin to *believe* in missions when we learn to know and believe in flesh and blood missionaries. The missionary growth of many a church may be dated from the visit of a dynamic missionary who told his or her story in the first person and made the missionary enterprise a living thing.

The work of the missionaries should be visualized. Words are inadequate to tell the story of need and opportunity, difficulty and progress on a mission field. Since not many of us can go to the mission fields, they must be brought to us. This can be done, of course, through pictures. Scarcely a month should pass in any church without the showing of missionary film slides or motion pictures. These pictures may be had at little or no cost from the denominational missionary headquarters. They can be used in many ways—in Sunday school and Training Union assembly, in the preaching and prayer services, in Woman's Missionary Union and Brotherhood programs, and in special classes and groups. Not only is the cause of missions promoted, but attractiveness is added to the meetings in which such pictures are used.

Special seasons should be set apart for missionary emphasis. The weeks of prayer for missions observed by the women's organizations are of inestimable value. At these special seasons the church as a whole should be called to join in prayer for missions. The church school of missions should be an annual affair and should be made a red-letter week in the church's calendar. Classes for all ages will be held, children of school age perhaps best coming in the afternoon for their study, following dismissal from school; other classes being for five successive evenings, with two study periods of about thirty-five minutes each, with a great inspirational period between classes during which all will assemble to hear a missionary or a missionary address by a local speaker or to see informing and inspiring missionary pictures. The school of missions should become an established event in the life of every church that would grow a great missionary constituency.

Missionary literature should be widely distributed. One or more missionary magazines should be found in the home of every church family. Readable missionary tracts should be secured and circulated among the members. Missionary posters can be made locally or secured from denominational headquarters. One of the most attractive sections in the church library should be that containing missionary books. Attention should be called to these books in a special way with a view to securing their widest possible circulation. A church that is intelligent concerning missions will be responsive to the call for missionary support.

A church may have a missions sanctuary. A room set apart for this purpose will contain a missionary map of the world, spot maps showing various mission fields, pictures of great missionaries, scenes from mission fields, curios and other objects illustrative of conditions and needs, Bibles in many languages, phonograph records on which may be the voices of living missionaries, missionary programs and hymns, missionary Bible readings and the like. To this room each Sunday school class may go in turn, so that a visit will be made at least once a year. The missionary room or sanctuary should be in charge of one or more persons who are especially qualified, having thorough knowledge of materials and exhibits, and being skilled in presenting missions on the level of interest and capacity of the various age groups. Such a plan will pay gratifying and continuous missionary dividends.

Inspirational and educational promotion of missions should always be accompanied by opportunities for expression. The missionary enterprise begins at home, and "the light that shines brightest at home shines farthest abroad." Local missionary projects should therefore be instituted in places of need and opportunity on or near the church's field. Occasions for sacrificial giving, over and above regular gifts through the budget, should be arranged, not as "specials" interfering with the church program of financing, but as planned events on the church calendar. These missionary love offerings may be sponsored by a particular group, as Sunday school or Woman's Missionary Union or Brotherhood, but participation should be invited from the whole church. Missions must never be allowed to become the monopoly of any segment of the church membership, but must be held up as the high privilege and duty of the whole church. A great missionary church is grown through intelligent giving to missions week by week through the church budget and then through sacrificial offerings on notable occasions.

There are many enterprises among men today worthy of investment of life and money. At the head of the list stands the missionary enterprise. Upon its success more than any other depends the future of individual churches and the denominations to which they belong. Indeed, the rescue of civilization from ruin and the rebuilding of a shattered world depend more upon Christian missions than upon any other activity known to men. If we fail to be missionary, we shall *fail*—as individual Christians, as churches, as denominations, and as a nation. The growing of missionary churches after the New Testament pattern is today's biggest business. In very truth "the mission of the church is missions."

A CHURCH EXTENDING ITS LOCAL OUTREACH

Almost every church has a local mission field. Somewhere in the community or the association is a field of opportunity for the church to carry out directly the missionary commission. It may be an isolated neighborhood whose people are not being reached, into which the church may go with its message and ministry. It may be a neglected area, where a branch Sunday school or a mission may be established. It may be a racial group, cut off from fellowship with the church, who need the gospel and Christian friendship. It may be a new community where no church has been yet formed, in which a beginning may be made with the help of a missionary-minded church. It may be a weak and struggling church whose success would be guaranteed by the timely assistance of the stronger neighboring church.

Jesus himself indicated the starting point in a church's missionary outreach when he said, "But ye shall receive power, when the Holy Spirit is come upon you: and ye shall be my witnesses both in Jerusalem, and in all Judaea and Samaria, and unto the uttermost part of the earth." The disciples were to begin where they were—in Jerusalem, perhaps the hardest spot in the world for them to win; and beyond Jerusalem they were to extend their witness throughout Judea, where they would meet prejudice and hostility at every turn. The obvious truth is that a church which cannot win at home is not likely to win abroad.

Not since the first three centuries has Christianity been faced with such powerful and violent opposition as in this twentieth century. The churches, as the organized expression of Christianity, are in many quarters on trial for their lives. Many signs indicate widespread awakening to the realization that the churches, built and conducted after the fashion of the New Testament pattern, are the hope of a confused and stricken world. Let it be recalled that it was in the context of his declaration, "I will build my church," that Jesus announced the basic life-principle: "For whosoever would save his life shall lose it: and whosoever shall lose his life for my sake shall find it." Applied to a church, this principle means that a church lacking missionary outreach and passion, seeking to save its life rather than losing it in an abandon of self-giving, is a dying church —and ought to die.

When the risen Lord of the church pushed aside everything of lesser moment and put at the center that which he counted of supreme importance, he said: "Go ye therefore, and make disciples of all the nations, baptizing them in the name of the Father and of the Son and of the Holy Spirit: teaching them to observe all things whatsoever I commanded you: and lo, I am with you always, even unto the end of the world." Has a church the right to be called a church that is not seeking to its utmost to carry out these marching orders of its Lord?

CHECKING UP ON THE CHURCH'S OUTREACH

Items for evaluation	Yes	No	To some extent	Don't know
1. Is the church well and favorably known beyond its immediate locality?				
2. Has the church a program of publicity?				
3. Are the principles of publicity studied and followed?				
4. Is a variety of publicity media used?				
5. If no present publicity plan, could one be wisely inaugurated?				
6. Does the church seem concerned about recruitment for the Christian ministry?				
7. Has the church furnished young men and women for full-time Christian service?				
8. Are there special occasions when this matter is given attention?				
9. Does the church follow its students to college and seminary?				
10. Does the church seem mindful of its social responsibility?				
11. Is the Christian ideal of society presented?				
12. Is interest stimulated in social and political issues?				
13. Is the church made aware of interracial problems?				
14. Is there evidence of intelligent Christian racial attitudes?				
15. Is the church concerned over specific local evils —gambling, drinking, prostitution, political corruption, etc.?				
16. Is the church's influence in these areas distinctly felt, even though indirectly?				
17. Does the church co-operate fully with the denomination?				
18. Does it take active interest in associational affairs?				
19. Does it share worthily in the denominational state program?				
20. Is it intelligently loyal to the Convention-wide program?				

Items for evaluation	Yes	No	To some extent	Don't know
21. Are the denominational causes presented educationally?				
22. Are messengers sent to denominational meetings?				
23. Is the denominational paper made available to heads of families?				
24. Is there a spirit of co-operation with other Christian bodies?				
25. Is the distinction between co-operation and organic church union clearly understood?				
26. Has the church worldwide missionary vision?				
27. Do many members manifest a spirit of indifference towards missions?				
28. Is there united support of foreign missions?				
29. Does the church recognize literally that its field is the world?				
30. Does the church accept its obligation to carry out Christ's great commission?				

Classified Bibliography

ADMINISTRATION

Blackwood, Andrew W., *Pastoral Leadership*. New York and Nashville: Abingdon-Cokesbury Press, 1949

Brand, N. F., *The Pastor's Legal Adviser*. New York and Nashville: Abingdon-Cokesbury Press, 1942

Cashman, Robert, *The Business Administration of the Church*. Chicago: Willett, Clark and Company, 1944

Cruzan, Rose Marie, *Practical Parliamentary Procedure*. Bloomington, Ill. McKnight & McKnight

Dimock, Marshall, *The Executive in Action*. New York: Harper and Bros., 1945

Dobbins, G. S., *Building Better Churches*. Nashville: Broadman Press, 1947

———. *A Ministering Church*. Nashville: Broadman Press, 1960

Landis, James M., *The Administrative Process*. New Haven: Yale University Press, 1938

Leach, William H., *Handbook of Church Management*. Englewood Cliffs, N. J.: Prentice-Hall, Inc., 1958

Leiffer, Murray H., *The Effective City Church*. New York and Nashville: Abingdon-Cokesbury Press, 1949

Mooney, J. C. and Reily, Alan C., *The Principles of Organization*. New York: Harper and Bros., 1947

Scott, Walter D. et al., *Personnel Management*. New York: McGraw-Hill Book Company, 1949

Shelton, Orman L., *The Church Functioning Effectively*. St. Louis: Christian Board of Publication, 1946

Smith, Howard, *Developing Your Executive Ability*. New York: McGraw-Hill Book Company, 1945

BUILDING AND EQUIPMENT

Conover, E. M., *The Church Builder*. New York: Harper and Bros., 1948

Harrell, W. A., *Planning Better Church Buildings*. Nashville: Broadman Press, 1948

Leach, Wm. H., *Protestant Church Building*. New York and Nashville: Abingdon-Cokesbury Press, 1948

Scotford, John R., *The Church Beautiful*. Boston: Pilgrim Press, 1945

CHILDREN AND YOUNG PEOPLE

Aldrich, Anderson and Mary, *Babies Are Human Beings*. New York: Macmillan Company, 1938

Chaplin, Dora P., *Children and Religion.* New York: Charles Scribner's Sons, 1948

Crawford, John E., and Woodward, Luther E., *Better Ways of Growing Up.* Philadelphia: Muhlenberg Press, 1948

Eakin, Mildred and Frank, *The Pastor and the Children.* New York: Macmillan Company, 1947

Ellenwood, James, *Just and Durable Parents.* New York: Charles Scribner's Sons, 1948

Jones, Mary Alice, *Guiding Children in Christian Growth.* New York and Nashville: Abingdon-Cokesbury Press, 1949

Ligon, Ernest M., *Toward a Greater Generation.* New York: Macmillan Company, 1948

Sherrill, Lewis J., *The Opening Doors of Childhood.* New York: Macmillan Company, 1939

Trent, Robbie, *Your Child and God.* Chicago: Willett, Clark and Company, 1941

THE CHURCH

Dana, H. E., *Christ's Ecclesia.* Nashville: The Sunday School Board of the Southern Baptist Convention, 1926

Flew, R. Newton, *Jesus and His Church.* New York: Abingdon Press, 1938

Hanson, Stig, *The Unity of the Church in the New Testament.* Almquist and Winksells Boktryckeri: Upsalla, 1946

Lindsay, Thomas M., *The Church and the Ministry in the Early Centuries.* London: Hodder and Stoughton, 1902

Miller, Park Hayes, *The New Testament Church.* Philadelphia: Westminster Press, 1926

Manson, T. W., *The Church's Ministry.* London: Hodder and Stoughton, Ltd., 1948

Moffatt, James, *The First Five Centuries of the Church.* Nashville: Cokesbury Press, 1938

Scott, Ernest F., *The Nature of the Early Church.* New York: Charles Scribner's Sons, 1941

Speer, Robert E., *When Christianity Was New.* New York: Fleming H. Revell Company, 1939

Walton, Robert C., *The Gathered Community.* London: Carey Press, 1946

THE COMMUNITY

Kincheloe, S. D., *The American City and Its Church.* New York: The Missionary Education Movement, 1938

Leiffer, Murray H., *City and Church in Transition.* Chicago: Willett, Clark and Company, 1938

Mims, Mary, *The Awakening Community.* New York: Macmillan Company, 1932

Morgan, Arthur E., *The Small Community.* New York: Harper and Bros., 1942

Mumford, Lewis, *City Development*. New York: Harcourt, Brace Company, 1945

Odum, H. W., and Moore, H. E., *American Regionalism*. New York: Henry Holt and Company, 1938

Young, Pauline, *Scientific Social Surveys and Research*. New York: Prentice-Hall, Inc., 1939

THE CONSTITUENCY

Allport, G. W., *Personality: A Psychological Interpretation*. New York: Henry Holt and Company, 1937

Boisen, Anton, *Problems in Religion and Life*. New York and Nashville: Abingdon-Cokesbury, 1946

Kardiner, A., *The Individual and His Society*. New York: Columbia University Press, 1944

Newstetter, W. I., Feldstein, M. J., and Newcombs, T. M., *Group Adjustment*. Cleveland: Western Reserve University, 1938

Wissler, C., *Man and Culture*. New York: Thomas Crowell Company, 1938

Murphy, Gardner, *Personality—A Bio-Social Approach*. New York: Harper and Brothers, 1947

ENLISTMENT AND SERVICE

Anderson, Wm. K., *Making the Gospel Effective*. New York and Nashville: Abingdon-Cokesbury Press, 1945

Binkley, Olin T., *The Churches and the Social Conscience*. Indianapolis: National Foundation Press, 1948

Corzine, J. L., *Fields of Service in the Church*. Nashville: The Sunday School Board of the Southern Baptist Convention, 1937

Gage, Albert H., *Increasing Church Attendance*. Grand Rapids: Zondervan Publishing House, 1942

Murray, Alfred L., *Reaching the Unchurched*. New York: Round Table Press, 1940

EVANGELISM

Barnette, J. N., *The Place of the Sunday School in Evangelism*. Nashville: The Sunday School Board of the Southern Baptist Convention, 1945

Blackwood, Andrew W., *Evangelism in the Home Church*. New York and Nashville: Abingdon-Cokesbury Press, 1942

Bryan, Dawson C., *A Workable Plan of Evangelism*. New York and Nashville: Abingdon-Cokesbury Press, 1945

Commission on Evangelism, *Towards the Conversion of England*. Toronto and Vancouver: J. M. Dent and Sons, Ltd.

Dobbins, G. S., *Evangelism According to Christ*. Nashville: Broadman Press, 1949

Muncy, W. L., Jr., *A History of Evangelism in the United States*. Kansas City: Central Seminary Press, 1945

Powell, Sidney W., *Toward the Great Awakening*. New York and Nashville: Abingdon-Cokesbury Press, 1949

Sangster, W. E., *Let Me Commend*. New York and Nashville: Abingdon-Cokesbury Press, 1948

Sweet, W. W., *Revivalism in America*. New York: Charles Scribner's Sons, 1944

LAY OFFICERS AND LEADERS

Barker, L. V., *Lay Leadership in Protestant Churches*. New York: Association Press, 1934

Burroughs, P. E., *Honoring the Deaconship*. Nashville: The Sunday School Board of the Southern Baptist Convention, 1936

Cooper, Alfred M., *How to Conduct Conferences*. New York: McGraw-Hill Book Company, 1942

Laird, Donald A., and Eleanor C., *The Technique of Building Personal Leadership*. New York: McGraw-Hill Book Company, 1944

Lindquist, Harold L., *Leadership for Christ*. Chicago: Moody Press, 1946

Tead, Ordway, *The Art of Leadership*. New York: McGraw-Hill Book Company, 1935

MARRIAGE AND THE FAMILY

Becker, Howard, and Hill, Reuben, *Marriage and the Family*. Boston: D. C. Heath Company, 1942

Burgess, Ernest, and Locke, H. J., *The Family*. New York: American Book Company, 1945

Burkhart, Roy A., *The Secret of a Happy Marriage*. New York: Harper and Bros., 1949

Goldstein, Sidney E., *Marriage and Family Counseling*. New York: McGraw-Hill Book Company, Inc., 1945

Groves, Ernest R., *Christianity and the Family*. New York: Macmillan Company, 1942

Popenoe, Paul B., *Modern Marriage*. New York: Macmillan Company, 1940

Wood, Leland Foster, *Pastoral Counseling in Family Relationships*. New York: The Commission on Marriage and the Home of the Federal Council of Churches, 297 Fourth Avenue, 1948

Wood, Leland Foster, *Harmony in Marriage*. New York: Round Table Press, 1939

MISSIONS

Anderson, Wm. K., Ed., *Christian World Missions*. Nashville: Commission on Ministerial Training, 1946

Cash, William Wilson, *The Missionary Church*. London: Church Missionary Society, 1939

Carver, Wm. O., *Christian Missions in Today's World*. New York: Harper and Bros., 1942

Goerner, Henry Cornell, *America Must Be Christian*. Atlanta: Home Mission Board, 1947

Harner, Nevin C., and Baker, D. D., *Missionary Education in Your Church*. New York: Missionary Education Movement, 1942

Latourette, Kenneth S., *The Christian Outlook*. New York: Harper and Bros., 1948

Soper, Edmund D., *The Philosophy of the Christian World Mission*. New York and Nashville: Abingdon-Cokesbury Press, 1943

Van Kirk, Walter W., *Christian Global Strategy*. New York: Willett, Clark and Co., 1945

ORGANIZED SERVICE

Ady, Cecilia M., *The Role of Women in the Church*. London: Press and Publication Board of the Church Assembly, 1948

Bacon, F. D., *Women in the Church*. London and Redhill: Lutterworth Press, 1946

Brunner, Heinrich Emil, *Justice and the Social Order*. New York: Harper and Bros., 1945

Mott, John R., *Liberating the Lay Forces of Christianity*. New York: Macmillan Company, 1932

PASTOR AND STAFF

Blackwood, Andrew W., *Pastoral Leadership*. New York and Nashville: Abingdon-Cokesbury Press, 1949

Hewitt, A. W., *Highland Shepherds*. Chicago: Willett, Clark and Company, 1939

Howse, W. L., *The Church Staff and Its Work*. Nashville: Broadman Press, 1959

Palmer, Albert W., *The Minister's Job*. New York: Harper and Bros., 1949

Schell, Erwin H., *The Technique of Executive Control*. New York: McGraw-Hill Book Company, 1946

Smith, Howard, *Developing Your Executive Ability*. New York: McGraw-Hill Book Company, 1946

PASTORAL CARE AND COUNSELING

Bonnell, John S., *Psychology for Pastor and People*. New York: Harper and Bros., 1949

Dicks, Russell and Cabot, Richard, *The Art of Ministering to the Sick*. New York: Macmillan Company, 1936

English and Pierson, *Emotional Problems of Living*. New York: W. W. Norton and Company, 1945

Hiltner, Seward, *Pastoral Counseling*. New York and Nashville: Abingdon-Cokesbury Press, 1949

May, Rollo, *The Art of Counseling*. Nashville: Cokesbury Press, 1939

Murphy, Gardner, *Personality—A Bio-Social Approach*. New York: Harper and Bros., 1947

Oates, Wayne E., *The Christian Pastor*. Philadelphia, Westminster Press, 1951
Rogers, C. R., *Counseling and Psychotherapy*. New York: Houghton Mifflin Company, 1942
Slavson, S. R., *An Introduction to Group Therapy*. New York: Commonwealth Fund, 1943
Trueblood, D. Elton, *The Predicament of Modern Man*. New York: Harper and Bros., 1944

PROMOTION AND PUBLICITY

Angell, Norman, *Let the People Know*. New York: Viking Press, 1943
Brodie, W. Austin, *Keeping Your Church in the News*. New York: Fleming H. Revell Company, 1942
Dollard, John, et. al., *Frustration and Aggression*. New Haven: Yale University Press, 1939
Dolloff, Eugene D., *Crowded Churches Through Modern Methods*. New York: Fleming H. Revell Company, 1946
Flesch, Rudolph, and Lass, A. H., *The Way to Write*. New York: Harper and Bros., 1947
Harral, Stewart, *Public Relations for Churches*. New York and Nashville: Abingdon-Cokesbury Press, 1945
Harral, Stewart, *Successful Letters for Church*. New York and Nashville: Abingdon-Cokesbury Press, 1946
Hutchinson, Eliot D., *How to Think Creatively*. New York and Nashville: Abingdon-Cokesbury Press, 1949
Wolseley, R. E., and Campbell, Laurence, *Exploring Journalism*. New York: Prentice-Hall, Inc., 1943

SPECIAL SERVICES AND OCCASIONS

Babbitt, Trond H., *The Pastor's Pocket Manual for Hospital and Sick Room*. New York and Nashville: Abingdon-Cokesbury Press, 1949
Church World Press (Cleveland, Ohio), *Handbook of Dedications*.
Glover, Carl A., *The Lectern: A Book of Public Prayers*. New York and Nashville: Abingdon-Cokesbury Press, 1949
Harmon, Nolan B., *Ministerial Ethics and Etiquette*. Nashville: Abingdon-Cokesbury Press, 1950
Keighton, Robert E., *The Minister's Communion Service Book*. Philadelphia: Judson Press, 1940
Leiffer, N. H., Ed., *In That Case: A Study of Ministerial Leadership Problems*. New York: Willett, Clark and Company, 1938
Leach, Wm. H., *Cokesbury Funeral Manual*. Nashville: Cokesbury Press, 1932
Leach, Wm. H., *Cokesbury Marriage Manual*. Nashville: Cokesbury Press, 1932
Maier, Walter Arthur, *For Better, Not for Worse—A Manual of Christian Matrimony*. St. Louis: Concordia Publishing House, 1936
Morrison, James Dalton, *Minister's Service Book*. Chicago: Willett, Clark and Company, 1937

Palmer, Gordon, *A Manual of Church Services*. New York: Fleming H. Revell Company, 1937

Van Buren, Maud, *Quotations for Special Occasions*. New York: H. W. Wilson Company, 1938

STEWARDSHIP AND FINANCE

Crowe, J. M. and Moore, Merrill D., *Church Finance Record System*. Nashville: Broadman Press, 1959

Long, Roswell C., *The Stewardship Parables of Jesus*. New York and Nashville: Abingdon-Cokesbury Press, 1947

McCall, Duke K., *God's Hurry*. Nashville: Broadman Press, 1949

McKeown, Boyd, *Achieving Results in Church Finance*. Nashville and New York: Abingdon-Cokesbury Press, 1942

Muncy, W. L., Jr., *Fellowship With God Through Christian Stewardship*. Kansas City: Central Seminary Press, 1949

Ownbey, Richard L., *A Christian and His Money*. New York and Nashville: Abingdon-Cokesbury Press, 1942

Rolston, Holmes, *Stewardship in the New Testament*. Richmond: John Knox Press, 1946

Versteeg, John M., *When Christ Controls*. New York and Nashville: Abingdon-Cokesbury Press, 1943

Williams, L. B., *Financing the Kingdom*. Grand Rapids: Wm. B. Eerdmans Publishing Company, 1939

THE SURVEY

Colcord, Joanna C., *Your Community*. New York: Russell Sage Foundation, 1939

Douglass, H. P., and Brunner, E. E., *The Protestant Church as a Social Institution*. New York: Harper and Bros., 1935

Hiscox, Ira V., *Community Health Organization*. New York: Commonwealth Fund, 1950

Odum, H. W., and Moore, H. E., *American Regionalism*. New York: Henry Holt and Company, 1938

Sanderson, Ezra D., *Leadership for Rural Life*. New York: Association Press, 1940

Smith, Rockwell, *The Church in Our Town*. New York and Nashville: Abingdon-Cokesbury Press, 1945

Young, Pauline, *Scientific Social Surveys and Research*. New York: Prentice-Hall, Inc., 1939

TEACHING AND TRAINING

Barnette, J. N., *A Church Using Its Sunday School*. Nashville: The Sunday School Board of the Southern Baptist Convention, 1937

Lotz, Philip Henry, ed., *Orientation in Religious Education*. New York and Nashville: Abingdon-Cokesbury, 1950

Dobbins, G. S., *The Improvement of Teaching.* Nashville: The Sunday School Board of the Southern Baptist Convention, 1943

Eakin, Mildred M., and Frank, *The Church-School Teacher's Job.* New York: Macmillan Company, 1949

Hensley, J. Clark, *The Pastor as Educational Director.* Kansas City: Central Seminary Press, 1946

Lambdin, J. E., *Building a Church Training Program.* Nashville: The Sunday School Board of the Southern Baptist Convention, 1946

Murch, James Deforest, *Christian Education and the Local Church.* Cincinnati: Standard Publishing Company, 1943

Rogers, W. L., and Vieth, P. H., *Visual Aids in the Church.* Philadelphia: Christian Education Press, 1946

WORSHIP

Blackwood, A. W., *The Fine Art of Public Worship.* New York and Nashville: Abingdon-Cokesbury Press, 1939

Coffin, Henry Sloan, *The Public Worship of God.* Philadelphia: Westminster Press, 1946

Kettring, Donald D., *Steps Toward a Singing Church.* Philadelphia: Westminster Press, 1948

McDormand, Thomas B., *The Art of Building Worship Services.* Nashville: Broadman Press, 1942

Myers, A. J. W., *Enriching Worship.* New York: Harper and Bros., 1949

Palmer, A. W., *The Art of Conducting Public Worship.* New York: Macmillan Company, 1939

Patterson, D. Tait, Ed., *The Call to Worship—A Book of Services.* London: Carey Press, 1938

Smith, Robert S., *The Art of Group Worship.* New York: Abingdon Press, 1938

Susott, Albert A., *A Practical Handbook of Worship.* New York: Fleming H. Revell Company, 1941

ADDITIONAL BOOKS

Tead, Ordway, *The Art of Administration.* New York: McGraw-Hill Book Company, 1951.

Dobbins, G. S., *Winning the Children.* Nashville: Broadman Press, 1953.

Beaver, Gilbert A., *Christ and Community.* New York: Association Press, 1950.

Morris, L. E., and Loth, David, *For Better or Worse.* New York: Harper and Bros., 1952.

Bedell, Clyde (Ed.), *How to Write Advertising That Sells.* New York: McGraw-Hill Book Company, 1952.

Grace, W. J., and J. C., *The Art of Communicating Ideas.* New York: Devin-Adair Co., 1952.

McCraw, Mildred C., *The Extension Department.* Nashville: Broadman Press, 1952.

Index